FAMOUS DUBLINERS

FAMOUS DUBLINERS

W.B. Yeats, James Joyce,
Jonathan Swift, Wolfe Tone,
Oscar Wilde, Edward Carson

Michael Stanley

WOLFHOUND PRESS

First published 1996 by WOLFHOUND PRESS Ltd
68 Mountjoy Square
Dublin 1
Ireland

© Michael Stanley 1996

British Library Cataloguing-in-Publication Data
A catalogue record for this book is available from the British Library

ISBN 0 86327 532 X

ACKNOWLEDGMENTS
At the end of each chapter is a bibliography listing the published works relied on for researching the lives and works of these famous Dubliners. I am indebted to the authors and publishers of those books, which can be recommended to readers seeking further information about these famous Dubliners.

I wish to thank Dublin Corporation's Gilbert Library, Pearse Street, for enabling me to obtain a photocopy of Wolfe Tone's pamphlet, *An Argument on Behalf of the Catholics of Ireland*, which is out of print. I also wish to thank the staff of the Royal Dublin Society's library for responding to my requests for particular books.

Cover photographs:
Cover design: Slick Fish Design, Dublin
(*Front*) Oscar Wilde, January 1882 (by Napoleon Sarony, New York, 1882. Library of Congress D.C.) W. B. Yeats, about 1911 (by Charles Beresford. National Portrait Gallery, London) James Joyce in Zurich, 1917 (Croessman Collection, University of Southern Illinois Library)
(*Back*) Swift (by Robert Wyse Jackson. By permission of the National Gallery of Ireland) Wolfe Tone (from Dr Madden's *The United Irishmen*. Courtesy of Peter Costello) Carson in 1919 (etching by J D Day 1919. National Portrait Gallery, London)
Typesetting: Wolfhound Press
Printed in the Republic of Ireland by Colour Books, Dublin

CONTENTS

List of Illustrations   6

Introduction   9

William Butler Yeats   13

James Joyce   51

Jonathan Swift   92

Wolfe Tone   128

Oscar Wilde   171

Edward Carson   219

Acknowledgements   274

LIST OF ILLUSTRATIONS

SECTION 1

Section pages

Yeats

Yeats in the early 1930s	1
W.B. Yeats, a portrait by his father John Butler Yeats	2
Yeats's Dublin birthplace	2
Lilly (Susan) Yeats by John Butler Yeats	2
Jack Yeats, the painter	2
Georgiana Hyde-Lees, Mrs Yeats	3
Yeats, with his childen Michael and Anne	3
Thoor Ballylee	3
Yeats the Magus	3
How the Poets Passed: the famous caricature of Yeats and AE as public figures.	4
Yeats during his last years	4

Joyce

James Joyce, a portrait by Pavel Tchelitchev	5
James Joyce as the youngest boy at Clongowes	6
Joyce with his college contemporaries	6
Nora Barnacle	7
James Joyce, photographed by his friend Con Curran	7
The Volta, Dublin's first cinematograph	7
Joyce in Trieste with his son Giorgio	8
Lucia Joyce, the Joyces' daughter	8
Four generations of Joyces	8

Swift

Dean Swift, portrait by Charles Jervas	9
The house in Hoey's Court behind Dublin Castle in which Swift was born	10
St Patrick's Cathedral	10
Esther Johnson, Swift's 'Stella'	11
Hester van Homrigh, Swift's 'Vanessa'	11
St Patrick's Hospital	11
Gulliver in Lilliput	12
Swift's memorial	12

SECTION 2

Section pages

Tone

Wolfe Tone in Irish Volunteer's uniform	1
Mrs Tone and her children	2
William Tone, who edited his father's memoirs	2
Irish rebels charge the cannons of the British	3
The defeat of 1798 at Vinegar Hill	3
Tone in French Army uniform	4
Aspects of Tone's death mask	4

Wilde

Oscar Wilde at the height of his fame, about 1894	5
Oscar as a child	6
Oscar Wilde's birthplace in Westland Row	6
The Wilde house in Merrion Square	6
Sir William Wilde	7
Jane Francesca Elgee, Lady Wilde	7
Wilde caricatured early in his career by *Punch*, June 1881	7
Lord Alfred Douglas as a young man	8
Constance Wilde	8
The arrest of Oscar Wilde at the Cadogan Hotel	8

Carson

Edward, Lord Carson, from a portrait by Sir John Lavery	9
Annette, Carson's first wife	10
Mr Carson cross-examining Wilde at the Old Bailey	10
Carson addressing an anti-Home Rule meeting 1913	10
Ruby, Carson's second wife	11
'The Ulster King-at-Arms' 1913 *Punch*	11
Ulster anti-Home Rule demonstration at South Derry	11
Sir Edward Carson putting his name to the Ulster Solemn League and Covenant	12
Memorial statue of Lord Carson in front of the parliament buildings at Stormont	12

(For a full list of acknowledgements see pages 274-5)

INTRODUCTION

Anybody writing a book containing biographies of a selected number of famous Dubliners has to make a decision at an early stage as to who to include and who to exclude, due to the large number of Dubliners who have made their mark in politics and literature. The six covered in this book would not be everybody's choice of the most famous six, and others could be selected from the following names without raising too many eyebrows: Edmund Burke, Bernard Shaw, J. M. Synge, Sean O'Casey, Patrick Pearse, Roger Casement, Arthur Griffith, John Field and Samuel Beckett. Nevertheless, the six covered are undoubtedly among the greatest of Dubliners.

The book attempts to give a concise but comprehensive biography of each of the Dubliners named. It also examines their writings, or other works, and opens the way to further study. It is hoped that the book will appeal to those who know a little about these famous people but who would like to know more. Students of Anglo-Irish history and literature will, I believe, find it a useful introduction to the lives and works of the six Dubliners chosen.

Firstly, we must raise the question: what is a Dubliner? In this study a Dubliner means a person who was born in Dublin and who spent a substantial part of his life there. The six chosen clearly come within this definition, though some people are inclined to regard W. B. Yeats as a Sligo man because his mother came from Sligo, he spent many happy periods there as a boy, and chose to be buried there. Nevertheless, Yeats was born in Dublin, spent some of his early years there (when his father moved the family between Dublin and London), and lived in Dublin for many years as an adult.

W. B. Yeats (1865–1939) was one of the greatest poets in the English language. He commenced writing poetry when he was about twenty years old and continued to write poetry of great merit until shortly before his death. His first volume of poetry, *The Wanderings of Oisin and Other Poems*, was published in 1899 and his final volume, *Last Poems*, in 1939, shortly after his death in January of that year. But his claim to fame does not depend solely on his poetry. With Lady Gregory and Edward Martyn he formed the Irish Literary Theatre in 1899, which led in 1904 to the foundation of the Abbey Theatre, of which Yeats was president for many years. He wrote several plays which were successfully produced. He fell in love with the beautiful Maud Gonne but his proposal of marriage (renewed in later years) was turned down. Yet out of his unrequited love came great love poems.

His paternal grandfather was a Church of Ireland clergyman, but his father, John Yeats, the painter, lost his Christian faith while he was still a student in Trinity College, and became a religious sceptic. William,however, believed in the existence of an occult world, and was intensely interested in fairies, ghosts and spirits, and developed a keen interest in theosophy, Buddhism and Hinduism. He spent many years searching for a religious philosophy that would explain all facets of human life, and wrote a book, *A Vision*, which set out his conclusions. It is a difficult book to understand but some of his religious ideas left a mark on his poetry, so that it is worthwhile knowing something of his religious and philosophical opinions.

James Joyce (1882–1941) is recognised as one of the dominant writers of modern fiction, particularly through his long novel *Ulysses*. His short stories, *Dubliners*, have been compared with those of Chekov. *A Portrait of the Artist as a Young Man* is a gripping, if slightly morbid, picture of a young man rebelling against the whole establishment in Ireland, including his family, his teachers (the Jesuits), the Catholic church and the Catholic faith, and Irish nationalism.

Ulysees recounts the happenings of one day in Dublin, in June 1904, through the movements, comments and thoughts of the principal characters in the story, particularly Leopold Bloom, a near-middle-aged converted Jew, and Stephen Dedalus, the same character as in *A Portrait* but some years older. Their itineraries cross two or three times during the day but they do not meet in the novel until night-time. Joyce tried to put into his story the inner thoughts of his main characters, including the stray and fleeting thoughts that pass through a person's mind as part of normal consciousness. Joyce was not the first writer to use this stream of consciousness' technique, but he was one of the first to utilise it in an advanced and extended form. *Ulysses* is not an easy book to read, as it has a few turgid sections, but it contains some excellent scenes of human behaviour.

Towards the end of his life Joyce spent many years writing *Finnegans Wake*, in a manner that stretched the English language to, or beyond, its limits. Many commentators, including some of his close friends, felt that his efforts in this book had not been worthwhile, but it is a highly influential work.

All Joyce's stories are located in Dublin city, but he himself became disenchanted with Dublin as a young man and left it in 1904, with Nora

Barnacle, to earn a living as a teacher of English (while also pursuing creative writing) in Trieste, in Zurich, during the First World War, in Paris between the world wars, and in Zurich again for a short while, where he died while taking refuge from the German occupation of France.

Jonathan Swift (1667–1745) was one of the greatest political and satirical writers in the English language, and his book *Gulliver's Travels* is still widely read. His *Drapier's Letters*, written as part of a campaign against the British government's proposal to grant a licence (which incidentally would financially benefit King George I's mistress) to mint copper coins for use in Ireland, is a classic example of successful political propaganda directed at an unpopular government scheme. It helped to make Swift's name as an Irish patriot, though he himself always felt cheated at having been born in Ireland rather than in England, the country of his parents.

Swift was a strange and disappointed man who none the less, had many friends, male and female. His liaisons with Stella and Vanessa became legendary. James Joyce said that Swift had muddled up two women's lives', which is fair comment, but there is more to these complex relationships than that.

Wolfe Tone (1763–1798) was not a literary figure like Swift, though he wrote several political pamphlets and kept a journal which showed writing talent; fundamentally he was a political organiser whose objective was the achievement of independence for Ireland, if necessary by revolutionary means. He was married (happily) at a very young age and qualified as a barrister, but lost interest in the legal profession. Instead, he devoted himself to Irish politics and was one of the founders of the United Irishmen in 1791. He spent almost the last three years of his short life (he died at the age of 35) in France, trying to persuade the French revolutionary government to invade Ireland for the purpose of achieving independence from British rule. Two French invasions were attempted, but (apart from the small landing at Killala) failed, and Tone lost his life as a result of the second invasion.

Tone summed up his political philosophy in the following famous passage, written in France in 1796:

> To subvert the tyranny of our execrable government, to break the connection with England, the never failing source of all our political evils, and to assert the independence of my country – these were my objects.

> To unite the whole people of Ireland, to abolish the memory of all past dissensions, and to substitute the common name of Irishmen, in the place of the denominations of Protestant, Catholic and Dissenter – these were my means.

Oscar Wilde (1854–1900) wrote essays, poems and plays, but his main claim to fame rests on his highly entertaining and witty plays, *Lady Windermere's Fan*, *A Woman of No Importance*, *An Ideal Husband*, and *The Importance of Being Earnest*, and also on the court trials which resulted in his being found guilty of acts of gross indecency (homosexuality) and sentenced to two years imprisonment with hard labour. This was a devastating experience for Wilde, and he was a broken man after serving his prison sentence. Ironically, he himself was largely to blame for his own downfall, by deciding to take action for criminal libel against the Marquess of Queensberry, father of Wilde's close but unreliable friend, Alfred Douglas. He had foolishly told his solicitor and counsel that there was no truth in Queensberry's allegation that he posed as a sodomite', and this untruth, when revealed in court, was his undoing.

Edward Carson (1854–1935) was born a few months earlier than Wilde, in a house only about a mile away; but they had little in common, apart from their brilliant minds. Wilde died at the age of 46, whereas Carson lived to be 81.

Carson spent the first 38 years of his life (except for terms in a boarding school at Portarlington) in Dublin, during which period he qualified as a barrister, practised assiduously at the Irish Bar, married at the age of 25, fathered four children, and became Crown Prosecutor in Ireland, all before he left Dublin to live in London. He moved his family from Dublin because, on his election as Member of Parliament for Trinity College in 1892, he decided to transfer his legal and political interests to England.

He rapidly made a name for himself at the English Bar and also in the House of Commons where, as a Liberal Unionist, he supported the Conservatives. He came to political prominence as chairman of the Irish Unionists from 1910 onwards, and took a leading part in opposing the Liberal Government's Home Rule Bill of 1912. He helped to found the Ulster Volunteers to preserve Ulster from Irish Home Rule, if necessary by force. During the First World War he was a member of the British government for a while, but resigned so that he could be free to continue to oppose Home Rule. He failed to defeat Home Rule for Ireland but did succeed in having the six north-eastern counties excluded from an all-Ireland parliament.

He became disillusioned with British party politics but was appointed to the House of Lords as a Lord of Appeal in 1921, when he ceased to be leader of the Ulster Unionists. His imposing statue stands outside the parliament buildings at Stormont in Belfast.

Mingling hands and mingling glances
Till the moon has taken flight;
To and fro we leap
And chase the frothy bubbles,
While the world is full of troubles
And is anxious in its sleep.
Come away, O human child!
To the waters and the wild
With a faery, hand in hand,
For the world's more full of weeping than you
  can understand.

Where the wandering water gushes
From the hills above Glen-Car,
In pools among the rushes
That scarce could bathe a star,
We seek for slumbering trout
And whispering in their ears
Give them unquiet dreams;
Leaning softly out
From ferns that drop their tears
Over the young streams.
Come away, O human child!
To the waters and the wild
With a faery, hand in hand,
For the world's more full of weeping than you
  can understand.

Away with us he's going,
The solemn-eyed:
He'll hear no more the lowing
Of the calves on the warm hillside
Or the kettle on the hob
Sing peace into his breast,
Or see the brown mice bob
Round and round the oatmeal-chest.
For he comes, the human child,
To the waters and the wild
With a faery, hand in hand,
From a world more full of weeping than he
  can understand.

Shortly afterwards Yeats wrote 'The Lake Isle of Innisfree', probably his most popular short poem, so popular that he tended to belittle it. But it is still worth reading:

I will arise and go now, and go to Innisfree,
And a small cabin build there, of clay and wattles made:
Nine bean-rows will I have there, a hive for the honey-bee,
And live alone in the bee-loud glade.

And I shall have some peace there, for peace comes dropping slow,
Dropping from the veils of the morning to where the cricket sings;
There midnight's all a glimmer, and noon a purple glow,
And evening full of the linnet's wings.

I will arise and go now, for always night and day
I hear lake water lapping with low sounds by the shore;
While I stand on the roadway, or on the pavements grey,
I hear it in the deep heart's core.

Another short poem from the same period is 'When You Are Old':

When you are old and grey and full of sleep,
And nodding by the fire, take down this book,
And slowly read, and dream of the soft look
Your eyes had once, and of their shadows deep;

How many loved your moments of glad grace,
And loved your beauty with love false or true,
But one man loved the pilgrim soul in you,
And loved the sorrows of your changing face;

And bending down beside the glowing bars,
Murmur, a little sadly, how Love fled
And paced upon the mountains overhead
And hid his face amid a crowd of stars.

An example of his romantic nationalism at that time is the poem 'To Ireland in the Coming Times':

Know, that I would accounted be
True brother of a company
That sang, to sweeten Ireland's wrong,
Ballad and story, rann and song;
Nor be I any less of them,
Because the red-rose-bordered hem
Of her, whose history began
Before God made the angelic clan,
Trails all about the written page.
When Time began to rant and rage
The measure of her flying feet
Made Ireland's heart begin to beat;
And Time bade all his candles flare
To light a measure here and there;
And may the thoughts of Ireland brood
Upon a measured quietude.

Nor may I less be counted one

With Davis, Mangan, Ferguson,
Because, to him who ponders well,
My rhymes more than their rhyming tell
Of things discovered in the deep,
Where only body's laid asleep.
For the elemental creatures go
About my table to and fro,
That hurry from unmeasured mind
To rant and rage in flood and wind;
Yet he who treads in measured ways
May surely barter gaze for gaze.
Man ever journeys on with them
After the red-rose-bordered hem.
Ah, faeries, dancing under the moon,
A Druid land, a Druid tune!

While still I may, I write for you
The love I lived, the dream I knew.
From our birthday, until we die,
Is but the winking of an eye;
And we, our singing and our love,
What measurer Time has lit above,
And all benighted things that go
About my table to and fro,
Are passing on to where may be,
In truth's consuming ecstasy,
No place for love and dream at all;
For God goes by with white footfall.
I cast my heart into my rhymes,
That you, in the dim coming times,
May know how my heart went with them
After the red-rose-bordered hem.

The above three poems were included in his book of verse *The Rose*, published in 1893. Several other volumes of verse were published at intervals up to the very end of his life.

THEOSOPHY AND OCCULTISM

Yeats's early religious beliefs were uncertain and undefined, probably due to his mixed upbringing: a pious mother and an agnostic father. He was not a Christian in the usual sense of the word (a person who believes that Christ was a divine person who had become man to redeem and save mankind); nor did he believe in any other specific form of religion. But he was not a materialist, and did not subscribe to the view that biology and physics can explain everything. He was convinced that another world existed outside the physical world, and was determined to find out what this other world was and what purpose it had. Hence his inquisitive, questioning approach to religion and his intellectual sallies into occultism in all its forms.

When he was about nineteen, his aunt, Isabella Pollexfen, gave him a book, *Esoteric Buddhism*, by A.P. Sinnett, which had just been published. It greatly interested him, particularly the references to Madame Blavatsky, one of the apostles of theosophy, who claimed a spiritual authority derived from ancient Tibetan teachers. He passed on the book to two of his friends, George Russell and Charles Johnson. Russell adopted a cautious attitude, but Johnson was enthusiastic and developed an interest in theosophy. (Theosophists believe that the human soul passes through various re-incarnations and purifications until it reaches a sublime stage called Nirvana.) Yeats and Johnson, with some other youths, formed the Dublin Hermetic Society in June 1885 and rented a room in York Street where they had discussions on theosophy and Eastern forms of religion; Johnson also read a paper on the subject to one meeting of the Hermetic Society.

A month before the Yeats family went back to London in May 1887, Madame Blavatsky herself arrived in London and founded the Blavatsky Lodge of the Theosophical Society. Yeats called on her and was persuaded to join the Lodge. Madame Blavatsky warned against meddling in black magic but Yeats, with his friend Katharine Tynan, attended a spiritualist seance, which they both found to be unnerving. Madame scolded him for this but nevertheless formed an Esoteric Section for members who were interested in psychical experimentation. Yeats joined this section, as he hoped that further investigations would help to explain ghosts, fairies, and other manifestations of the other world. He remained a member of the Blavatsky Lodge for about three years, but then resigned at Madame's request. His biographer, A. Norman Jeffares, comments:

> He was always longing for evidence and was too involved in experimentation for the taste of the other members. What he got from the Theosophists was a means of accepting and adapting theories of evolution and reincarnation which had the great benefit from his point of view of being based upon secret traditional doctrines. This linked it with his interest in Irish mythology and traditional folklore. What he got from Madame Blavatsky herself was an example of someone making their own philosophy out of many sources – something he was later to do when he wrote *A Vision*.[1]

Shortly before resigning from the Blavatsky Lodge, however, Yeats had become a member of a similar organisation called the Hermetic Students of the Golden Dawn. It had secret rituals and emphasised the rebirth of the individual through magical practice and training. As part of this ritual he took an oath to:

Bind myself that I will to the uttermost lead a pure and unselfish life and will prove myself a faithful and devoted servant of the Order; that I will keep secret all things connected with this Order and its secret knowledge from the whole world ... I further solemnly promise and swear that with the Divine permission I will from this day forward apply myself unto the great work which is so to purify and exalt my spiritual nature that with the Divine Aid I may at length attain to be more than human, and thus gradually raise and unite myself to my Magus and Divine Genius, and that in this event I will not abuse the great power entrusted to me.[2]

Yeats's willingness to take such an oath is evidence of his seriousness. In fact, for the rest of his life he had a profound interest in occultism, in the soul's destiny, and in the search for an Absolute to which all life was destined.

His father made it clear he felt that William was wasting his time in searching for the occult world, had but to no avail. John O'Leary also questioned the value of such research, and received a very definite response, in a letter where Yeats said: 'If I had not made magic my constant study I could not have written a single word of my Blake book nor would *The Countess Cathleen* have ever come to exist. The mystical life is the centre of all that I do and all that I think and all that I write.'

MAUD GONNE

When Yeats returned to London in 1887, aged 22, he was a shy, self-conscious, unhappy young man. Domestic circumstances did not help. His mother suffered a stroke that year which rendered her an invalid for the remaining twelve years of her life. His father was usually short of money. One of his problems was that he spent far too much time painting a portrait, as he never seemed to be satisfied with what he had done, and kept trying to improve it.

On 30 January 1899 a tall, beautiful young woman, of about Yeats's own age, with reddish-brown hair, knocked on the door of their house in Bedford Park, with a letter of introduction to John Butler Yeats from John O'Leary. In discussions during the following few days she made clear her ardent support for Irish independence, though she herself had been born in Aldershot of an English mother and a father of Irish descent, who was a colonel in the British army. Her mother had died when she was only five years old, and a nurse and governess had taken care of her and her sister when their father was posted overseas. She had spent some years in Ireland and had become involved in the campaign to prevent evictions and was virulently anti-British in her political outlook.

Yeats was captivated by her beauty, her strong personality and independent mind, and quickly fell in love with her. They became great friends, with many common interests, but Maud had no romantic interest in him. In fact, unknown to Yeats at that time and for some years afterwards, she was in love with a French political activist and journalist, Lucian Millevoye, by whom she had two children. One, a son born in January 1890, died from meningitis in July 1891, and the second, a girl named Iseult, was born in 1895. (Iseult herself afterwards had a chequered career in Ireland.) M. Millevoye was a supporter of French right-wing movements which sought the recovery of Alsace-Lorraine from Germany and which regarded Britain as an arch enemy of France. Millevoye's political opinions, especially his anti-English views, appealed to Maud Gonne but eventually she became disillusioned with him, and their relationship ended in 1899. Only then did she inform Yeats of her relations with Millevoye, about which he had simply heard rumours.

In later years Yeats described the effect of his first meeting with Maud Gonne:

> I was twenty-three years old when the troubling of my life began. I had heard from time to time in letters from Miss O'Leary, John O'Leary's old sister, of a beautiful girl who had left the society of the Viceregal Court for Dublin nationalism. In after years I persuaded myself that I felt premonitory excitement at the first reading of her name. Presently she drove up to our house in Bedford Park with an introduction from John O'Leary to my father. I had never thought to see in a living woman so great beauty. It belonged to famous pictures, to poetry, to some legendary past. A complexion like the blossom of apples, and yet face and body had the beauty of lineaments which Blake calls the highest beauty because it changes least from youth to age, and a stature so great that she seemed of a divine race. Her movements were worthy of her form and I understood at last why the poet of antiquity, where we would but speak of face and form, sings, loving some lady, that she paces like a goddess.[3]

Yeats met Maud Gonne many times thereafter and proposed marriage to her in 1891, but was not accepted. Maud Gonne then lived mainly in France, but visited Ireland periodically to pursue campaigns for the protection of tenant farmers and for the supply of school meals to children, about which she developed a particular interest. (A significant event happened in 1908, according to Ellmann[2], who says than when he was researching Yeats's journals he came across an obscure passage relating to Yeats's meeting with Maud Gonne in France in 1908. He asked Mrs Yeats about it and she confirmed, with some reluctance, that Yeats and Maud Gonne had been lovers at that time, though apparently only for a short while.)

Yeats retained a loving interest in Maud Gonne and when Major John MacBride, whom she married in Paris in 1903, was executed in 1916 for his part in the Easter Rising, he proposed marriage to her again, but still without success.

Her marriage to John MacBride was a failure and lasted only two years. In the meantime they had a son, Sean, born in 1904, who lived to become a noted Senior Counsel in Ireland and a member of the Irish Government (Minister for External Affairs) from 1948 to 1951.

LIFE IN LONDON

In London, Yeats began to take an interest in literary activities. He felt the need for a forum where young poets could meet to discuss their ideas and, with his friends Ernest Rhys and T.W. Rolleston, formed the Rhymers Club in 1891, whose meetings were held above the Cheshire Cheese pub in Fleet Street. In the same year he founded the Irish Literary Society in London, and the following year in Dublin. He wrote the play *The Countess Cathleen*, which depicts a beautiful young noblewoman who sells her soul to the devil in order that her people may be saved from starvation. This theme caused public controversy when the play was staged in the Antient Concert Rooms, Brunswick Street (now Pearse Street) in Dublin in 1899.

During all this time, Yeats was living with his parents at Blenheim Road in London, but in 1895, when he was 30 years of age, things changed as a result of meeting an attractive, well-educated young English woman named Olivia Shakespear. She had been married in 1885 to a man fourteen years her senior, had a daughter (Dorothy, who later married Ezra Pound), but found her married life to be unsatisfactory. She had seen Yeats's new play, *The Land of Heart's Desire*, in 1894, and having seen Yeats at a dinner with mutual friends, arranged to be introduced to him. She was a friendly, outspoken woman and made it clear that she was interested in him as a man as well as a poet. Yeats had had a number of female friends, but apparently, apart from his idealised and unrequited love for Maud Gonne, had no passionate interest in any woman up to then.

After a number of meetings in art galleries and railway carriages, Mrs Shakespear (afterwards called Diana Vernon by Yeats, as a cloak) expressed her love for him, which put him in a quandary because of his continuing infatuation with Maud Gonne. Mrs Shakespear was uncertain whether to separate from her husband or simply deceive him. She decided on the latter course as her husband was aghast at the idea of a separation. Yeats rented rooms in a house in Woburn Buildings (where he remained a tenant until 1919). Yeats and Olivia Shakespear met regularly in these rooms for almost a year, apparently to their mutual satisfaction, but the affair ended when Mrs Shakespear felt that he was still more interested in Maud Gonne than in her. She ceased meeting him for some time but they became friends again, a friendship that lasted the rest of their lives. She died only a few months before he did.

Yeats's next volume of verse, *The Wind Among the Reeds*, was published in 1899.

William Blake's poems greatly interested Yeats. In 1893 he participated in the preparation of a three-volume edition of Blake's works, and he published a selection of Blake's poems in 1906.

From 1894 to 1899 Yeats spent most of his time in London, though he made several trips to Ireland. In 1894 he compiled *A Book of Irish Verse*, and two years later he became associated with the Irish Republican Brotherhood, no doubt under the influence of John O'Leary, though he was not exclusively republican in his outlook. He took part in efforts to commemorate the centenary of Wolfe Tone's death in 1798, and spoke at a Wolfe Tone banquet in London. After 1898 his interest in active politics waned and he became more concerned about Irish culture and literature.

LADY GREGORY

In 1896 Yeats travelled to Ireland with Arthur Symons, a close English friend, who had never been to Ireland before. They visited Sligo and the Aran Islands and then called on Edward Martyn in Tulira Castle, County Galway. Martyn, a devout Catholic, lived in the castle with his mother. He had an organ on which he played church music. As Yeats was practically tone deaf it is doubtful whether he enjoyed these musical interludes.

During their stay in Tulira Castle, Lady Gregory called and invited them to lunch at her own large house, Coole Park, a few miles away. This meeting between Yeats and Lady Gregory turned out to be one of the most important of their lives, as it led to the formation, with Edward Martyn, of the Irish Literary Theatre in 1899 and to the establishment, with J.M. Synge, of the Abbey Theatre in 1904, by which stage Martyn had dropped out because of disagreements.

At first the plays they produced for a short period each year were staged in different theatres, using English actors. The first production was in the Antient Concert Rooms in Dublin for the week commencing 8 May 1899, when Yeats's *The Countess Cathleen* and Edward Martyn's *The Heather Field* were staged. The theme of both plays was the land problem in Ireland. In the following two years they booked the Gaiety

Theatre, where Douglas Hyde's play in Irish, *Casadh an tSugain* (The Twisting of the Rope), was performed.

In 1902 Yeats allowed his play *Cathleen ní Houlihan* to be produced by a Dublin amateur dramatic group run by two brothers, Frank and William Fay, who had a great love for the theatre. The Fays staged this play, together with George Russell's *Deirdre*, in St Teresa's Hall, with Maud Gonne in the main part of Cathleen. This production was a great success and led the Fays to form the Irish National Theatre Society in 1903, with Yeats as president. The company had a short tour in London that year and the English critics praised the naturalistic style of acting of the Irish players.

ABBEY THEATRE

An historic event occurred in 1904, when a wealthy English lady, Miss Annie Horniman (an acquaintance of Yeats and an admirer of his poetic drama; she was also interested in occultism) offered to help the Society by agreeing to pay the cost of converting the old Mechanics Institute in Abbey Street into a small theatre with about 500 seats. The stage facilities were limited, but it provided a permanent home for the production of plays by Irish authors. The Abbey Theatre opened in December 1904 with two one-act plays: *Spreading the News*, a comedy by Lady Gregory, and *On Baile's Strand*, a verse play by Yeats about the mythical Irish warrior, Cuchulain. The Abbey Theatre has been producing plays ever since, despite financial and other difficulties, and a fire that destroyed the old building in 1951.

In 1906 the Irish National Theatre Society was changed into a limited company with Yeats, Lady Gregory and J.M. Synge as directors. In 1908 the Fays left because of disputes about who should have control over the actors.

Lady Gregory discovered that she had a hidden talent for writing humorous plays about Irish peasant life, the best known of which are the one-act plays *Spreading the News* (1904), *The Rising of the Moon* and *The Workhouse Ward* (1908). Yeats had also developed a facility for writing plays and, perhaps just as important, a capacity for managing the theatre company and defending it against reactionary groups who felt that some of the plays were too critical of Irish life. Among such critics, strangely enough, were Maud Gonne and Arthur Griffith, who wished to have Irish national characters depicted in a pleasing light.

Lady Gregory (1852–1932), whose maiden name was Persse, had been born into landed gentry in County Galway, where she spent most of her life. When she was 28 years of age she married Sir William Gregory, a widower aged 63, who lived on a nearby estate. Sir William had been educated at Harrow and Oxford and was a Member of Parliament from 1842 to 1871, when he was appointed Governor of Ceylon. He retired from public service in 1877 and went to live on the family estate at Coole Park. He died in 1892. Their only son, Robert, was killed in the First World War while an airman in Italy. Yeats had a very high regard for Robert Gregory and wrote the following poem about him in 1918:

AN IRISH AIRMAN FORESEES HIS DEATH

> I know that I shall meet my fate
> Somewhere among the clouds above;
> Those that I fight I do not hate,
> Those that I guard I do not love;
> My country is Kiltartan Cross,
> My countrymen Kiltartan's poor,
> No likely end could bring them loss
> Or leave them happier than before.
> Nor law, nor duty bade me fight,
> Nor public men, nor cheering crowds,
> A lonely impulse of delight
> Drove to this tumult in the clouds;
> I balanced all, brought all to mind,
> The years to come seemed waste of breath,
> A waste of breath the years behind
> In balance with this life, this death.

One night in February 1903, shortly before he was due to give a lecture, Yeats received a letter from Maud Gonne telling him that she had married Major John MacBride in Paris. This completely unexpected news shocked him deeply. When he had asked Maud Gonne to marry him she had led him to believe that she was not interested in marrying anyone – but now she had married MacBride, a man whose main claim to fame at the time was that he had joined the Irish Brigade in support of the Boers and had attained the rank of Major. Yeats tried to understand what had happened, and why, but did not succeed. His rejection by Maud Gonne had a profound effect on him, but did not end his love for her.

He continued to press ahead with literary work, though during the following few years he wrote little poetry. Instead he concentrated on essays and plays, including a book of essays called *Ideas of Good and Evil* and the plays *On Baile's Strand*, *The King's Threshold*, *The Golden Helmet*, *Deirdre*, and *The Player Queen*.

Yeats went on a lecture tour in the United States and Canada from November 1903 to March 1904, speaking mainly in universities. He described one of these in a letter to Lady Gregory:

> I was entirely delighted by the big merry priests of Notre Dame – all Irish and proud as Lucifer of their success in getting Jews and Noncon-formists to come to their college, and of the fact that they have no endowments. I did not succeed in my first lecture. I began of a sudden to think, while I was lecturing, that these Catholic students were so out of the world that my ideas must seem the thunder of a battle fought in some other star. The thought confused me and I spoke badly, so I asked if I might go to the literary classes and speak to the boys about poetry and read them some verses of my own. I did this both at Notre Dame and St Mary's, the girls' college near, and delighted them all. I gave four lectures in one day and sat up late telling ghost stories with the Fathers at night ... They belong to an easygoing world that has passed away – more's the pity perhaps – but certainly I have been astonished at one thing, the general lack of religious prejudice I found on all sides here.

The lecture tour, though tiring, was financially rewarding. It also improved his lecturing skill.

J.M. SYNGE

Synge (1871–1909) was the greatest of the early Abbey playwrights. He was educated at Trinity College and decided to be a musician, for which purpose he went to Germany. Then he turned to literature and went to live in Paris, with occasional trips home, including a visit to the Aran Islands. Yeats met him in Paris and advised him to go back to Aran to write about the way of life of the people there. Synge spent the summers of 1899 to 1902 on the islands and wrote a book, *The Aran Islands*, which was published in 1907. In the meantime he wrote a number of outstanding plays, including *In the Shadow of the Glen* (1903), *Riders to the Sea* (1904) and *The Playboy of the Western World* (1907). *In the Shadow of the Glen* was criticised because it depicted a young wife of an old farmer leaving home with a sweet-talking travelling man; this was regarded by some as a reflection on Irish womanhood. The production of *The Playboy* was greeted with shouts and the blowing of trumpets by those who regarded it as a reflection on the people of the west of Ireland, because it depicted them as welcoming a strange young man who told them he had killed his father with the blow of a shovel. The protests continued for a week and Yeats, who had been in Scotland, returned hurriedly to confront the objectors. In agreement with Lady Gregory he called in the police to maintain order so that the play could proceed. This only increased the fury of the objectors and Yeats decided to call a public meeting in the Abbey Theatre. He spoke with determination to a largely critical audience in defence of the right of free speech and the right of individuals to attend plays without being obstructed by others. *The Playboy* has since been recognised as one of the best plays written and produced in Ireland.

In 1910 Yeats was granted a Civil List pension by the government. He had received confirmation that its acceptance would not inhibit his political comments, but he was criticised by some nationalists for accepting a pension from the British government. In the same year he was appointed to the Academic Committee of the Royal Society of Literature.

Yeats's father had returned to Dublin in 1901 in response to a request by Sir Hugh Lane (a nephew of Lady Gregory) to paint a series of portraits of prominent Irish literary and political figures, and went to live with his two daughters (who had a small hand-press and embroidery business) in Dundrum, County Dublin. The old man grew restive again, however, and in 1908 went on a rather prolonged visit to America with his daughter Lily. They stayed in New York where John Butler had a close American friend, John Quinn, a successful company lawyer, who had previously commissioned him to paint portraits of John O'Leary and George Russell. Lily returned to Ireland but her father remained in New York, where he had settled into a boarding house on West 29th Street run by three French sisters. Because it was popular with actors and actresses, dinner was served at 6 p.m. every day, and it became a custom for a number of John Butler's friends to attend a weekly dinner with him, where he sat at the head of the table, with a sketch book, and became known as the best conversationalist in New York. Despite requests from members of his family, including William, to return to Dublin (in view of his age) he never did so, and died in New York on 3 February 1922, aged almost 83 years.

MASKS

From around 1909 Yeats became captivated with the idea that individuals have a mask of another self (called their anti-self) which they can utilise to hide their inner feelings and to protect and promote their real personality. He began keeping a journal and in January 1909 wrote:

> There is a relation between discipline and the theatrical sense. If we cannot imagine ourselves as different from what we are and try to assume that second self, we cannot impose a discipline upon ourselves, though we may accept one from others. Active virtue as distinguished from the passive acceptance of a current code is therefore theatrical, consciously dramatic, the wearing of a mask. It is the condition of arduous full life. One constantly notices in very active natures a tendency to pose, or a preoccupation with the effect they are producing if the pose has become a second self.

A journal entry in March 1909 reads:

> I think all happiness depends on having the energy to assume the mask of some other self, that all joyous or creative life is a rebirth as something not oneself, something created in a moment and perpetually renewed in playing a game like that of a child where one loses the infinite pain of self-realization, a grotesque or solemn painted face put on that one may hide from the terrors of judgment, an imaginative Saturnalia that makes one forget reality. Perhaps all the sins and energies of the world are but the world's flight from an infinite blinding beam.

In his analysis of Yeats's concept of the mask, Ellmann[2] says that at its simplest the mask is the social self, behind which we face both the world and the beloved. A closely related meaning, Ellmann says, is that:

> the mask includes all the differences between one's own and other people's conception of one's personality. To be conscious of the discrepancy which makes a mask of this sort is to look at oneself as if one were somebody else. In addition, the mask is defensive armour: we wear it, like the light lover, to keep from being hurt. So protected, we are only slightly involved no matter what happens. This theory seems to assume that we can be detached from experience like actors from a play. Finally, the mask is a weapon of attack; we put it on to keep up a noble conception of ourselves; it is a heroic ideal which we try to live up to.

Another literary critic, John Unterecker, in his *Reader's Guide to William Butler Yeats*[4], says that although Yeats was right in believing that his genius lay in 'personal utterance', he recognised that personal utterance alone could not organise a body of lyric poetry and drama into the organic structure he hoped to build. Yeats's problem therefore was to discover a technique by which the personal could somehow be objectified, be given the appearance of impersonal 'truth' and yet retain the emotive force of privately felt belief. A partial solution, Unterecker says, was the theory of the Mask which, perhaps compounded from popular psychology on one hand and occult material on the other, was used by Yeats to make public his secret selves.

Daniel Albright, in his introduction to *W.B. Yeats: The Poems*[5], comments:

> It is important to note that, for Yeats, art is not self-expression – the self is too shifty and evanescent – but a search for impersonal beauty. By 1909 this feeling that the proper subject matter of art is the opposite of oneself developed into the doctrine of the Mask. In the poem 'Ego Dominus Tuus' (1915) and the essay 'Per Amica Silentia Lunae' (1917), Yeats expounded the belief that every man has an ideal counterpart, an intimate double, an anti-self in whom every trait is the opposite of his own. Poets, according to this doctrine, gain imaginative intensity through the struggle to realize in their poems a vision of this Mask ...

To Yeats, the fundamental self is what a man strives to become, not what he originally is.

We are all prepared to accept that we have the same human nature as other human beings, though we realise that we are distinct and separate persons. Personal feelings are deep and sensitive, hence our inclination to adopt a countenance – a mask – which protects or conceals our private personal feelings; and this mask can vary depending on who we are with at the time. However, Yeats's concept of the mask goes much further. For him, the mask is another self, an opposite or anti-self, which we must pursue to develop our personality.

Yeats himself seems to have adopted a pose or a mask of solemnity as part of his everyday behaviour. Micheál MacLiammóir, actor and writer, who knew Yeats, described him as follows in the book about Yeats which he co-authored with Eavan Boland[6]:

> In his manner to strangers he was courteous, stately and formal; at times he seemed remote, behind a mask of exaggerated dignity. With people whom he liked and felt he understood he would unbend and become by turns eloquent, turbulent and laughing. But never, as far as the present writer can remember, was there any humorous warmth of intimacy in his demeanour. All that he did or said had an air of ceremony; one could not imagine him engaged in shopping, or mending the fire, or taking an inquiring stranger by the arm and showing him the quickest way to O'Connell Street, though he himself might ask the way in a voice which suggested that he spoke from a great distance.

SPIRITUALISM

As mentioned earlier, Yeats had attended a spiritualist seance around 1887, and the experience was so upsetting that he did not investigate spiritualism further for many years. However, when lecturing in America in 1911 he met a lady spiritualist whose messages from the occult world renewed his interest. In London the following year he came across a young woman whose automatic writing seemed to contain information that was outside her own knowledge and experience. This intrigued him and he began to attend seances regularly, including some in the Hampstead home of an American medium, Mrs Wreidt, whose efforts brought him into touch with a spirit claiming to be Leo Africanus, an Italian geographer and traveller, who said he was Yeats's attendant spirit. When Yeats discovered that Leo Africanus had been a poet, this increased his interest and raised in his mind the question whether the spirit Leo Africanus might be an attendant anti-self. The poem 'Ego Dominus Tuus' ('I am your Lord') was apparently influenced by the Leo Africanus episode. The poem is in the form of a dialogue and the last verse reads as follows:

Because I seek an image, not a book.
Those men that in their writings are most wise
Own nothing but their blind, stupefied hearts.
I call to the mysterious one who yet
Shall walk the wet sands by the edge of the stream
And look most like me, being indeed my double,
And prove of all imaginable things
The most unlike, being my anti-self,
And, standing by these characters, disclose
All that I seek; and whisper it as though
He were afraid the birds, who cry aloud
Their momentary cries before it is dawn,
Would carry it away to blasphemous men.

This is an example of Yeats's ability to mix language, imagination and mystery to create a poetic world of wonder.

POETIC DEVELOPMENT

When Yeats reached his forties his poetic style began to change and mature. Maud Gonne's marriage to John MacBride had greatly upset him, and he became disillusioned with Irish politicians and with the unreasonable public opposition to some of the Abbey plays. Also, as a bachelor without a stable family life, he became more aware of his isolation as an individual. These factors tended to embitter his outlook, and his poems became introspective and the wording less lyrical and more terse. An example of his new style, from the volume *Responsibilities*, published in 1914 is, 'September 1913':

What need you, being come to sense,
But fumble in a greasy till
And add the halfpence to the pence
And prayer to shivering prayer, until
You have dried the marrow from the bone?
For men were born to pray and save:
Romantic Ireland's dead and gone,
It's with O'Leary in the grave.
Yet they were of a different kind,
The names that stilled your childish play,
They have gone about the world like wind,
But little time had they to pray
For whom the hangman's rope was spun,
And what, God help us, could they save?
Romantic Ireland's dead and gone,
It's with O'Leary in the grave.

Was it for this the wild geese spread
The grey wing upon every tide;
For this that all that blood was shed,
For this Edward Fitzgerald died,
And Robert Emmet and Wolfe Tone,
All that delirium of the brave?
Romantic Ireland's dead and gone,
It's with O'Leary in the grave.

Yet could we turn the years again,
And call those exiles as they were
In all their loneliness and pain,
You'd cry, 'Some woman's yellow hair
Has maddened every mother's son':
They weighed so lightly what they gave.
But let them be, they're dead and gone,
They're with O'Leary in the grave.

Unknown to Yeats when he wrote that poem, revolutionary plans were being prepared in secret by the Irish Republican Brotherhood (who had infiltrated the Irish Volunteers, founded in November 1913), and these led to the Easter Rising of 1916. The Volunteers seized several public buildings in Dublin and proclaimed an Irish Republic; but the Rising lasted only a week because of misadventures and lack of support. The Easter Rising came as a great surprise to Yeats, as it did to many others, but made a profound impression on him, particularly when fifteen of the leaders were tried by court-martial and executed by firing squad in Dublin within the following few weeks.

Between May and September 1916 he wrote his famous poem 'Easter, 1916', which was published in the volume *Michael Robartes and the Dancer* in 1921:

I have met them at close of day
Coming with vivid faces
From counter or desk among grey
Eighteenth-century houses.
I have passed with a nod of the head
Or polite meaningless words,
Or have lingered awhile and said
Polite meaningless words,
And thought before I had done
Of a mocking tale or a gibe
To please a companion
Around the fire at the club,
Being certain that they and I
But lived where motley is worn:
All changed, changed utterly:
A terrible beauty is born.

That woman's days were spent
In ignorant good-will,
Her nights in argument
Until her voice grew shrill.
What voice more sweet than hers
When, young and beautiful,
She rode to harriers?
This man had kept a school
And rode our wingèd horse;
This other his helper and friend
Was coming into his force;
He might have won fame in the end,
So sensitive his nature seemed,
So daring and sweet his thought.
This other man I had dreamed
A drunken, vainglorious lout.
He had done most bitter wrong
To some who are near my heart,
Yet I number him in the song;
He, too, has resigned his part
In the casual comedy;
He, too, has been changed in his turn,
Transformed utterly:
A terrible beauty is born.

Hearts with one purpose alone
Through summer and winter seem
Enchanted to a stone
To trouble the living stream.
The horse that comes from the road,
The rider, the birds that range
From cloud to tumbling cloud,
Minute by minute they change;
A shadow of cloud on the stream
Changes minute by minute;
A horse-hoof slides on the brim,
And a horse plashes within it;
The long-legged moor-hens dive,
And hens to moor-cocks call;
Minute by minute they live:
The stone's in the midst of all.

Too long a sacrifice
Can make a stone of the heart.
O when may it suffice?
That is Heaven's part, our part
To murmur name upon name,
As a mother names her child
When sleep at last has come

On limbs that had run wild.
What is it but nightfall?
No, no, not night but death;
Was it needless death after all?
For England may keep faith
For all that is done and said.
We know their dream; enough
To know they dreamed and are dead;
And what if excess of love
Bewildered them till they died?
I write it out in verse –
MacDonagh and MacBride
And Connolly and Pearse
Now and in time to be,
Wherever green is worn,
Are changed, changed utterly:
A terrible beauty is born.

The following notes on the individuals referred to in that poem may he helpful.

'That woman' in line 17 is Constance Markiewicz, *née* Gore-Booth (1868–1927), who was active in Irish revolutionary politics. Her death sentence for her part in the 1916 Rising was commuted to life imprisonment, and she was released in the general amnesty of June 1917. After her death Yeats wrote a poem about her and her sister Eva, who had died the previous year, reflecting on the happy times he had spent in their family home, Lissadell in County Sligo, many years earlier, and lamenting what he regarded as their wasted lives. That poem is quoted further on.

'This man' in line 24 is Patrick Pearse (1879–1916), Gaelic scholar and schoolteacher, and Commander-in-Chief of the rebel forces. He was executed on 3 May 1916.

'This other his helper and friend' in line 26 is Thomas MacDonagh (1876–1916), who was a poet and a teacher of English in University College, Dublin. He was also executed on 3 May 1916.

'This other man' in line 31 is John MacBride (1865–1916), who married Maud Gonne. He was executed on 5 May 1916.

'Connolly' in the fifth last line is James Connolly (1870–1916), trade-union leader and organiser of the workers' Citizen Army. He was executed on 12 May 1916.

In the same volume, *Michael Robartes and the Dancer*, there is a rather strange short poem called 'The Second Coming', which Yeats wrote in January 1919. He had become very interested in world history, particularly the rise and fall of civilisations, and came to believe that history is cyclical and that civilisations rise and fall every 2,000 years or so. That may help to explain the thinking behind this poem:

Turning and turning in the widening gyre
The falcon cannot hear the falconer;
Things fall apart; the centre cannot hold;
Mere anarchy is loosed upon the world,
The blood-dimmed tide is loosed, and everywhere
The ceremony of innocence is drowned;
The best lack all conviction, while the worst
Are full of passionate intensity.

Surely some revelation is at hand;
Surely the Second Coming is at hand.
The Second Coming! Hardly are those words out
When a vast image out of *Spiritus Mundi*
Troubles my sight: somewhere in sands of the desert
A shape with lion body and the head of a man,
A gaze blank and pitiless as the sun,
Is moving its slow thighs, while all about it
Reel shadows of the indignant desert birds.
The darkness drops again; but now I know
That twenty centuries of stony sleep
Were vexed to nightmare by a rocking cradle,
And what rough beast, its hour come round at last,
Slouches towards Bethlehem to be born?

The despondent (and fundamentally anti-Christian) note in that poem may have arisen, not only from his religious-philosophical opinions, but from the appalling loss of life in the First World War (which had just ended) and from the unsettled conditions in Ireland at the time.

This is the text of 'In Memory of Eva Gore-booth and Con Markiewicz,' mentioned earlier, written in 1927 and included in the volume *The Winding Stair and Other Poems*, published in 1933:

The light of evening, Lissadell,
Great windows open to the south,
Two girls in silk kimonos, both
Beautiful, one a gazelle.
But a raving autumn shears
Blossom from the summer's wreath;
The older is condemned to death,
Pardoned, drags out lonely years
Conspiring among the ignorant.
I know not what the younger dreams –
Some vague Utopia – and she seems,
When withered old and skeleton-gaunt,
An image of such politics.
Many a time I think to seek
One or the other out and speak
Of that old Georgian mansion, mix

Pictures of the mind, recall
That table and the talk of youth,
Two girls in silk kimonos, both
Beautiful, one a gazelle.

Dear shadows, now you know it all,
All the folly of a fight
With a common wrong or right.
The innocent and the beautiful
Have no enemy but time;
Arise and bid me strike a match
And strike another till time catch;
Should the conflagration climb,
 Run till all the sages know.
We the great gazebo built,
They convicted us of guilt;
Bid me strike a match and blow.

MARRIAGE

When Maud Gonne became a widow as a result of the execution of John MacBride, Yeats went to visit her in France in 1917 and asked her once again to marry him. She turned down his proposal but made it clear that she wished to continue their friendship. A few days later he asked her whether she would object if he proposed to her daughter Iseult, then aged 22. She was, of course, surprised and mentioned that Iseult might not take him seriously. Nevertheless, he proposed to Iseult, who was flattered but, after an interval, decided against.

Yeats was not really a philanderer (except perhaps towards the end of his life) but, in addition to his relationship with Mrs Shakespear in 1895, he had a few other affairs. His friends Lady Gregory and Mrs Shakespear felt that this was not a satisfactory situation for him and encouraged him to get married. Lady Gregory even introduced him to some women who might be suitable, but without success. Mrs Shakespear felt that a young woman named Georgie Hyde-Lees, already known to Yeats, would be a very suitable wife for him. Georgie was an English woman, 27 years younger than Yeats, who had first met Yeats in 1911 and who was attracted to him. They had a common interest in philosophy and occultism, and Yeats had encouraged her to join the Golden Dawn in 1914. She was attractive, intelligent and well educated, and had a sense of humour.

Yeats, now aged 52, was in favour of marrying and felt that Georgie Hyde-Lees, who was fond of him, would be a good wife; they were married in a London registry office on 20 October 1917. Ezra Pound, friend of Yeats and Joyce, was best man.

For a brief period after the marriage Yeats had doubts about the wisdom of his decision, but these soon disappeared and they had a happy married life together. They had two children: Anne, born in Dublin in 1919 and Michael, born in Thame, near Oxford, in 1921.

Within a few days of their marriage Mrs Yeats began to try automatic writing, i.e. the writing of messages purporting to come from a spirit who took control of the medium's writing hand. Yeats describes it as follows in his Introduction to *A Vision* (*A Vision* itself will be discussed in more detail later):

> On the afternoon of October 24th 1917, four days after my marriage, my wife surprised me by attempting automatic writing. What came in disjointed sentences, in almost illegible writing, was so exciting, sometimes so profound, that I persuaded her to give an hour or two day after day to the unknown writer, and after some half-dozen such hours offered to spend what remained of life explaining and piecing together those scattered sentences. 'No,' was the answer, 'we have come to give you metaphors for poetry.' The unknown writer took his theme at first from my just published *Per Amica Silentia Lunae*. I had made a distinction between the perfection that is from a man's combat with himself and that which is from a combat with circumstance, and upon this simple distinction he built up an elaborate classification of men according to their more or less complete expression of one type or another.

Yeats exhorted his wife to continue this automatic writing, but she became bored with it and suggested that he should write more poetry, an aspect of his life that he was tending to neglect. However, Yeats continued to devote time to these explorations of the spirit world.

The newly married couple lived at first in Oxford, where they took a house in Broad Street in January 1918. Later that year they crossed to Ireland and lived in Dublin for a while. A few years earlier Yeats had purchased from the Congested Districts Board an old ruined tower, with a cottage attached to it, near Gort in County Galway, only a few miles away from Coole Park. They decided to renovate the old tower, called Thoor Ballylee, and use it as a summer home. To meet the cost of the restoration work he undertook another lecture tour in America, with his wife, from October 1919 to May 1920. He spoke about his own poetry, which was widely acclaimed.

In February 1921 Yeats was one of the speakers at an Oxford Union debate on a motion 'That this House would welcome self-government for Ireland and condemns reprisals'. He supported the motion and criticised the British government for the atrocities carried out by the Black and Tans. He was applauded and the motion was carried by a large majority.

A Treaty between the British government and representatives of the 'elected Government of the Republic of Ireland' was signed on 6 December 1921, providing for the establishment of an Irish Free State, covering 26 of the 32 counties in Ireland, within the British commonwealth. (Northern Ireland had been established a few months earlier by the British Parliament, under the Government of Ireland Act, 1920.) There was, however, strong opposition to this Treaty by the more extreme republicans, led by Eamonn De Valera, and this resulted in a murderous civil war during 1922 and 1923.

Yeats favoured the Treaty and accepted an invitation by the Irish Government to become a member of the new Irish Senate, to which he was appointed for a period of six years. He was pleased with this honour and took his position as Senator seriously. He spoke on many occasions in the Senate, including a speech in 1925 strongly criticising the Government for bringing in a Bill prohibiting divorce in the Free State. Yeats regarded this Bill as an infringement of the civil rights of Protestants in the State and put his point as follows:

> We [Protestants] against whom you have done this thing are no petty people. We are one of the great stocks of Europe. We are the people of Burke: we are the people of Grattan: we are the people of Swift, the people of Emmet, the people of Parnell. We have created the most of the modern literature of this country. We have created the best of its political intelligence.

The Yeatses lived in Oxford until early in 1922, when they bought one of the Georgian houses (No. 82) in Merrion Square, Dublin.

In 1923 he was awarded the Nobel Prize for literature which brought him a useful sum of money. After the conferring ceremony he spoke to the Swedish Royal Academy on the subject of the Irish Dramatic Movement. The first paragraph of this speech encapsulates his thoughts about the beginnings of the Irish theatre:

> The modern literature of Ireland, and indeed all that stir of thought which prepared for the Anglo-Irish war, began when Parnell fell from power in 1891. A disillusioned and embittered Ireland turned from parliamentary politics; an event was conceived; and the race began, as I think, to be troubled by that event's long gestation. Dr Hyde founded the Gaelic League, which was for many years to substitute for political argument a Gaelic grammar, and for political meetings village gatherings, where song were sung and stories told in the Gaelic language. Meanwhile I had begun a movement in English, in the language in which modern Ireland thinks and does its business; founded certain societies where clerks, working men, men of all classes, could study the Irish poets, novelists and historians who had written in English, and as much of Gaelic literature as had been translated into English. But the great mass of our people, accustomed to interminable political speeches, read little, and so from the very start we felt that we must

have a theatre of our own. The theatres of Dublin had nothing about them that we could call our own. They were empty buildings hired by the English travelling companies, and we wanted Irish plays and Irish players. When we thought of these plays we thought of everything that was romantic and poetical, because the nationalism we had called up – the nationalism every generation had called up in moments of discouragement – was romantic and poetical. It was not, however, until I met in 1896 Lady Gregory, a member of an old Galway family, who had spent her life between two Galway houses, the house where she was born, the house into which she married, that such a theatre became possible. All about her lived a peasantry who told stories in a form of English which has much of its syntax from Gaelic, much of its vocabulary from Tudor English, but it was very slowly that we discovered in that speech of theirs our most powerful dramatic instrument, not indeed until she herself began to write. Though my plays were written without dialect and in English blank verse, I think she was attracted to our movement because their subject-matter differed but little from the subject-matter of the country stories.[7]

In the same year, the Abbey Theatre produced the first of Sean O'Casey's highly successful plays, *The Shadow of a Gunman*, a tragi-comedy in two acts. This was followed by *Juno and the Paycock* in 1924 and by *The Plough and the Stars* in 1926, both of which were acclaimed. (*The Plough* is regarded by many as one of the best plays of the twentieth century.)

There was some criticism of O'Casey's plays by people who felt they showed Irish characters, and their motives, in a bad light. The strongest objection was to *The Plough*, which was booed and hissed by many in the audience who tried to stop its performance. During the tumult Yeats came on to the stage and said to the objectors: 'You have disgraced yourselves again. Is this to be an ever-recurring celebration of the arrival of Irish genius? Synge first, and then O'Casey. The news of the happenings of the past few minutes will go from country to country. Dublin has once more rocked the cradle of genius.' His remarks could not be heard but were published in the *Irish Times*.

Early in 1928 Yeats and his family went to stay in Rapallo, Italy, to recuperate from congestion of the lungs and influenza. He continued to be subject to lung congestion and spent several winters abroad in sunnier climes.

The volume *The Tower*, published in 1928, contains some of his best poetry, including poems which show Yeats in a dissatisfied frame of mind, despite his achievements. One of the best-known poems in it is 'Sailing to Byzantium':

> That is no country for old men. The young
> In one another's arms, birds in the trees,
> – Those dying generations – at their song,

The salmon-falls, the mackerel-crowded seas,
Fish, flesh, or fowl, commend all summer long
Whatever is begotten, born, and dies.
Caught in that sensual music all neglect
Monuments of unageing intellect.

An aged man is but a paltry thing,
A tattered coat upon a stick, unless
Soul clap its hands and sing, and louder sing
For every tatter in its mortal dress,
Nor is there singing school but studying
Monuments of its own magnificence;
And therefore I have sailed the seas and come
To the holy city of Byzantium.

O sages standing in God's holy fire
As in the gold mosaic of a wall,
Come from the holy fire, perne in a gyre,
And be the singing-masters of my soul.
Consume my heart away; sick with desire
And fastened to a dying animal
It knows not what it is; and gather me
Into the artifice of eternity.

Once out of nature I shall never take
My bodily form from any natural thing,
But such a form as Grecian goldsmiths make
Of hammered gold and gold enamelling
To keep a drowsy Emperor awake;
Or set upon a golden bough to sing
To lords and ladies of Byzantium
Of what is past, or passing, or to come.

The volume also includes the following two poems which show his ability to write poetry on simple themes: one about his restored tower at Thoor Ballylee and the other about his two young children.

MY HOUSE

An ancient bridge, and a more ancient tower,
A farmhouse that is sheltered by its wall,
An acre of stony ground,
Where the symbolic rose can break in flower,
Old ragged elms, old thorns innumerable,
The sound of the rain or sound
Of every wind that blows;
The stilted water-hen
Crossing stream again
Scared by the splashing of a dozen cows;

A winding stair, a chamber arched with stone,
A grey stone fireplace with an open hearth,
A candle and written page.
Il Penseroso's Platonist toiled on
In some like chamber, shadowing forth
How the daemonic rage
Imagined everything.
Benighted travellers
From markets and from fairs
Have seen his midnight candle glimmering.

Two men have founded here. A man-at-arms
Gathered a score of horse and spent his days
In this tumultuous spot,
Where through long wars and sudden night alarms
His dwindling score and he seemed castaways
Forgetting and forgot;
And I, that after me
My bodily heirs may find,
To exalt a lonely mind,
Befitting emblems of adversity.

MY DESCENDANTS

Having inherited a vigorous mind
From my old fathers, I must nourish dreams
And leave a woman and a man behind
As vigorous of mind, and yet it seems
Life scarce can cast a fragrance on the wind,
Scarce spread a glory to the morning beams,
But the torn petals strew the garden plot;
And there's but common greenness after that.

And what if my descendants lose the flower
Through natural declension of the soul,
Through too much business with the passing hour,
Through too much play, or marriage with a fool?
May this laborious stair and this stark tower
Become a roofless ruin that the owl
May build in the cracked masonry and cry
Her desolation to the desolate sky.

The Primum Mobile that fashioned us
Has made the very owls in circles move;
And I, that count myself most prosperous,
Seeing that love and friendship are enough,
For an old neighbour's friendship chose the house
And decked and altered it for a girl's love,
And know whatever flourish and decline
These stones remain their monument and mine.

An important event in 1928 was the submission to the Abbey of a new play by Sean O'Casey called *The Silver Tassie*. O'Casey, having had three plays successfully produced at the Abbey, was understandably annoyed when Yeats turned down his new play on the grounds that its theme (the First World War) was outside O'Casey's own experience and that therefore the play was based on opinions. O'Casey, who was then living in London, was furious and published the rejection letter from Yeats. As a result of this disagreement, O'Casey's attitude towards the Abbey Theatre became vengeful and continued so for many years afterwards. (The Abbey did eventually stage *The Silver Tassie*, which is a good play but not as captivating as his earlier plays).

Yeats's term of office as Senator ended in 1928, which meant that his allowance of £360 a year ceased. They decided to sell their house at 82 Merrion Square as it was too large for their needs. For the following few years they stayed in a flat in Fitzwilliam Square (with winter periods abroad) and, in 1932, leased an old farmhouse, with beautiful gardens, at Rathfarnham, on the south side of Dublin city, overlooked by the Dublin mountains. It was to be his last residence.

After wintering in Rapallo they returned to Ireland in the spring of 1929, and Yeats paid his last visit to Thoor Ballylee. During the following winter in Rapallo he contracted Maltese fever and had to stay in bed for several weeks. By the spring he had recovered sufficiently to embark on writing another play, *The Words upon the Window Pane*, which was successfully performed at the Abbey in December 1930. The play portrays a seance in an old house in Dublin conducted by a medium, Mrs Henderson, which is attended by six people with different motives for taking part. Through the medium's mouth the spirits of Swift, Stella and Vanessa speak. Swift is quoted as saying, 'I have something in my blood that no child must inherit,' to explain why he had refused to marry Vanessa. Other quotes reflect Swift's loneliness and isolation in old age. Yeats, as he grew older, came to have a high regard for Swift. Indeed, he held eighteenth-century Ireland, when Swift, Berkeley, Burke and Goldsmith were alive, to be the high point of Anglo-Irish culture.

When *The Words upon the Window Pane* was published shortly afterwards he wrote a lengthy introduction in which he praised Swift's political ideas and went on to comment on the credibility of seances. He clearly believed that such spirits exist and can contact human beings through a medium. He posed the following rhetorical question to himself: 'If I had allowed some character [in the play] to speak my thoughts, what would he have said?', and answered:

It seems to me that after reading many books and meeting many phenomena, some in my own house, some when alone in my room, I can see clearly at last. I consider it certain that every voice that speaks, every form that appears, whether to the medium's eyes and ears alone or to some one or two others or to all present, whether it remains a sight or sound or affects the sense of touch, whether it is confined to the room or can make itself apparent at some distant place, whether it can or cannot alter the position of material objects, is first of all a secondary personality or dramatisation created by, in, or through the medium[7]

To confirm his belief in the authenticity of these manifestations he wrote at the end of the introduction:

The Indian pilgrim has not deceived us; he did hear the bed where the sage of his devotion slept a thousand years ago creak as though someone turned over in it, and he did see – he himself and the old shrine-keeper – the blankets all tossed about at dawn as if someone had just risen; the Irish country-woman did see the ruined castle lit up, the bridge across the river dropping; those two Oxford ladies did find themselves in the garden of the Petit Trianon with Marie Antoinette and her courtiers, see that garden as those saw it; the gamekeeper did hear those footsteps the other night that sounded like the footsteps of a stag where stag has not passed these hundred years. All about us there seems to start up a precise inexplicable teeming life, and the earth becomes once more, not in rhetorical metaphor, but in reality, sacred.

But a sceptic may reasonably enquire what worthwhile knowledge or insight is derived from the sound of creaks or footsteps or other such phenomena.

TOWARDS OLD AGE

During the winters of 1930 and 1931 Yeats did not go abroad because Lady Gregory's health was poor and he wished to be at hand in case of need. During the autumn and winter of 1931–32 he spent most of his time in Coole. Lady Gregory's health deteriorated and she died, aged 80, on 22 May 1932, while Yeats happened to be in Dublin on business. They had been great friends since their first meeting in 1896 and he grieved for her. Her prolonged personal interest in him had transformed his life, particularly as regards playwriting.

A few months later he undertook another lecture tour in America to raise funds for the Irish Academy of Letters, which he, Shaw and Russell had founded. (Joyce was asked to become a founding member but refused.)

In 1933 the volume *The Winding Stair and Other Poems* was published. He continued to pay visits to London where he had many friends, and where he was recognised as a poet of genius. He took care of his appearance and was always well dressed, usually with a large hat.

Under the influence of the dictators Mussolini and Hitler, Fascism as a political creed was then a matter of political controversy. Many people were dazzled by its successes, which were more apparent than real. In Ireland a movement commonly called 'The Blueshirts' came into being in 1933, under the leadership of General Eoin O'Duffy, who had been sacked as Commissioner of Police by President De Valera. Yeats favoured government by people of education and status rather than by the multitude, and was sympathetic towards the Blueshirts whom he considered defenders of public order, though he changed his opinion of them later.

In 1934 Yeats began to worry about his declining sexual potency, which he feared might also diminish his poetic power. One of his friends suggested that he might consider an operation for rejuvenation which an Austrian physiologist, Eugen Steinach, had introduced some years earlier. Yeats consulted a London surgeon who had carried out a number of these operations (which were, in fact, vasectomies) and agreed to go ahead with it. He believed the result of the operation was successful, both sexually and poetically, but whether this was psychological rather than physical is uncertain. Yeats had affairs with a few women in his later years, which his understanding and patient wife tolerated because of her belief in his genius.

He accepted an invitation to compile and edit *The Oxford Book of Modern Verse* and spent many months reading the poetry written since Tennyson's death. The anthology was published in 1936 and was criticised as being too much influenced by personal friendships. For example, it contained several poems by his friends Oliver St John Gogarty and Dorothy Wellesley, but none by Austin Clarke or Wilfred Owen. Jeffares says, 'It remains an eccentric book.' Yeats's introduction to this anthology is contained in Jeffares's prose selection[7].

Yeats reached 70 years of age in 1935 and, though his health was not good, he continued to write with undiminished vigour. In November 1935 he went to Majorca to assist an Indian sage, Shri Purohit Swami, to write a new English translation of the *Upanishads*. He was seriously ill in January 1936 but recovered, and in April wrote to Olivia Shakespear: 'I have no consciousness of age, no sense of declining energy, no conscious need of rest.'

A VISION

The first edition of this extraordinary book appeared in 1926, based largely on the messages and answers obtained from Mrs Yeats's automatic writing and from things she said in her sleep. In the first edition Yeats did not disclose his wife's role as a medium, but when he prepared a revised edition later on he informed readers of his wife's automatic writing. She had raised objections to this being revealed but Yeats prevailed upon her to agree. The revised edition was published in 1937.

Yeats regarded *A Vision* as one of his most important works, in which he set out the religious and philosophical conclusions he had reached over the years. It is a difficult book to understand, but it is clear Yeats believed that people's personalities are linked to the different phases of the moon (though he does not explain clearly how this occurs). The book is divided into sections. Book 1 is entitled 'The Great Wheel' and contains a detailed commentary on each of the 28 phases of the moon and their connection with different types of personality. For instance, Yeats nominates Walt Whitman as an example of phase six; for phase seven Alexandre Dumas and Thomas Carlye are examples; for phase eight the example is 'the idiot of Dostoieffsky perhaps'; for phase nine it is 'an unnamed artist'; for phase ten it is Parnell; for phase eleven the examples are Spinoza and Savonarola, and for phase twelve it is Nietzsche. And so on. No example is given for phase fifteen (Full Moon), which Yeats says is a phase of 'complete beauty'.

After further sections on different aspects of his philosophic system, there follows a one-page epilogue entitled 'The End of the Cycle' in which Yeats expresses a mood of reflection, or perhaps uncertainty, as follows:

> Day after day I have sat in my chair turning a symbol over in my mind, exploring all its details, defining and again defining its elements, testing my convictions and those of others by its unity, attempting to substitute particulars for an abstraction like that of algebra. I have felt the convictions of a lifetime melt though at an age when the mind should be rigid, and others take their place, and these in turn give way to others. How far can I accept socialistic or communistic prophecies? I remember the decadence Balzac foretold to the Duchesse de Castries. I remember debates in the little coach-house at Hammersmith or at Morris' supper-table afterwards. I remember the Apocalyptic dreams of the Japanese saint and labour leader Kagawa, whose books were lent me by a Galway clergyman. I remember a Communist described by Captain White in his memoirs ploughing on the Cotswold Hills, nothing on his great hairy body but sandals and a pair of drawers, nothing in his head but Hegel's *Logic*. Then I draw myself up into the symbol and it seems as if I should know all if I could but banish such memories and find everything in the symbol.

> But nothing comes – though this moment was to reward me for all my toil. Perhaps I am too old. Surely something would have come when I meditated under the direction of the Cabalists. What discords will drive Europe to that artificial unity – only dry or drying sticks can be tied into a bundle – which is the decadence of every civilisation? How work out upon the phases the gradual coming and increase of the counter-movement, the antithetical multiform influx:

> Should Jupiter and Saturn meet,
> O what a crop of mummy wheat!

Then I understand. I have already said all that can be said. The particulars are the work of the Thirteenth Cone or cycle which is in every man and called by every man his freedom. Doubtless, for it can do all things and knows all things, it knows what it will do with its own freedom but it has kept the secret.

Shall we follow the image of Heracles that walks through the darkness bow in hand, or mount to that other Heracles, man, not image, he that has for his bride Hebe, 'The daughter of Zeus the mighty and Hera shod with gold'?

One must admire Yeats for the amount of effort he put into the writing of *A Vision*, but it is an exceedingly difficult work to comprehend or to make sense of.

One helpful attempt to explain it is *The Mystery Religion of W.B. Yeats by Graham Hough*[8]. The following are short quotations from that book:

It is thus possible to see, behind the bewildering accumulation of lists, spells, exotic nomenclature and incantation with which the Golden Dawn snowed up its neophytes, the outline of a system of correspondences which is in principle capable of absorbing the religions of the world, because it goes deeper than the particulars of any of them, down to their psychic roots. In short, what we are offered by these central Cabalistic presuppositions of the Golden Dawn is a sort of ground-plan, a skeleton outline, on which an immense range of myth, religion and speculative philosophy can be projected. The value of this to Yeats was inestimable. From childhood on he had been assembling a miscellany of legendary material from which he hoped to extract a philosophy of life. Here he found an organising principle capable of bringing all together, capable too of satisfying both sides of his nature – the propensity to dream, and to expand his dream until it included everything; and the other propensity, much less noted in commentary on Yeats, to systematise, to order, to bring all the vagaries of reverie under a single rule.

It is this fusion of a free exploration of all the varieties of human experience with a predestined cosmic scheme that gives all Yeats's poetry, from the first to the last, its peculiar density and weight. Much later, at the time of the first version of *A Vision*, he came to realise clearly the object of his occult researches: 'I wished for a system of thought that would leave my imagination free to create as it chose, and yet make all that it created, or could create, part of one history, and that the soul's.'

Some literary critics, who otherwise admired Yeats's writings, have referred to *A Vision* as muddled or exasperating. A recent critical introduction to Yeats by Professor Stan Smith of Dundee University includes the following comments on it: 'This much rewritten book is in reality a fascinating and infuriating mish-mash of many traditional ideas, including much half-baked historical and metaphysical speculation and a great amount of intellectual garbage.[9]

LAST POEMS

Though his health was declining in old age, Yeats continued to write poetry. The volume *Parnell's Funeral and other Poems* was published in 1935, followed by *New Poems* in 1938.

His final volume, *Last Poems*, was published posthumously in 1939. This last volume contains 'Under Ben Bulben', the last two verses of which are well known:

> Irish poets, learn your trade,
> Sing whatever is well made,
> Scorn the sort now growing up
> All out of shape from toe to top,
> Their unremembering hearts and heads
> Base-born products of base beds.
> Sing the peasantry, and then
> Hard-riding country gentlemen,
> The holiness of monks, and after
> Porter-drinkers' randy laughter;
> Sing the lords and ladies gay
> That were beaten into the clay
> Through seven heroic centuries;
> Cast your mind on other days
> That we in coming days may be
> Still the indomitable Irishry.
>
> Under bare Ben Bulben's head
> In Drumcliff churchyard Yeats is laid,
> An ancestor was rector there
> Long years ago, a church stands near,
> By the road an ancient Cross.
> No marble, no conventional phrase,
> On limestone quarried near the spot
> By his command these words are cut:
>
> *Cast a cold eye*
> *On life, on death*
> *Horseman, pass by!*

During 1937 he broadcast several times on BBC radio. In the following year he wrote a one-act play, *Purgatory*, and was present at its production in the Abbey in August, when he addressed the audience from the stage for the last time. Maud Gonne visited him in Rathfarnham and afterwards wrote that he was 'sitting in his armchair from which he could rise only with great effort'. His close friend, Olivia Shakespear, died in October 1938, aged 75.

Kidney trouble confined him to his room for a while, but after a visit to England he and his wife left to spend the winter on the Riviera. Their son Michael came to visit them, and they also met several Irish and English friends there. Yeats enjoyed these visits but tired easily. In a letter to Lady Elizabeth Pelham (a friend of the Indian Swami) dated 4 January 1939 he wrote: 'When I try to put all into a phrase I say, "Man can embody truth but cannot know it." I must embody it in the completion of my life. The abstract is not life and everywhere draws out its contradictions. You can refute Hegel but not the Saint or the Song of Sixpence.'

He completed the poem 'The Black Tower' on Saturday, 21 January, and read it to his wife and some friends. By Thursday his condition was poor and his speech wandered. Next day he was given morphia to relieve pain, and was very breathless. He died on Saturday, 28 January 1939.

He was buried at Roquebrune cemetery, pending later transfer to Ireland, but due to the Second World War his remains were not brought back to Ireland, for burial in Drumcliff, County Sligo, until September 1948.

BIBLIOGRAPHY

(1) A. Norman Jeffares, *W.B. Yeats: A New Biography*. Hutchinson, London, 1988.

(2) Richard Ellmann, *Yeats: The Man and the Masks*. Macmillan, 1949, Norton & Co, 1979 (with new preface), and Penguin Books, 1979.

(3) Denis Donoghue (ed.), *W.B. Yeats: Memoirs*. Macmillan, London, 1972.

(4) John Unterecker, *A Reader's Guide to William Butler Yeats*. Thames & Hudson, London, 1959.

(5) Daniel Albright, *W.B. Yeats: The Poems*. Dent & Sons, London, 1990.

(6) Micheál MacLiammoir and Eavan Boland, *W.B. Yeats and his World*. Thames & Hudson, London, 1971.

(7) A. Norman Jeffares (ed.), *W.B. Yeats: Selected Criticism and Prose*. Pan Books, 1980.

(8) Graham Hough, *The Mystery Religion of W.B. Yeats*. Harvester Press, Sussex, 1984.

(9) Stan Smith, *W.B. Yeats: A Critical Introduction*. Gill & Macmillan, Dublin, 1990.

JAMES JOYCE
(1882–1941)

James Joyce is widely regarded as one of the twentieth century's out-standing writers. His fame is based to a large extent on his novel *Ulysses*, not only because of the many and varied characters it depicts against the background of Dublin city in the year 1904, but because of the manner in which the story was written. He recounted the movements, moods and comments of his principal characters, particularly Leopold Bloom and Stephen Dedalus, and also the thoughts and associated ideas that passed through their minds. He wrote sections of the book in different literary styles. *Ulysses* is not an easy book to read but is well worth the effort involved. It contains many scenes of daily life in Dublin at that time which are remarkably true to life, and passages of great humour.

Joyce wrote two other notable works before he tackled Ulysses: a collection of short stories, entitled *Dubliners*, and a novel about youthful life called *A Portrait of the Artist as a Young Man*. His final work, *Finnegans Wake*, on which he spent many years, is a completely different literary effort: tortuously written and extremely difficult to understand, it is nevertheless regarded as one of the most important books of the century.

Joyce himself was an interesting character. From an early age he was determined to become a great writer, and succeeded, but not without a great deal of effort and many disappointments, not least being his own serious eye troubles and his daughter's schizophrenia.

Joyce's father, John Stanislaus Joyce (1849–1931), was an only child, born and reared in Cork city, where he received a good education, including three years in Queen's College, Cork, studying medicine (unsuccess-fully). At college he took a keen interest in sports and amateur dramatics. When John's father died in 1866, at the age of 39, he left a number of small properties in Cork which gave John an income of about £315 a year, reasonable amount at that time. Also, when John reached 21 years of age, four years later, he received £1,000 from his grandfather's estate. In other words, James Joyce's father was fairly well off before he got married, but this comparative affluence deteriorated in later years, due to drink, loss of employment, improvidence, and the expense of rearing a large family.

Around 1874 John's widowed mother decided to leave Cork and live in Dublin, with her son. She got a house in Dalkey, then a quaint coastal village just south of Dublin city, where John had his own boat. He had a good tenor voice and took singing lessons. He was also interested in politics and became secretary of the United Liberal Club in Dublin. After helping in the election of two Liberal members to the British House of Commons in 1880, he was rewarded by being nominated by the new Lord Lieutenant as a Rates Collector in Dublin, at a good salary.

Around that time John usually sang in the choir during Sunday Mass at the Church of the Three Patrons, Rathgar, where he met and fell in love with a young woman named Mary Jane Murray (1859–1903), who lived in Clanbrassil Street. Her father, John Murray, a Longford man, was an agent for wines and spirits. She was educated in a small private school at Usher's Island (which was to be the location of Joyce's famous short story 'The Dead') and learned the piano, singing and dancing. Like many other mothers of large families she turned out to be the stable centre of the Joyce household, where her husband was careless and too fond of drink.

Mary Murray's father tried to discourage her from marrying John Joyce, because he was already a heavy drinker. John Joyce's mother strongly disapproved of the marriage, because she felt that Mary Murray was not good enough for her son. However, the couple liked each other and were married in the Catholic Church in Rathmines, on 5 May, 1880. They lived for a short while at 13 Ontario Terrace, Rathmines, and then at 47 Northumberland Avenue, Dun Laoghaire (then called Kingstown). In 1882 they moved to 41 Brighton Square, Rathgar; in 1884, to 23 Castlewood Avenue, and in 1887 to 1 Martello Terrace, Bray. In subsequent years they moved to several other addresses on the north side of the city, where rents were lower. Mr Joyce's difficulties in meeting arrears of rent were the main cause of these moves. It is not surprising that James would become very familiar with the different parts of Dublin city.

James Augustine Joyce was born on 2 February 1882, at 41 Brighton Square, Rathgar, a small house in a residential area of the south side of Dublin city. He was the eldest of ten children, four boys and six girls, all born between 1882 and 1893. (Another baby boy was born before James, but survived only a few weeks.) James was baptised on 5 February in St Joseph's Catholic Church, Terenure.

Some of the children disliked their father. Stanislaus, the second son, almost three years younger than James, despised him, as is clear from his book *My Brother's Keeper*[1], but James was fond of his father. He loved his mother, but when he lost his religious faith during adolescence his attitude towards her was rather hard-hearted.

CLONGOWES

John Joyce was anxious that his sons should have a good education and decided to send James to one of the best schools in Ireland, Clongowes Wood, a residential college standing in its own spacious grounds, near Clane, County Kildare, which was staffed by the Jesuit Fathers (Society of Jesus). The parents brought him to Clongowes on 1 September, 1888, when he was six and a half years old (which was six months below the usual minimum age for admission) and he was accepted at a reduced fee of £25 a year, an amount which Mr Joyce could readily afford at that time. The parents' decision to send James to be educated by the Jesuits turned out to be pivotal in the writer's intellectual and artistic development, a point which he himself recognised in later years, even though he rejected their religious teachings.

Joyce was the youngest and the smallest boy in Clongowes. He was a good pupil, though apparently not an outstanding one. Cricket and gravel football (a form of loosely organised football on a gravel pitch, which had been imported from Stonyhurst, the Jesuits' college in Lancashire, and which the young Joyce, probably as a result of his small physique, disliked) were popular games in Clongowes during his time there. Rugby had just been introduced to the college and soon replaced gravel football. Clongowes had its own swimming pool and Joyce became a good swimmer. He was, however, more interested in languages and literature than in games, as is evident from the semi-autobiographical pages of A Portrait of the Artist as a Young Man, in which his interior and exterior experiences in Clongowes (and also Belvedere) are portrayed acutely.

Religious instruction and the fulfilling of religious duties (confession, attendance at Mass, visits to the chapel for prayer) were essential features of school life in Clongowes. (Kevin Sullivan, in his book about Joyce's school and college education, *Joyce among the Jesuits*[2], comments: 'At Clongowes Wood the child was immersed in a deeply religious atmosphere, almost monastic in its intensity.')

The importance of gentlemanly behaviour was also emphasised by the Jesuits. The rules governing behaviour in college were read out regularly to the pupils. One of these rules was:

All are reminded of the very great importance they should attach to politeness and good manners. Politeness and good manners are absolutely essential for a gentleman and equally so for success in life. Great care should be taken to correct faulty pronunciation, slouching gait, and any other defect of the kind ... Politeness requires that all raise their caps when they meet any member of the Community. A gentleman should not require to be reminded of this point of civility ... All should be careful to conduct themselves in a gentlemanly manner while outside the College; therefore throwing stones, climbing trees, shouting, whistling and such like are to be avoided ... Whistling, romping and every sort of rude play are prohibited, likewise slang words and all ungentlemanly and unbecoming language.

Another rule reminded the boys that they were 'expected to show on all occasions that they are no less anxious to be good Irish Catholics than they are to acquire knowledge'.

Joyce spent three years in Clongowes and probably would have remained there to complete his preparatory studies had not his father been informed, in 1891, that his job as a Rates Collector was being abolished, under new civic arrangements. In consequence, Mr Joyce felt he could not afford to continue paying for his son in Clongowes, and the boy was withdrawn from the college towards the end of 1891. Early in 1892 the family moved to 23 Carysfort Avenue, Blackrock, and, about a year later, to 14 Fitzgibbon Street, off Mountjoy Square, on the north side of the city.

For some months after leaving Clongowes, Joyce stayed at home, trying to keep in touch with his education by personal study and reading. The other children of school-going age attended local convent schools.

Only a few hundred yards from Fitzgibbon Street, at North Richmond Street, was a very successful day school for boys run by the Irish Christian Brothers. About the same distance from Fitzgibbon Street, in the opposite direction, was Belvedere College, a Jesuit day-school for boys. Fees were normally payable in Belvedere, whereas the Christian Brothers school in Richmond Street was free. The objective of the Christian Brothers was to educate boys for suitable employment and to teach them the Catholic religion, aims which they successfully achieved for thousands of boys throughout Ireland whose parents were not well off. The Jesuits were also good teachers and paid great attention to Christian doctrine and practice; their scheme of education was directed towards preparing boys to be well-educated Catholic gentlemen, perhaps professional gentlemen. This meant that the boys in Belvedere were expected to continue their education until they could, where feasible, proceed to university. In the 1890s only a small proportion of families, even with the aid of scholarships, could afford to send their sons or daughters to university.

BELVEDERE

After a while Mr Joyce decided to send James and Stanislaus to the nearby Christian Brothers school, but they remained there for only some months. It transpired in the meantime that Mr Joyce met Father John

Conmee, who had been rector of Clongowes while Joyce was there and who had just been transferred to Belvedere. Father Conmee agreed to see what could be done about James and Stanislaus being accepted in Belvedere without having to pay fees. This was accomplished and James and Stanislaus were enrolled as pupils of Belvedere on the same day, 6 April 1893. James was then eleven and remained in Belvedere for five years. (The two other younger Joyce boys, Charles and George, were also accepted into Belvedere without fees.)

With regard to the payment of fees in Clongowes and Belvedere, it is interesting to note the information given by Fr Bruce Bradley, SJ, who was attached to those schools in recent years, in his book *James Joyce's Schooldays*[3]. He says that Joyce was admitted to Clongowes at a special inclusive fee of £25 a year until September 1890 (i.e. two years later), when the full fee of 40 guineas would apply, plus extra payments for schoolbooks, haircuts and piano lessons (Joyce took piano lessons in his last year there).

The school bills were sent to parents twice a year, in September and February. Fr Bradley says that the Clongowes bill sent to Mr Joyce in September 1891, for nearly £30, was not paid, but adds that Mr Joyce's bill 'was very far from being the only bill unpaid and it was certainly not the largest. Apart from accounts not settled, there was also quite a number of pupils who had been received free.' Mr Joyce does not seem to have made approaches to Clongowes about reducing or remitting the fees. This may have been because he knew the financial position of the college was not strong. The provincial of the Order had written to the new rector of Clongowes in September 1891 expressing alarm at the large debt on Clongowes and mentioning the absolute necessity for economies.

Though fees were normally payable in Belvedere, Joyce's admission without fees was not unusual. Fr Bradley says that the Cash Book for 1893–94 shows that several boys in Joyce's class paid no fees and quite a number paid reduced fees. (The fees at that time were £3 per term, for three terms per year.)

The Belvedere prospectus for the year 1888 contained the following information:

BELVEDERE College, Great Denmark Street, is conducted by the Fathers of the Society of Jesus. To parents resident in or near the City of Dublin, who desire to combine in the education of their sons the discipline and teaching of a public school with the very important influences of home life, it offers the advantages of a High Class Grammar School.

The Course of Education comprises the usual Grammar School subjects. In the three Higher Forms boys are prepared for the Intermediate

Examinations. Candidates are also prepared for the Entrance Examinations of the College of Surgeons, for Civil Service Examinations,
Preliminary Examinations for Solicitors' Apprentices etc.

The prospectus gave the following details of the religious exercises in the
college:

EVERY DAY: 9.30 am Mass. 12 am Beads or Instruction.
TUESDAYS: 9 am Sodality of the Holy Angels.
SATURDAYS: 9 am Sodality meeting of Congregation of BVM.
10 to 12 am Confessions. 12 am Benediction of M.H. Sacrament.
First FRIDAY of the month: Benediction of the M.H. Sacrament.
Annual First Communion on the Feast of the Sacred Heart.
ANNUAL RETREAT: Beginning on the 6th October and ending on
the 10th, Feast of St Francis Borgia.

Parents are earnestly requested to co-operate, in the following particulars, with the Master of the College:

Where apparent remissness in the discharge of religious duties is
observable, especially in the frequentation of the Sacraments, or attendance at daily Mass, the Superior is to be acquainted of it without delay.

If sufficient diligence be not shown in the performance of home-work,
the Prefect of Studies is to be at once informed.

Apologies for school lessons, or absence from College, should not be
sent without grave reason.

The Monthly-Judgment, which will be sent henceforward, will facili-
tate attention to these particulars. Parents are invited to sign it, and, if
necessary, comment on it.

It is quite clear from the above that during the entire school year there
was a strong religious background to the academic studies of the pupils.

Joyce was an exceptionally good student in Belvedere, learning English, Latin, French, Italian and mathematics. He had a number of teachers,
religious and lay, in particular Mr George Dempsey, teacher of English,
who served in Belvedere from 1884 to 1923, a period far longer than any
other teacher there. Joyce won a number of prizes under the annual
examinations conducted by the Intermediate Education Board for Ireland. In 1894 he won an exhibition prize of £20 for his overall total marks.
His total marks in 1895 just squeezed him into the exhibition winners
(164th place for 164 exhibition prizes), which gained him a prize of £20
for three years. In 1897 he won a prize of £3 for the best composition in
Middle Grade and also an exhibition prize of £30 for three years. In 1898
he won a prize of £4 for an essay, though his marks for other subjects
were lower than in previous years.

He was pious and became a member of the Sodality of the Blessed
Virgin Mary. In 1896, age fourteen, he became prefect of the sodality and

tried to live up to the religious and moral standards of the Catholic Church but, like most youths of that age, he experienced strong sexual urges and began to realise the difficulties of harmonising religious faith with sexual desire. It seems that, at the age of sixteen, when he was walking home from the Gaiety Theatre one night, he met a prostitute on the banks of the canal and indulged himself. (Stephen's encounter with a prostitute is described briefly in *A Portrait*.) It seems that this was not an isolated occurrence in the early life of Joyce. His brother Stanislaus, who was a fan of James and very close to him, makes a few references to this matter[1], without going into detail. He mentions James's 'precocious sexual experience', that 'his promiscuous sexual life was open and deliberate', and that his brother 'disliked prostitutes though he had recourse to them'. (Stanislaus himself, though an unbeliever, frowned on such activities.)

In *A Portrait* Joyce devoted 30 pages to a description of the annual retreat for pupils, including long extracts from the sermons about the awfulness of hell. The basis for this account was a retreat given by Fr Cullen in Belvedere in 1896, though Fr Bradley shows that the sermons as quoted in *A Portrait* are more likely to have been taken from a tract about hell written by a seventeenth-century Italian Jesuit, an English translation of which was published in Dublin in 1868. The retreat had a demoralising effect on Joyce and he tried to lead a more chaste life for a while, but the improvement did not last.

In his last year in Belvedere, Joyce and three other students did not turn up for the catechetical examination conducted by the rector, Fr Henry. The latter was furious at this deliberate omission and threatened to exclude them from the entire Intermediate examination. However, the French teacher intervened on their behalf and no action was taken.

Joyce experienced the usual ups and downs with his schoolmates in Belvedere but seems to have got on fairly well with most of them, despite the rather gloomy scenario depicted in *A Portrait*. During his last two years there he became very friendly with the sons and daughters of David Sheehy, a Member of Parliament, two of whose sons attended Belvedere. One son, Richard Sheehy, who knew Joyce in Belvedere and in University College, and who afterwards became a Circuit Court Judge, mentions in his memoirs[5] that Joyce's mood 'alternated between cold, slightly haughty, aloofness and sudden boisterous merriment', that he was fond of practical jokes and had an impish sense of humour.

The Sheehy family held regular social evenings which James and Stanislaus often attended, and at which James sang songs in his excellent tenor voice. He became very fond of one of the Sheehy daughters, Mary, but nothing came of it apart from good-natured friendship. (She afterwards married Thomas Kettle, who is mentioned further on.)

Another school and college friend of Joyce, William G. Fallon, (who became a barrister) recalls that Joyce's antics in the gymnastic class in Belvedere could be most amusing, that he was a good walker and an expert swimmer, and that, though he seemed a little too distant to be a close friend, he always entered into the spirit of things.[5]

Joyce left Belvedere in 1898 and enrolled in University College at 86 St Stephen's Green, which had been placed under the management of the Jesuits in 1883. Kevin Sullivan points out[2] that the Jesuits, 'though burdened with the responsibility of a college, at no time possessed an authority commensurate with their responsibility. They had not, for example, an entirely free hand even in the preparation of the curriculum.' He adds: 'The truth is that the Jesuits, during their quarter of a century on Stephen's Green (1883–1909), were little more than educational caretakers.' The degree examinations were conducted by the Royal University of Ireland until the National University was set up in 1909.

JOYCE AND RELIGION

Even though Joyce came to reject the religious doctrines he had been taught in Clongowes and Belvedere, his writings are permeated with religion. The characters in his books are often portrayed as selfish, sinful Catholics (apart from Leopold Bloom, who is a converted Jew) going about their ordinary lives in Dublin, but they are set against a background that raises in the reader's mind, perhaps unconsciously, the question whether there is any purpose in life other than day-to-day living. Joyce himself, having discounted a religious purpose, concluded that being an artist gave his life a purpose.

On the religious element in Joyce's writings, it is of interest to note the comments made by Thomas Merton, an American convert to Catholicism who became a Cistercian monk, in his outstanding autobiography *Seven Storey Mountain*[6]:

> So then I continued to read Joyce, more and more fascinated by the pictures of priests and Catholic life that came up here and there in his books. That, I am sure, will strike many people as a strange thing indeed. I think Joyce himself was only interested in rebuilding the Dublin he had known as objectively and vitally as he could. He was certainly very alive to all the faults in Irish Catholic society, and he had practically no sympathy left for the Church he had abandoned: but in his intense loyalty to the vocation of artist for which he had abandoned it (and the two vocations are not per se irreconcilable: they only became so because of peculiar subjective circumstances in Joyce's own case) he meant to be as accurate as he could in rebuilding his world as it truly was.

Therefore, reading Joyce, I was moving in his Dublin, and breathing the air of its physical and spiritual slums: and it was not the most Catholic side of Dublin that he always painted. But in the background was the Church, and its priests, and its devotions, and the Catholic life in all its gradations, from the Jesuits down to those who barely clung to the hem of the Church's garments. And it was this background that fascinated me now, along with the temper of Thomism that had once been in Joyce himself. If he had abandoned St Thomas, he had not stepped much further down than Aristotle.

Loss of religious faith for a Catholic can be a profound personal upheaval, because it means that one's whole attitude to the meaning of human life has been fundamentally changed. No longer is life seen as having an eternal purpose, but as a finite life on earth to be enjoyed as best one can. Loss of faith sometimes arises out of the conflict between the attractions of the flesh and the teachings of the Church on chastity. It seems clear that Joyce found himself in a dilemma of this kind. In a letter dated 29 August 1904 to Nora Barnacle (which is quoted more fully later on) he said: 'Six years ago I left the Catholic Church, hating it most fervently. I found it impossible for me to remain in it on account of the impulses of my nature.'

Another factor in Joyce's loss of faith may have been the strong anti-clericalism of his father, apparently stemming from the time (1890) when the Irish Catholic clergy spoke out against Parnell, after the Irish Party had split following the Kitty O'Shea divorce case. Parnell died in October 1891, after he had married Mrs O'Shea, leaving a legacy of political bitterness behind him, as is reflected in a scene in *A Portrait*. Some comments by Stanislaus lend credence to this view: 'In his (Jim's) childhood, the vaguely understood drama of Parnell had not stirred any feelings of patriotism or nationalism in his heart; rather, under his father's influence, it had implanted there an early spirit of revolt against hypocrisy and clerical authority and popular servility to it.'[1] Stanislaus, who was strongly attached to James and who lived with the Joyces on the continent for many years, also lost his faith at an early age and became fiercely critical of the Catholic Church.

Kevin Sullivan[2] propounds a different reason for Joyce's loss of faith:

During his four years on Stephen's Green he had lost the faith of his boyhood. Why he lost it is a question to which there can be no simple answer. Part of the answer, however, must surely lie in Father Browne's confession [Father Henry Browne, SJ, professor of Latin and Greek and director of the university sodality when Joyce was there] that religious training at University College 'was defective on the intellectual side', that the students 'had not been in a position to think out its philosophical basis'. Joyce, whose will was as firmly harnessed to his intellect as that of any Jesuit, could never have brought himself 'to do the right deed for the wrong reason' – or, what is worse, for no reason at all. But it must not be thought that he 'rejected' the faith as he had once rejected a vocation to the Jesuit order. The one was a decisive act, clean-cut, definite, and irrevocable. Loss of faith is a slow, wearing-out process, the gradual unravelling of the garment of belief into the strings and threads of skepticism. One can never be sure just when faith is lost, one is sure only that it has been lost.

It is difficult to ascertain when precisely Joyce ceased being a practising Catholic. Joyce's letter to Nora in August 1904 says he ceased believing in the Catholic Church six years earlier, i.e. in 1898. However, William G. Fallon (mentioned above), who knew Joyce in UCD, says he was still a member of the College Sodality in his third year there.

An interesting feature of Joyce's irreligion was that, though he disdained the teachings of the Catholic Church and tried to have his children and grandchildren brought up without being baptised, he maintained an interest in the church's liturgy, and often attended the Easter Week church ceremonies in later years.

UNIVERSITY COLLEGE, DUBLIN

When Joyce became a student at UCD in 1898 it was a small but developing university college, for day pupils, at 86 St Stephen's Green (the same premises where the short-lived Catholic University of Ireland had been established in 1854, with John Henry Newman as its rector; short-lived because it had no endowments and its degrees were not recognised). The chief university in Dublin was Trinity College, which had been established in 1592, but this was attended almost exclusively by Protestants. Catholics were not admitted until 1873, and were discouraged by the Catholic clergy from applying.

At UCD Joyce continued his study of languages and became proficient in Latin, French, Italian and German; he also gained sufficient Norwegian to enable him to read Ibsen's plays in the original. He enjoyed the new-found freedom of a university. He was a good student but adopted a rather condescending attitude towards those in charge of the college. He did not monopolise attention, however, as there were several other outstanding students in UCD during Joyce's four years there. Three of the more noteworthy, for different reasons, were the following:

Thomas Kettle (1880–1916), who was called to the Bar in 1905, became Professor of National Economics in UCD in 1908, elected MP in 1906, toured the USA on behalf of the Irish Nationalist Party, joined the Irish Volunteers in 1913, became an officer in the Dublin Fusiliers after the outbreak of the First World War and was killed in the battle of the Somme in 1916.

Francis Skeffington (1878–1916), a socialist, pacifist and feminist; married Hanna Sheehy (a sister of Mary, who had married Kettle) in 1903; became active in the Irish labour movement and was for a while associated with the Irish Citizen Army. He disagreed with the 1916 Rising and took no part in it except to try to stop looting; nevertheless, he was arrested by the British military under Captain Bowen-Colthurst and, the following morning, without any trial, was executed. Because he was well known as a pacifist there was a public outcry against this murder and demands for an inquiry. Bowen-Colthurst, who had also committed other atrocities, was eventually found guilty but insane.

George Clancy (1879–1921), who was a close friend of Joyce in UCD and became a model for 'Davin' in *A Portrait*; helped to form a branch of the Gaelic League to give lessons in the Irish language, which Joyce attended for a while; he was elected mayor of Limerick in January 1921 but was shot dead at his home by the Black and Tans on 7 March 1921, four months before the truce between British and Irish military forces.

Three other friends of Joyce in UCD were: Constantine Curran, who later became Registrar of the High Court and who took the famous photograph of Joyce as a young man, wearing a cap, with hands in his trouser pockets, standing among potted plants with his back to a garden green house; Vincent Cosgrave, whom Joyce had also known in Belvedere, clever but lazy and who often accompanied Joyce on long walks – later he was drowned in the Thames, apparently by suicide; John Francis Byrne, whom he had also known in Belvedere, good-looking, athletic, clever and self-possessed, and a good listener; his mother died shortly after he entered Belvedere and he went to live with a middle-aged cousin in Essex Street. They later moved to 7 Eccles Street, which became the home of Leopold and Molly Bloom in *Ulysses*; he became 'Cranly' in the *Portrait*.

Joyce joined the UCD Literary and Historical Society and, in January 1900, read a paper on 'Drama and Life'. Shortly before reading this paper he had written to the editor of the *Fortnightly Review* in London enquiring whether he would accept an article about Ibsen's plays. The editor replied that he did not need an article about Ibsen but would consider a review of his new play, *When We Dead Awaken*. Joyce set to work and in April 1900 the *Fortnightly Review* published an article by James A. Joyce entitled 'Ibsen's New Drama', for which he was paid twelve guineas. It was a notable achievement for a youth of eighteen years, and his UCD critics were amazed. To add to Joyce's delight, Henrik Ibsen himself wrote to his English translator, William Archer, thanking the author of the article, which message Archer passed on to Joyce. Joyce wrote to Archer on 28 April, 1900, from his then current address of 13 Richmond Avenue, Fairview, as follows:

> Dear Sir – I wish to thank you for your kindness in writing to me. I am a young Irishman, eighteen years old, and the words of Ibsen I shall keep in my heart all my life. Faithfully yours, Jas. A. Joyce.

He gave £1 from the twelve guineas to his mother and, with the remainder, he and his father went to London, where they enjoyed the theatre and the music halls. He made it his business to call on William Archer.

Shortly afterwards Joyce tried his hand at writing a play, called A Beautiful Career, and sent it to Archer for appraisal. The latter replied at some length, trying to be helpful in his comments, but saying it puzzled him a great deal. Joyce destroyed the play later; he wasn't really a playwright, though his play Exiles, published in 1918, gained some recognition. He tried writing poems and sent them to Archer, who said there was 'as yet more temperament than anything else in your work'. This was at a time when W.B. Yeats (seventeen years older than Joyce) was fast developing his reputation as a poet of genius; his third volume of lyrics, The Wind Among the Reeds, which Joyce greatly admired, had been published in 1899. Joyce was only moderately successful at writing poetry.

In 1899 the Irish Literary Theatre was founded by Lady Gregory, W.B. Yeats and Edward Martyn, and this led to the establishment of the Abbey Theatre in Dublin in 1904. Joyce was more interested in continental playwrights than in the plays about rural Ireland which Martyn and Gregory favoured, and in October 1901 he wrote an article criticising the Irish Literary Theatre for its provincialism. The editor of the college magazine, *St Stephen's*, refused to publish it and, as an article by Francis Skeffington (about equal rights for women in the university) had also been refused, the two young men arranged with a printer to publish the two articles jointly, at their own expense. Joyce's article was called 'The Day of the Rabblement', in which he said that the Irish rabblement, 'the most belated race in Europe', must be countered and not appeased. He went on to find fault with both Yeats and Moore, and was obviously out of sympathy with the then emerging Irish theatre – though he later made some amends.

In November 1901 a society called the Academy of St Thomas Aquinas was set up in UCD and Joyce attended some of its meetings. Joyce was particularly interested in a philosophy of art and aesthetics that could explain the beautiful. His writings, particularly *A Portrait*, indicate that he had a high regard for the thinking of Thomas Aquinas (1226–74). [Joyce's interest in Aquinas is examined in *Joyce and Aquinas* by William T. Noon S.J.[8]].

At a meeting of the Literary and Historical Society in February 1902, he read a paper on the Irish poet James Clarence Mangan (1803–49).

Soon afterwards his young brother, George, not yet fifteen, died from typhoid fever, much to the family's distress. Joyce wrote one of his 'epiphanies' about him:

> They are all asleep. I will go up now ... He lies on my bed where I lay last night; they have covered him with a sheet and closed his eyes with pennies ... Poor little fellow! We have often laughed together. He bore his body very lightly ... I am very sorry he died. I cannot pray for him as the others do. Poor little fellow! Everything else is so uncertain.

After completing his degree in modern languages in mid-1902, Joyce started to attend St Cecilia's Medical School in Dublin, hoping that becoming a doctor might supplement his career as a writer, but he soon lost interest. In November he wrote to Lady Gregory (from 7 St Peter's Terrace, Cabra) informing her that he would be leaving Dublin by the night boat on Monday, 1 December, on his way to study medicine at the University of Paris. He ended his letter with these words:

> I am not despondent however for I know that even if I fail to make my way such failure proves very little. I shall try myself against the powers of the world. All things are inconstant except the faith in the soul, which changes all things and fills their inconstancy with light. And though I seem to have been driven out of my country here as a misbeliever I have found no man yet with a faith like mine.

This was probably the first time he alleged that he was 'driven out' of Ireland, a theme that recurred subsequently, perhaps without much justification.

Lady Gregory replied suggesting that he should consider studying medicine in Trinity College, Dublin, but Joyce was not inclined in that direction. She also suggested that he should call on the editor of the Dublin *Daily Express* (whom she notified), who might be able to give him some work reviewing books – which in fact he did. She wrote to Yeats in London asking him to meet Joyce when he was passing through London and give him a meal. Yeats spent the whole day with Joyce, bought him breakfast, lunch and dinner, and introduced him to Arthur Symons, who afterwards helped to get Joyce's poems published.

PARIS

In Paris he succeeded in getting a provisional card of admission to the Medical School to attend a certificate course in physics, chemistry and biology, but his interest waned rapidly and, in letters home, he began to complain of feeling unwell, and raised the question of going home for

Christmas. The effect of this was that his father had to raise a loan to pay for his trip home. One of his mother's letters to him at that time shows her concern:

> My dear Jim,
>
> If you are disappointed in my letter and if as usual I fail to understand what you would wish to explain, believe me it is not from any want of a longing desire to do so and speak the words you want but as you so often said I am stupid and cannot grasp the great thoughts which are yours much as I desire to do so. Do not wear your soul out with tears but be as usually brave and look hopefully to the future. Let me have a letter by return and for God's sake take care of your health and if you get the little stove be very careful with it.

Joyce arrived home in Dublin on 23 December 1902. Shortly afterwards he had his first meeting with Oliver St John Gogarty (1878–1957). Gogarty had attended UCD but transferred to Trinity College to study medicine. He was a talented, witty young man, who wrote poetry and became a well-known surgeon. Joyce later used him as a model for Buck Mulligan in *Ulysses*.

Joyce returned to Paris on 17 January and eked out an existence giving English lessons to students, while he himself read Ben Jonson's plays and Aristotle's *Metaphysics* and *Poetics*. His mother sent him small sums of money from time to time, apparently raised from the sale of household items, and his father sent him enough to purchase a stove, a saucepan, a plate, a cup and saucer, a knife, fork and spoon, and some groceries.

On 6 March, John Millington Synge arrived in the same hotel (Hotel Corneille) and stayed a week. Synge had already spent a few summers in the Aran Islands, observing the people and learning their modes of speech, and had started writing plays, including the recently completed *Riders to the Sea*. He lent a copy to Joyce, who found fault with its construction as a tragedy. Ellman says they 'parted amicably, respecting and disdaining each other'.

RETURN TO DUBLIN

On Good Friday, 10 April, he received a telegram which said: MOTHER DYING COME HOME FATHER. One of his pupils was good enough to lend him 375 francs and he left Paris next morning. He found his mother to be very ill but not as bad as he had feared. Her doctor thought she was suffering from cirrhosis of the liver, but it transpired she had cancer, from which she died on 13 August 1903, aged 44. When James returned from Paris she tried to persuade him to fulfil his Easter duty by going to Confession and Communion, but he refused. When she was in a coma

Yeats in the early 1930s

Above left: W.B. Yeats, a portrait by his father, John Butler Yeats

Above right: Yeats's Dublin birthplace, 5 Sandymount Avenue

Below: Jack Yeats, the painter, as formidable a talent as his brother

Lilly (Susan) Yeats by John Butler Yeats

Above right: Yeats, with his children Michael and Anne, in the garden at Thoor Ballylee in the 1920s
Above left: Georgiana Hyde-Lees, Mrs Yeats

Below right: Yeats the Magus, the engraved frontispiece by Edmund Dulac for *A Vision*
Below left: Thoor Ballylee, Yeats's symbolic home in Galway

How the Poets Passed: the famous caricature of Yeats and AE as public figures. It was said that Yeats set out from 82 Merrion Square to call on AE, just as AE left 84 Merrion Square to call on Yeats. Neither found the other at home...

Yeats during his last years

James Joyce, a portrait by Pavel Tchelitchev

James Joyce (sitting on the ground in the centre) as the youngest boy at Clongowes

Joyce (standing 2nd from the left) with his college contemporaries

Above: Nora Barnacle, photographed in Galway in 1903, the year before she ran away with Joyce

Above right: James Joyce, photographed by his friend Con Curran. Asked what he was thinking, he replied, 'I was wondering if you would lend me five shillings.'

Right: The Volta, Dublin's first cinematograph, opened by Joyce in 1909

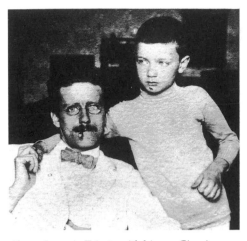

Above: Joyce in Trieste with his son Giorgio

Below right: Four generations of Joyces. James Joyce (on left) with son, Giorgio, and grandson, Stephen (on right), beneath a portrait of his father.
Below left: Joyce's contribution to *Two Essays* was an attack on Yeats and Lady Gregory's National Theatre Movement

Above: Lucia Joyce, the Joyces's daughter, with other student dancers in Paris

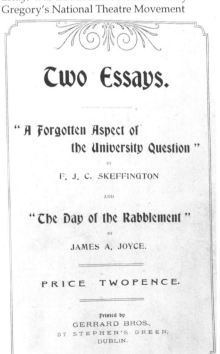

Two Essays.

"A Forgotten Aspect of the University Question"

BY

F. J. C. SKEFFINGTON

AND

"The Day of the Rabblement"

BY

JAMES A. JOYCE.

PRICE TWOPENCE.

Printed by
GERRARD BROS.,
87 STEPHEN'S GREEN,
DUBLIN.

Dean Swift, portrait by Charles Jervas

Left: The house in Hoey's Court behind Dublin Castle in which Swift was born

Below: St Patrick's Cathedral by W. H. Bartlett

Above right: Esther Johnson, Swift's 'Stella'; portrait by James Lathem
Above left: Hester van Homrigh, Swift's 'Vanessa' by Philip Hussey

Above: St Patrick's Hospital, the original aspect photographed at the turn of the century before the recent modernisation

Above: Gulliver in Lilliput: inflatable model of Gulliver landed on Dollymount beach during the Dublin Millenium celebrations in 1988

Left: Swift's memorial, with its famous inscription in St Patrick's Cathedral:
Here lies the body of Jonathan Swift, Dean of this Cathedral, where savage indignation no longer lacerates his heart. Go traveller and imitate, if you can, his strenuous vindication of human liberty

Hic depositum est Corpus
IONATHAN SWIFT S.T.D.
Hujus Ecclesiæ Cathedralis
Decani,
Ubi sæva Indignatio
Ulterius
Cor lacerare nequit.
Abi Viator
Et imitare, si poteris,
Strenuum pro virili
Libertatis Vindicatorem.

Obiit 19 Die Mensis Octobris
A.D. 1745. Anno Ætatis 78.

before dying the members of the family knelt at the bedside, praying for her, but James and Stanislaus did not kneel. Mrs Joyce's brother, John Murray, who was present, told the two sons to kneel down with the others, but they refused to do so. Nevertheless Joyce tried to console his youngest sister, Mabel, aged nine, by telling her: 'You must not cry like that because there is no reason to cry. Mother is in heaven. She is far happier now than she has ever been on earth, but if she sees you crying it will spoil her happiness. You must remember that when you feel like crying. You can pray for her if you wish; mother would like that. But don't cry any more.' [Sad to relate, Mabel died from typhoid eight years later].

The house at 7 St Peter's Terrace had been purchased by Mr Joyce with £900 raised by selling half his pension, but some of the money had been spent foolishly. After Mrs Joyce's death the household became disorganised. Mr Joyce, in desperation, sold the family piano, an act that infuriated James. There were still nine children in the house: three boys (James, Stanislaus and Charles) and six girls (Margaret, May, Florence, Eileen, Eva and Mabel). The eldest girl, Margaret, became responsible for looking after the others, helped by Aunt Josephine. (In 1909 Margaret became a nun in the Sisters of Mercy in New Zealand and died there in 1964.)

Joyce remained in Dublin after his mother's death, still reading and writing. His father often found fault with James and Stanislaus for their indolence. (Stanislaus had given up his job as a clerk in the Apothecaries Hall in January 1904.) In the same month Joyce learned that a new intellectual journal was about to be published in Dublin, and he wrote an autobiographical essay called *A Portrait of the Artist*, which proved to be unacceptable to the editors of the new journal. Nevertheless this story-essay became significant in his literary development, as he later expanded it considerably into *Stephen Hero*, which he jettisoned and re-wrote as *A Portrait of the Artist as a Young Man*. Ellman's comments about this story-essay were : 'At the age of twenty-one Joyce had found he could become an artist by writing about the process of becoming an artist, his life legitimising his portrait by supplying the sitter, while the portrait vindicated the sitter by its evident admiration for him.'[4]

Though Joyce's main ambition was to become a serious writer, he also at times felt he could become a singer. John McCormack, who became a world-famous Irish tenor, had entered for the Feis Ceoil in Dublin in 1903 and had won a scholarship for a year's voice tuition in Italy. This was a headline for Joyce and in 1904 he took some singing lessons, with borrowed money. He sang two set pieces in a charming manner at the Feis Ceoil, but when given a piece of music to sing at sight he left the platform, much to the disappointment of the judge, Professor Denza, who had come from London to adjudicate and who thought very highly of Joyce's voice. In his report Denza recommended that Joyce should study singing seriously. But Joyce left it at that, though he afterwards enjoyed singing at parties.

For a few months early in 1904, Joyce worked as an assistant teacher in a private preparatory school in Dalkey, an experience which he used to good effect when writing the second episode in *Ulysses*.

NORA BARNACLE

On 10 June 1904 Joyce was walking along Nassau Street when he noticed a tall young woman on her own. He spoke to her and she responded agreeably; as he was wearing a nautical cap she thought at first he was a sailor. He discovered that she was a Galway girl who had come to Dublin only six months earlier and was working as a chambermaid and waitress in Finn's Hotel, a small hotel in Leinster Street, a continuation of Nassau Street. After a chat they agreed to meet on 14 June at the corner of Merrion Square, outside the house where the Wildes had lived. To his great disappointment she did not turn up, but he decided not to let matters rest at that. He sent her a rather humble note from his new address at 60 Shelbourne Road, where he had recently rented a room. It read:

> I may be blind. I looked for a long time at a head of reddish-brown hair and decided it was not yours. I went home quite dejected. I would like to make an appointment but it might not suit you. I hope you will be kind enough to make one with me if you have not forgotten me!
> James A. Joyce
> 15 June 1904

Nora responded and they met on 16 June, and went for a walk towards Ringsend, near the mouth of the river Liffey. Joyce was glad to find that Nora, then aged twenty, was a lively, sensual woman of good sense. She was tall, good-looking, with auburn hair, good deportment and a pleasant voice. She was no intellectual but had an independent mind, which she was prepared to express. Joyce was so impressed with the significance of that day's meeting with Nora that the date 16 June, 1904 became the date for the events in *Ulysses*, and has since become known as Bloomsday.

Nora Barnacle came from a large family and, for several years, had been raised by her grandmother. Her father, a baker, was a heavy drinker, with the result that Nora's parents eventually separated. She attended the local convent school of the Sisters of Mercy until she was twelve or thirteen and then got work as a porteress at the Presentation Convent in Galway. She enjoyed adolescent life with her friends as best she could in a rather strict family, and had three boyfriends, two of whom died at the age of sixteen; which indicates how young Nora was when she had boyfriends. Nora felt that she was too strictly controlled at home, particularly by her Uncle Tommy who took on the role of guardian by watching out for her around the town to make sure she did not get into any mischief. When she was about nineteen she, like thousands of other young women from the provinces, went to Dublin to find work. Her employment in Finn's Hotel brought her into the area of the city where Joyce and his friends perambulated.

Joyce's and Nora's love for each other transformed their existences and they were faithful to each other for the rest of their lives. Despite his irreligious views Joyce was almost entirely orthodox in his moral behaviour. When he was told (wrongly) that Nora had been intimate with one of his friends before he met her, he was profoundly hurt and jealous.

They met frequently and exchanged many letters. After a few weeks she was addressing him as 'My Precious Darling' and he, though slower to utter such endearments, also wrote in an amorous fashion. On 15 August he wrote:

My dear Nora,

It has struck one. I came in at half past eleven. Since then I have been sitting in an easy chair like a fool. I could do nothing. I hear nothing but your voice. I am like a fool hearing you call me 'Dear'. I offended two men today by leaving them coolly. I wanted to hear your voice, not theirs. When I am with you I leave aside my contemptuous suspicious nature. I wish I felt your head over my shoulder now. I think I will go to bed. I have been a half-hour writing this thing. Will you write something to me? I hope you will. How am I to sign myself? I won't sign anything at all, because I don't know what to sign myself.

A fortnight later he wrote her a long letter in which he tried to explain his outlook on life, part of which was as follows:

I may have pained you tonight by what I said but surely it is well that you should know my mind on most things. My mind rejects the whole present social order and Christianity – home, the recognised virtues, classes of life, and religious doctrines. How could I like the idea of home? My home was simply a middle-class affair ruined by spendthrift habits which I have inherited. My mother was slowly killed, I think, by my father's ill-treatment, by years of trouble, and by my cynical frankness of conduct. When I looked on her face as she lay in the coffin – a face grey and wasted with cancer – I understood that I was looking on the face of a victim and I cursed the system which had made her a victim. We were seventeen in family. My brothers and sisters are nothing to me. One brother alone is capable of understanding me.

Six years ago I left the Catholic Church, hating it most fervently. I found it impossible for me to remain in it on account of the impulses of my nature. I made secret war upon it when I was a student and declined to accept the positions it offered me. By doing this I made myself a beggar but I retained my pride. Now I make open war upon it by what I write and say and do. I cannot enter the social order except as a vagabond.

Joyce's reference to the 'positions offered' by the Church was probably the offer made to him by Sheehy Skeffington in September 1893 (when the latter became Registrar of UCD) to teach French in evening classes.

Nora was a believing and practising Catholic when she met Joyce and found it difficult to understand his complete rejection of religion and the Church, but this did not deter her from committing herself to him. Nora's life with Joyce is described in detail in Brenda Maddox's book *Nora: A Biography of Nora Joyce*[9].

LITERARY WORK

Though Joyce spent a lot of his time with Nora he continued to write prose and poetry. He managed to write much of *Stephen Hero* in 1904 and also some poems which he collected under the title of *Chamber Music*, although the book would not be published for three years. In July he was asked to write a short story for the *Irish Homestead* magazine and immediately produced 'The Sisters' under the pseudonym Stephen Dedalus. It was published on 13 August and he received one guinea. The theme of the story, seen through the eyes of a sensitive teenage boy, is the death of a retired sickly, old priest who was being looked after by his two sisters in a small house over a drapery shop. The very first paragraph shows Joyce's early skill as a writer:

> There was no hope for him this time: it was the third stroke. Night after night I had passed the house (it was vacation time) and studied the lighted square of window: and night after night I had found it lighted in the same way, faintly and evenly. If he was dead, I thought, I would see the reflection of candles on the darkened blind, for I knew that two candles must be set at the head of a corpse. He had often said to me: 'I am not long for this world,' and I had thought his words idle. Now I knew they were true. Every night as I gazed up at the window I said softly to myself the word paralysis. It had always sounded strangely in my ears, like the word *gnomon* in the Euclid and the word *simony* in the Catechism. But now it sounded to me like the name of some maleficent and sinful being. It filled me with fear, and yet I longed to be nearer to it and look upon its deadly work.

Within the following months Joyce wrote two more short stories for the *Irish Homestead*, and he conceived the idea of writing other stories depicting scenes of life in Dublin, which could be published in one volume.

After many publishing and printing delays (the alleged immorality of some of the stories was raised as a problem), the collection would be eventually published as *Dubliners* in 1914. Joyce had at last made an impact as a writer of short stories, particularly with the last story in the collection, 'The Dead'. Anybody with doubts about Joyce's ability to write a good story in orthodox English should read 'The Dead'. (An extract from it is quoted further on.)

At the beginning of September 1904 he had to leave his room in Shelbourne Road because the occupiers of the house closed it while they were away on holidays. He stayed two nights with a married couple in Sandymount, then a few nights with his Aunt Josephine, then a night with a medical student, and then, on 9 September, with Oliver St John Gogarty in the old Martello tower at Sandycove, which Gogarty had rented from the Office of Public Works for £8 a year. (This tower became the location of the opening scene in *Ulysses*. It is now the Joyce Museum.) He didn't stay there long because another guest, Samuel Trench, was neurotic and had nightmares, during one of which he fired his pistol at an imaginary black panther in the fireplace, beside which Joyce was trying to sleep. When Gogarty fired another shot at the 'panther', to try to pacify Trench, Joyce decided that this was too much and left.

For some time previously he had been thinking of going back to Paris to free himself from the constraints he felt in Irish life and to improve his prospects of becoming a serious writer. The incident at the Martello tower seems to have sharpened his thoughts and, the very next day, he met Nora and explained his wish to go abroad, with her if possible. She agreed. A day or two later he wrote her a letter in the course of which he said: 'The fact that you can choose to stand beside me in this way in my hazardous life fills me with great pride and joy ... Allow me, dearest Nora, to tell you how much I desire that you should share any happiness that may be mine and to assure you of my great respect for that love of yours which it is my wish to deserve and to answer.' (Neither of them could have foreseen the trials and troubles that lay ahead.)

The problem of getting a job on the continent had to be tackled. He answered an advertisement which claimed to be able to find teaching jobs for applicants who paid two guineas. He sent off this sum and received a telegram on 4 October advising him to go to the Berlitz language school in Zurich. He succeeded in raising some contributions (including £5 from Lady Gregory) to cover the fare to Paris. Some members of the family came to the North Wall to see him embark for England on 8 October, unaware that Nora was also travelling. Joyce and Nora boarded the ship separately. The die was cast, at age 22 for Joyce and age twenty for Nora.

EXILE

They passed through London without an overnight stay and, in Paris, Joyce managed to borrow 60 francs from a Frenchman he had met two years earlier, to enable them to continue their journey to Zurich. When they reached Zurich on 11 October he booked into a small hotel and went to the Berlitz School to let them know he had arrived to take up his position as a teacher of English. To his consternation the director knew nothing about his arrival and had no vacancy. He was sympathetic, however, and said he would make enquiries about possible vacancies elsewhere. When he told them that he thought there was a vacancy in Trieste they went there, only to be disappointed again. Luckily the director of the school at Trieste, an Austrian, had been instructed to set up a new school in the town of Pola, about 150 miles further south, on the coast, where the Austrian government (who were then in control of that whole area as part of the Austro-Hungarian Empire) had a naval base. He offered Joyce a job in Pola, teaching the naval officers for sixteen hours a week for a weekly wage of two pounds, which he readily accepted. They found a furnished room and kitchen in a house only a few doors from the school, where they settled down to something like normal married life. (They were not legally married, as Joyce did not believe in such requirements.)

The deputy director at Pola school was an Italian from Florence named Alessando Francini, only four years older than Joyce, who had a wife and a young child. Francini had had a Catholic upbringing similar to Joyce's, and his wife had been a singer before marriage. With the aid of these common interests the Joyces and the Francinis became close friends; at one stage they shared an apartment together. In a short memoir written in 1947, Francini displayed an obvious affection for Joyce:

> Although we were poles apart in our religious beliefs, we were always friends. Joyce tenaciously held to his ideas and I remained steadfast in my opposition to them. Joyce had a personable and good-natured disposition. So far as his genius was concerned, one could say he was sovereign. In the more worldly and less significant matters, however, Joyce was naive and almost childlike.[10]

In the summer of 1905 Joyce and Francini had to leave Pola as undesirable aliens (due to a suspected spy plot in the area) and were fortunate enough to be given work at the Berlitz school in Trieste. Joyce continued teaching English in Trieste for most of the time up to June 1915, when he had to leave and go to neutral Switzerland (Zurich) after the outbreak of the First World War, because Austria and Italy were on opposite sides. Joyce himself took little interest in the war.

Though Trieste was then in Austrian territory the common language of the city was Italian and, with his previous knowledge of Italian, Joyce soon acquired an excellent written and oral facility in the language, which Francini acknowledged. (He also acknowledged that Joyce became too fond of drink; Joyce and Nora frequented restaurants and Joyce liked to drink white wine in the evening; he didn't care for red wine.) Dante became one of Joyce's favourite authors, in particular his *Divine Comedy*.

A SON AND DAUGHTER

The Joyces' only son, Giorgio, was born on 27 July 1905. When Joyce wrote to his brother Stanislaus in Dublin, informing him of this birth, he said there would be no baptism. (This was correct but, unknown to Joyce, Giorgio was surreptitiously baptised in 1912, in his aunt's house in Dublin.) Stanislaus, then aged twenty, agreed to come to Trieste, at Joyce's prompting, to take up a post in the Berlitz school, and arrived in October 1905. To save money he shared accommodation with his brother, his wife and their young son. Stanislaus continued to live in Trieste for the remainder of his life, apart from interruptions during the First and Second World Wars.

In the following year the director of the school in Trieste told them that he could not afford to employ both brothers during the slack summer months and, as a result, Joyce, Nora and Giorgio went to Rome, where Joyce obtained a job as a foreign correspondence clerk in a bank. He disliked the job and the city.

Nora became pregnant again and they decided to return to Trieste, where Nora gave birth to a baby girl, Lucia, on 26 July 1907. Lucia was born with a squint in one eye, which was an embarrassment to her when she grew up, and unfortunately she became the source of much anguish in the Joyce family in later years when her mind became deranged due to schizophrenia.

Joyce's knowledge of Italian was now good enough to enable him to write some articles about Ireland for a local paper; he also delivered a public lecture at a local college. His book of poems, *Chamber Music*, was published in May 1907. He contracted rheumatic fever and spent part of July and August in hospital. In September he finished writing 'The Dead'.

In May 1908 he suffered from inflammation of the iris of the eye, for which leeches were applied. Thereafter, and for the rest of his life, he suffered from serious and often painful eye troubles, for which he underwent many operations, which were only partially successful. In

June he decided to become a commission agent in Trieste for Irish tweeds, for which he got occasional orders. He also wrote the first few chapters of *A Portrait*.

He wrote a sympathetic article about Oscar Wilde which was published in a local journal in March 1909. In a further effort to have *Dubliners* published he sent it to another publisher in Dublin (Maunsel & Co.) but this didn't succeed. He decided to make a trip to Ireland, bringing Giorgio with him, and leaving Nora, Lucia and Stanislaus in Trieste. The two arrived in Dublin on 29 July, where they met the Joyce family, then staying in 44 Fontenoy Street. They also visited Nora's mother in Galway.

He met a number of his former college friends, including Cosgrave, who was still leading an aimless life. Apparently out of envy or spite, Cosgrave told him that while Nora had been meeting Joyce in Dublin every second night in 1904 (because she had to work in the hotel on the other nights) she was actually, he alleged, meeting Cosgrave and going for long walks with him. Joyce was devastated by this story and immediately wrote a heart-broken letter to Nora enquiring if the allegations were true, saying that his heart was full of bitterness and despair. The following morning he wrote a follow-up letter asking whether Giorgio was his son and enquiring what exactly had happened between her and his 'friend' when they lay down on the banks of the Dodder river. He ended: 'O, Nora, is there any hope yet of my happiness? Or is my life to be broken? They say here that I am in consumption. If I could forget my books and my children and forget that the girl I loved was false to me and remember her only as I saw her with the eyes of my boyish love I would go out of life content. How old and miserable I feel!'

He walked around Dublin all day tortured by these thoughts. That afternoon he called on Byrne, his trusted friend, at 7 Eccles Street, and unburdened his soul to him. Byrne's immediate reaction was that Cosgrave's account was a complete lie, concocted to upset Joyce. This response was a great relief to Joyce, who began to feel ashamed of himself for doubting Nora. Meanwhile, Nora had shown Joyce's letters to Stanislaus, who was able to inform Joyce that one night in 1904 he had met Cosgrave in a pub, looking very morose. When asked what was wrong Cosgrave told him, in strict confidence, that he had tried to ingratiate himself with Nora but had been rebuffed. When Joyce heard this news he was re-assured and wrote abject letters of apology to Nora.

While Joyce was in Dublin, Shaw's play *The Shewing-Up of Blanco Posnet* had its premiere in the Abbey Theatre, and Joyce wrote a review of it for the Trieste paper, the *Piccolo*. He didn't think much of the play (it is not one of Shaw's best).

His sister Margaret was about to leave to become a Sister of Mercy in

New Zealand, which still left five sisters in the house. He arranged singing lessons for Eileen, to be paid for by Stanislaus and himself, and also decided to bring one of the other sisters (Eva) to Trieste with him. He arrived back in Trieste in September.

Eva, then aged eighteen, was homesick for Dublin but enjoyed going to the cinemas in Trieste. When she remarked how strange it was that Dublin, a larger city, had not even one cinema, Joyce saw this as an opportunity to make some badly needed money. He got in touch with some local businessmen who ran a few cinemas in Trieste and Bucharest and, when they expressed an interest in opening a cinema in Dublin (and perhaps also in Belfast and Cork), he entered into a contract with them to go to Dublin (expenses paid) to hire a suitable hall and to make all the necessary preliminary arrangements. As a result, Joyce was back in Dublin on 21 October and, a week later, discovered a suitable hall at 45 Mary Street. The partners sent Joyce £50 to book the hall and two of them arrived in Dublin soon afterwards, by which time Joyce had an estimate of the cost of installing electricity in the building. The three partners visited Belfast and Cork but found no place suitable. The cinema, named the 'Volta', was opened on 20 December, but it did not prosper under their management and some months later was sold to an English company, who made a success of it.

Before he left Dublin Joyce visited Finn's Hotel and was shown the room which Nora had occupied. He found the experience very moving and in his next letter to Nora he revealed an underlying religious attitude to human life:

> I could have knelt by that little bed and abandoned myself to a flood of tears. The tears were besieging my eyes as I stood looking at it. I could have knelt and prayed there as the three kings from the East knelt and prayed before the manger in which Jesus lay. They had travelled over deserts and seas and brought their gifts and wisdom and royal trains to kneel before a little new-born child and I had brought my errors and follies and sins and wondering and longing to lay them at the little bed in which a young girl had dreamed of me.

Joyce returned to Trieste in January 1910, this time with his sister Eileen. Now there were four members of the Joyce family in the city, not counting Nora, Giorgio and Lucia. But Eva didn't like Trieste and returned to Dublin in July 1911.

By this time Joyce had ceased teaching in the Berlitz school and relied mainly on giving private lessons, plus occasional articles for the press. The Joyces were always short of money in Trieste, and Stanislaus often had to rescue James, something which led to heated arguments.

In 1912 Nora, who had been corresponding with her family in Ireland, expressed a wish to go to Galway and it was agreed that she should go there with Lucia. Joyce asked Nora to call on George Roberts, managing director of Maunsel & Co. in Dublin, to enquire about the possible publication of *Dubliners*. On 8th July Nora and Lucia arrived in Dublin where they were met by the Joyce family, some of whom Nora brought with her when she called on Roberts. This visit achieved nothing. A few days later Joyce decided to follow Nora, with Giorgio, and they all succeeded in having an enjoyable holiday in Galway, including attendance at Galway races and a trip to the Aran Islands.

Joyce met Roberts several times to discuss alleged risks of litigation that could arise from the publication of some of the stories in *Dubliners*, i.e. that public houses were referred to by their real names and that some of the stories could be regarded as morally objectionable. Joyce was prepared to make certain amendments but regarded some of the alterations requested by Roberts as quite unjustified. He engaged a solicitor to support his view, but the solicitor's qualified clearance was not much help. The argumentation got nowhere and Joyce returned to Trieste in a state of frustrated fury, feeling that this was another example of the way Ireland treated her artists. He did not visit Ireland again.

While Joyce and Nora were absent from Trieste a problem about arrears of rent on their flat came to a head; the landlord informed Eileen that they would have to leave at the end of the quarter, in nine days' time. She told Stanislaus, who wrote to Joyce in Ireland, who replied explaining that he had thought the notice to quit had been revoked and ending by saying: 'Take possession of the house till I return. Don't let my debts trouble you. Tell them I am away and will return in the month of September.' Stanislaus, who was confronted with the immediate problem, adopted a more sensible approach and rented a smaller, newer flat, in which the Joyces lived for the rest of their time in Trieste.

In 1913 Joyce, with the assistance of his friends in Trieste, succeeded in obtaining an appointment as teacher in the local commercial high school. He taught in this school in the mornings and took his private pupils in the afternoons. His financial position became a bit easier as a result.

DUBLINERS AND *A PORTRAIT OF THE ARTIST*

Towards the end of 1913 Joyce received two welcome letters, one from the London publisher Grant Richards requesting to see the script of *Dubliners* once again, the other from an American friend of Yeats, Ezra Pound, who was in London, offering to help in trying to have his poems and stories published, as he had contacts with a number of magazines in

England and America. He added that Yeats had shown him Joyce's poem 'I Hear an Army', which he said he was prepared to include in an anthology and would pay for it. This poem reads as follows:

I hear an army charging upon the land
And the thunder of horses plunging, foam above their knees.
Arrogant, in black armour, behind them stand,
Disdaining the reins, with fluttering whips, the charioteers.
They cry unto the night their battlename:
I moan in sleep when I hear afar their whirling laughter.
They cleave the gloom of dreams, a blinding flame,
Clanging, clanging upon the heart as upon an anvil.
They come shaking in triumph their long green hair:
They come out of the sea and run shouting by the shore.
My heart, have you no wisdom thus to despair?
My love, my love, my love, why have you left me alone?

Joyce thereupon sent Pound the script of *Dubliners* and also the first chapter of *A Portrait*. Pound was impressed by both, and the *Egoist* magazine in England agreed to publish *A Portrait* in instalments, commencing in February 1914. Joyce was sufficiently heartened by this to write to Grant Richards asking for an immediate decision on whether he would publish *Dubliners*. Richards at long last agreed and an edition of 1,250 copies was published in June 1914. It got good reviews, though some reviewers thought the stories displayed a cynical view of life in Dublin. The legal risks foreseen by Maunsel & Co. did not arise. But Joyce did not make much money from *Dubliners* at first.

The last, and longest, story in *Dubliners* is 'The Dead', which has been highly praised ever since. Anybody interested in Joyce should certainly read it, as it shows Joyce at his best as a short-story writer. The scene of the story is the annual dance, or family party, given in a house on Usher's Island by two spinster sisters for their close friends. Among those invited are Mr Gabriel Conroy and his wife Gretta. During the festivities a song called 'The Lass of Aughrim' is sung, which deeply affects Gretta. When Gabriel asks her about it later that night, during their overnight stay in the Gresham Hotel, he discovers, for the first time in his life, that Gretta had loved a young man in Galway, named Michael Furey, before her marriage, and that this young man had died at the age of seventeen. He finds this experience upsetting. The following are brief extracts from the very end of the story:

She was fast asleep. Gabriel, leaning on his elbow, looked for a few moments unresentfully on her tangled hair and half-open mouth, listening to her deep-drawn breath. So she had had that romance in her life: a man had died for her sake. It hardly pained him now to think how poor a part he, her husband, had played in her life. He watched her while she slept, as though he and she had never lived together as man and wife. His curious eyes rested long upon her face and on her hair; and, as he thought of what she must have been then, in that time of her first girlish beauty, a strange, friendly pity for her entered his soul. He did not like to say even to himself that her face was no longer beautiful, but he knew that it was no longer the face for which Michael Furey had braved death.

Perhaps she had not told him all the story. His eyes moved to the chair over which she had thrown some of her clothes. A petticoat string dangled to the floor. One boot stood upright, its limp upper fallen down: the fellow of it lay upon its side. He wondered at his riot of emotions of an hour before. From what had it proceeded? From his aunt's supper, from his own foolish speech, from the wine and dancing, the merry-making when saying good night in the hall, the pleasure of the walk along the river in the snow. Poor Aunt Julia! She, too, would soon be a shade with the shade of Patrick Morkan and his horse. He had caught that haggard look upon her face for a moment when she was singing 'Arrayed for the Bridal'. Soon, perhaps, he would be sitting in that same drawing-room, dressed in black, his silk hat on his knees. The blinds would be drawn down and Aunt Kate would be sitting beside him, crying and blowing her nose and telling him how Julia had died. He would cast about in his mind for some words that might console her, and would find only lame and useless ones. Yes, yes: that would happen very soon ....

A few light taps upon the pane made him turn to the window. It had begun to snow again. He watched sleepily the flakes, silver and dark, falling obliquely against the lamplight. The time had come for him to set out on his journey westwards. Yes, the newspapers were right: snow was general all over Ireland. It was falling on every part of the dark central plain, on the treeless hills, falling softly upon the Bog of Allen and, further westwards, softly falling into the dark mutinous Shannon waves. It was falling, too, upon every part of the lonely churchyard on the hill where Michael Furey lay buried. It lay thickly drifted on the crooked crosses and headstones, on the spears of the little gate, on the barren thorns. His soul swooned slowly as he heard the snow falling faintly through the universe and faintly falling, like the descent of their last end, upon all the living and the dead.

The decision to publish *A Portrait* in instalments meant that Joyce had to knuckle down and complete the novel, which up to this had been left unfinished. With the outbreak of war in August 1914 the postal service between Britain and Austria was suspended and Joyce had to arrange for the final instalments to be posted from across the border in Italy. The last pages of *A Portrait* did not reach Pound until July 1915.

The editor of the *Egoist* who had agreed to publish *A Portrait* was Dora Marsen, who was succeeded shortly afterwards by Miss Harriet Shaw Weaver, who subsequently gave considerable financial assistance to Joyce. She paid £25 for serialising the book and advanced another £25 when she agreed to publish *A Portrait* in book form. A publisher in New York, Mr B.W. Huebsch, agreed to publish it in the USA and paid Joyce £54 in advance royalties. It appeared in America on 29 December 1916 (Huebsch had also published the first American edition of *Dubliners* a few weeks earlier). The first English edition of *A Portrait* consisted of 750 copies published by the Egoist press in February 1917; all these copies were sold by that summer. Joyce had at last arrived on the literary scene as a serious writer.

In the meantime, things were happening in Trieste. His sister Eileen had become engaged to a Czech bank cashier, Frantisek Schaurek, and they had been married in Trieste on 12th April 1915, with Joyce as best man in a borrowed dress suit. The married couple left for Prague, where they spent the war years. Italy entered the war against Austria and Germany in May 1915 and the situation in Trieste became very difficult, because of the city's large Italian population. The Austrians interned Stanislaus for the duration of the war, as he was regarded as a troublemaker, but James was allowed to leave Trieste and go to neutral Switzerland, where the Joyces arrived by train in Zurich in June 1915.

ZURICH

By the time Joyce left Trieste for Zurich he had spent eleven years in Trieste, during which he had succeeded in having *Chamber Music* and *Dubliners* published, had written a long semi-autobiographical novel called *Stephen Hero*, which he re-wrote in a shorter and much improved version as *A Portrait of the Artist as a Young Man*; he had written the play *Exiles* and had begun writing *Ulysses*. He liked living in Trieste, where his excellent command of Italian facilitated social and cultural contacts. The Joyces had become part of the Trieste community, and both Giorgio and Lucia spoke Italian.

The sudden transfer to German-speaking Zurich caused difficulties. Joyce himself was fairly proficient in German but Nora, Giorgio and Lucia had no knowledge of it. As a result, when Giorgio and Lucia began attending school in Zurich they were put back two years in their grading. Nevertheless, Joyce made many new friends in Zurich, where expatriates had assembled during the war. The theatre was very lively in Zurich, which suited Joyce.

He began to give private lessons in English but his income from this source was not large. Nora's uncle in Galway, Michael Healy, sent them fifteen pounds and later sent similar amounts. Yeats and Pound, who were concerned about Joyce's isolation in Zurich, made representations to the Royal Literary Fund in England, which assisted writers in distress, and the Fund awarded him £75. Yeats and Pound also made a case in favour of Joyce to the British Prime Minister, Mr Asquith, who approved a grant of £100 to him from the Civil List in August 1916. Further good news reached Joyce in 1917 when a London firm of solicitors wrote to tell him that an anonymous admirer had agreed to send him a cheque for £50 every quarter until the end of the war. The anonymous donor turned out to be Harriet Shaw Weaver (who later donated much larger sums to him: £2,000 in 1920, £1,500 in 1922 and £12,000 in 1923). In 1918 an American lady named Mrs Harold McCormick, then resident in Zurich, who was a daughter of John D. Rockefeller the multimillionaire, arranged for a bank to pay him 1,000 Swiss francs per month for a period of eighteen months. His financial situation improved noticeably from this time onwards.

Joyce's work on *Ulysses* was interrupted for many weeks during 1917 by severe and painful attacks of glaucoma, which necessitated an operation on his right eye that permanently impaired his vision. Pound continued to help by encouraging Harriet Weaver to publish *Ulysses* in instalments in the Egoist magazine and by arranging to have episodes published in *The Little Review* in New York, commencing in March 1918.

It was in Zurich that Joyce met Frank Budgen, an Englishman who worked for the Ministry of Information in the British consulate there. Mr Budgen had gone to sea at an early age and had educated himself by reading widely. He had learned to paint in Paris. Joyce and Budgen became firm friends, so much so that Joyce devoted quite a lot of his time to explaining the writing of *Ulysses* to him. When Joyce returned to Trieste in 1919 he missed Budgen, but kept in touch with him by correspondence; and later, when Joyce moved to Paris, Budgen visited him occasionally. Budgen then wrote the well-known account of their friendship and about the writing of *Ulysses*, which was published in 1934[11].

An unusual development in 1918 was the formation of a company of actors called The English Players to stage plays in Zurich. Joyce took a prominent part behind the scenes. Their first production in April was Wilde's *The Importance of Being Earnest*, followed in June by three one-act plays, including Synge's *Riders to the Sea*. In this play one of the minor parts was acted by Nora, whose Galway accent suited the role.

RETURN TO TRIESTE

After the armistice in November 1918 the Schaureks returned to Trieste, which had been annexed by Italy. Stanislaus joined them not long afterwards. In October of the following year Joyce, Nora and their two children also returned to Trieste, and moved into the Schaureks' flat, much to Stanislaus's annoyance, as he was also there. Joyce resumed teaching in the commercial high school, now classified as the University of Trieste, for one hour a day, but did not resume private lessons. It soon became noticeable that Trieste as an Italian port was not as lively as it had been when it was the main Austrian shipping port on the Adriatic. The Joyce family decided to leave Trieste and go to Paris. However, Stanislaus and the Schaureks remained in Trieste.

In fact, Stanislaus remained in Trieste for most of the rest of his life, until he died in 1955 at the age of 70. Frantisek Schaurek committed suicide in 1926 while his wife Eileen was on a visit to Dublin, an unexpected event which devastated her.

PARIS

Joyce, Nora and the two children arrived in Paris in July 1920, at which stage Giorgio was fifteen and Lucia thirteen years of age. The children's lives so far had been very unsettled due to changes of home, changes of school and changes of language; now they had to face another upheaval. Giorgio finished his schooling when he was sixteen years old and tried to make singing his career. He had a good baritone voice but did not succeed as a professional singer. Lucia tried singing and dancing, and also turned her hands to designing artistic lettering for printing, but without lasting success, due to her unbalanced mind.

The Joyces remained in Paris until 1940, when the Germans invaded France and occupied the greater part of the country for a few years. During this long period in Paris Joyce met many internationally famous people, together with a few individuals who assisted him in various ways. Among the latter were Samuel Beckett, a fellow Dubliner, who afterwards became a great writer in his own right, and Paul Leon, who had emigrated from Russia and settled in Paris in 1921. From about 1930 on Leon willingly acted as a sort of unpaid secretary for Joyce.

One of Joyce's most fortunate meetings in 1920 was with a young American woman, Sylvia Beach, who had a bookshop in Paris named Shakespeare & Co. He became very friendly with Miss Beach who, not long afterwards, became the agent for the first publication of *Ulysses* in book form. In a BBC radio broadcast in February 1950 Miss Beach gave her recollection of the first meeting with Joyce:

> It was in the autumn of 1920 that I went to a party with Adrienne Monnier to the house of the poet Andre Spier in Neuilly. When we got there we found Ezra Pound and he brought James Joyce and Mrs Joyce.

Andre Speir had come rushing up to me and told me in great excitement, 'The Irish writer, James Joyce, is here!' I was quite overwhelmed; it was so unexpected for me to come suddenly face to face with one for whom I had such a deep admiration, and I was quite trembling. After lunch I got up the courage to speak to him, however, and he soon put me at my ease. He was a very easy man to talk to. His manners were so courteous and he was very gentle, slightly humorous, and rather melancholy at the same time. I thought he was delightful; his musical voice, his long fingers, with several rings on them (and somehow they didn't seem to make him look effeminate either), his fair skin – he was always blushing – and his very small feet, and his way of drooping against a bookcase.[7]

Around the same time, T.S. Eliot and Wyndham Lewis called to see Joyce. He invited them to dinner in a nearby restaurant, accompanied by his son Giorgio, who now preferred to be called George. Lewis wrote an amusing account of this dinner, in the course of which he said Eliot handed over a brown paper parcel which Pound had asked him to bring to Joyce. When opened it was found to contain a pair of old brown boots (no doubt for Joyce to wear). Lewis's description of Joyce was: 'I found an oddity, in patent-leather shoes, large powerful spectacles, and a small gingerbread beard; speaking half in voluble Italian to a scowling schoolboy; playing the Irishman a little overmuch perhaps, but in amusingly mannered technique.' Eliot thought that Joyce was arrogant and excessively polite on first acquaintance, but he was always an admirer and praised *Ulysses* highly.

An eminent French literary critic, Valery Larbaud, became enthusiastic after seeing the published extracts from *Ulysses* and decided to write about Joyce in the *Nouvelle Revue Francaise*, one of France's literary periodicals, and to deliver a lecture about him. Joyce thus became the subject of literary comment in Paris. M. Larbaud's favourable review spurred Joyce to complete the remaining sections of *Ulysses*, which was accomplished by the end of October 1921.

ULYSSES

The publication of sections of Ulysses in the *American Little Review* led to the publishers of that journal being charged with publishing obscene material in the July–August 1920 issue, which contained the 'Nausicaa' episode, where Bloom has lecherous feelings when watching Gerty MacDowell on Sandymount strand. The case was heard before three judges in February 1921 and the editors were found guilty and fined $50 each. When Mr Huebsch, publisher of the American edition of *A Portrait*, heard this news he made it known that he could not publish *Ulysses* without some alterations being made in it. When this was refused he withdrew his offer to publish. This upset Joyce, who feared that he would now have similar difficulties and delays in publishing Ulysses as he had experienced with Dubliners. When he told Miss Beach about the disappointing news from Mr Huebsch she enquired whether he would allow Shakespeare & Co. to publish Ulysses. Joyce readily agreed and as a result the first edition of Ulysses was printed and published in France. Joyce sent instalments of the script to the printer in Dijon and, when the proofs were ready, proceeded to make copious changes in them, mainly additions, which added substantially to the length of the book. This of course annoyed the printer, but nevertheless a few advance copies of Ulysses reached Paris on 2 February 1922, Joyce's fortieth birthday.

Miss Weaver agreed to have an edition of 2,000 copies published by the Egoist Press in London, but printed in France by using the plates that had been made for Miss Beach's edition. Copies of *Ulysses* were posted from Paris to individuals and shops known to be interested in obtaining the book, but many copies were confiscated by the American and British customs authorities, because the book was regarded as obscene.

Ulysses had a mixed reception, even among literary people. Some critics praised it highly but others disparaged it. Bernard Shaw told Miss Beach he was not prepared to send money to buy a copy but that, having read several of the published extracts, he felt it was a revolting, but truthful, record of a disgusting phase of civilisation. Virginia Woolf said it was 'the book of a self-taught working man'. Ernest Hemingway referred to it as 'a most goddamn wonderful book'. Yeats admired it but confessed later that he had not been able to finish reading it. Stanislaus liked parts of it but disliked the brothel scene and Molly Bloom's soliloquy. Arnold Bennett said that these two episodes were superb. George Moore said: 'But *Ulysses* is hopeless; it is absurd to imagine that any good end can be served by trying to record every single thought and sensation of any human being.' D.H. Lawrence did not like it; he regarded the last section as indecent. (Joyce didn't think much of Lawrence's books either.) Nora never read the book; neither did Joyce's father, though having looked at it he remarked to his daughter Eva, 'He's a nice sort of blackguard.'

As a novel, *Ulysses* depicts the events and thoughts of Leopold Bloom, a man nearly 40 who is a Jew, though a baptised one, and of Stephen Dedalus (the same character as in *A Portrait* but slightly older), as they traverse Dublin city on their separate perambulations during one particular day (16th June 1904). Their itineraries cross two or three times but they did not meet until night time. During that day they each meet various different characters, most of whom are ordinary working people.

The book is called *Ulysses* because Joyce tried to link the events of that day in Dublin to the adventures of the Greek hero Odysseus (or Ulysses as he is known in the Latin version) during his long journey after the Trojan wars back to his island home, where his faithful wife, Penelope, had waited patiently for him for years. *Ulysses* can be appreciated without reading Homer's *Odyssey*, but some knowledge of the adventures that befell Odysseus can help the reader to understand the changes of scene in Joyce's novel, where Bloom echoes Odysseus and Dedalus echoes Odysseus's son, Telemachus.

The various Dublin characters are brought vividly to life by many scenes, such as the funeral procession to Glasnevin cemetery (Hades), the short scenes in the city centre during the afternoon (Wandering Rocks) which depict a multiplicity of different personalities, and the long scene in the bar of the Ormond Hotel (Sirens). However, some of the chapters in the second half of the book seem over-written, and the changes of literary style in these chapters can be confusing to the reader.

Difficulties of comprehension arose at a very early stage. In a letter to Joyce on 6 July 1919 Harriet Shaw Weaver referred to the Sirens episode, which she had just received from Pound, and commented that 'the episode seems to me not quite to reach your usual pitch of intensity'. Joyce was disappointed and wrote her two letters within the following few weeks. In the first of these he said: 'If the Sirens have been found so unsatisfactory I have little hope that the Cyclops or later the Circe episode will be approved of; and moreover it is impossible for me to write these episodes quickly. The elements needed will fuse only after a prolonged existence together. I confess that it is an extremely tiresome book but it is the only book which I am able to write at present.' In the second letter he said: 'I understand that you may begin to regard the various styles of the episodes with dismay and prefer the initial style much as the wanderer did who longed for the rock of Ithaca. But in the compass of one day to compress all these wanderings and clothe them in the form of this day is for me possible only by such variation which, I beg you to believe, is not capricious.'

Joyce tried to put into his script the inner thoughts of his leading characters, including the stray thoughts and associated ideas that pass through a person's mind as part of normal consciousness. Joyce tried to give significance to the mundane events and thoughts of everyday life, and his story exists as much in the minds of the characters as in their activities and spoken words. At the time of its publication, Ulysses was a new approach to the writing of a novel about ordinary human beings going about their daily tasks, without accomplishing much apart from being inhabitants of a particular city on a particular day in time.

In his book *Joyce and Aquinas*[8] Fr Noon makes some helpful comments on *Ulysses*:

> To come back to Ulysses, we see that though Joyce succeeds in presenting a searching and exhaustive critique of contemporary society (as reflected in Dublin on the day of June 16, 1904) the tone of the novel is nowhere that of *saeva indignatio*. Religious mores are satirized and burlesqued, sentimental patriotism is parodied, modern science is mocked, contemporary commercialism and journalism are presented as fraudulent – but at the same time there is an absence of anger. Joyce's own tone is nowhere pleading. He does not set out to deplore the evil; he is content with making us see these deviations from the norm as absurdities. If he throws the light of reason on the dark places in human behaviour, he chooses to filter the light through a comic screen so that it does not hurt. For the mature reader, this effort at detachment appears too in the nice neutrality which the novel shows in focus: its light is impartial and evenly dispersed ....
>
> Stephen and Bloom and Molly undergo no purification from the encounter with the evil with which they collide as the day wears away. No one is brought to a vision of peace after pain. There is no integration of character. There are moments when resolution of discords seems imminent: when Bloom calls Stephen by his first name, when Stephen and Bloom gaze without speaking into the mirror. But these moments pass. There is no abiding communication. Stephen goes away alone into the darkness; Bloom takes his dumb misery with him into the same old adulterous bed; Molly confusedly remembers the events of the day, which fuse formlessly with similar events of other similar days, but the void is not filled by her memories. The curtain slowly descends, and we see that there has been no growth for any of these Dubliners on this day.

One of the early literary assessments of *Ulysses* was that by the eminent American critic, Edmund Wilson, who devoted a chapter of his book *Axel's Castle: A Study in the Imaginative Literature of 1870–1930* to an analysis of *Ulysses*. It is a chapter well worth reading and can be found, with several other helpful essays, in the book *Joyce: A Collection of Critical Essays*, edited by William M. Chace[12]. Wilson found some faults with *Ulysses* (for example, he felt that Joyce elaborated too much and tried to put too many things into it) but nevertheless praised it as a work of modern literature. His comments include the following:

> Yet the more we read *Ulysses*, the more we are convinced of its psychological truth, and the more we are amazed at Joyce's genius in mastering and in presenting, not through analysis or generalization, but by the complete recreation of life in the process of being lived, the relations of human beings to their environment and to each other; the nature of their perception of what goes on about them and of what goes on within themselves; and the interdependence of their intellectual, their physical, their professional and their emotional lives. To have

traced all these interdependencies, to have given each of these elements its value, yet never to have lost sight of the moral through preoccupation with the physical, nor to have forgotten the general in the particular; to have exhibited ordinary humanity without either satirizing it or sentamentalizing it – this would already have been sufficiently remarkable; but to have subdued all this material to the uses of a supremely finished and disciplined work of art is a feat which has hardly been equalled in the literature of our time.

In 1933 a submission was made to the US District Court in New York that *Ulysses* was not obscene, and papers and witnesses were presented in support of this contention (one of the papers submitted was by Edmund Wilson). After due consideration Judge John M. Woolsey concluded, in a lengthy and analytical judgment, that it was not obscene and therefore could be sold in the USA. An appeal by the state against Judge Woolsey's opinion was rejected, and Random House published the American edition of *Ulysses* in January 1934. The British publisher John Lane decided to publish it in England but copies of this edition did not appear until 1936.

FINNEGANS WAKE

In 1923 Joyce began writing *Finnegans Wake*, a difficult and tortuous work, which was not completed until November 1938. In the meantime sections of it were published in magazines under the title of 'Work in Progress'. When the complete book was published in May 1939 simultaneously in London (by Faber & Faber) and in New York (by Viking Press) it received an even more mixed reception than *Ulysses* did, because of the difficulty of deciphering the language used in its composition. It seemed as if Joyce had gone as far as he could in re-constructing words to suit his particular purpose. When Joyce saw the reviews he became a bit despondent that his experimental effort might have been a failure, but he was encouraged by a few critics who were impressed by what he was trying to do. He particularly liked a review by an American named Harry Levin, who afterwards wrote a perceptive study of Joyce's writings[13].

Levin said:

The stream of unconsciousness in *Finnegans Wake* begins at the very point where the stream of consciousness in *Ulysses* left off – the point of falling asleep. For the last time we return to Dublin, where we spent an exhaustive day with Mr Bloom, to enjoy an exhausting night with Mr Earwicker. All of his adventures, like those of Bloom and Stephen under the spell of Circe, take place in the twilight regions of psychic fantasy.

Ellmann made the following comments on *Finnegans Wake*[4]:

In retrospect, it seems clear that the 'monster', as Joyce several times called *Finnegans Wake* in these days, had to be written, and that he had to write it. Readers may still sigh because he did not approach them more directly, but it does not appear that this alternative was open to him. In *Dubliners* he had explored the waking consciousness from outside, in *A Portrait* and *Ulysses* from inside. He had begun to impinge, but gingerly, upon the mind asleep. There lay before him, as in 1922 he well knew, this almost totally unexplored expanse ...

The language of the new book was as necessary to it as the verbal arrangements of his previous works to them. He had already succeeded in adapting English to suit states of mind and even times of day, but chiefly by special arrangements and special kinds of words in different chapters. Now, for *Finnegans Wake*, a polyglot language had to be brought, even more daringly, to its own making-house. To imitate the sophistication of word- and image-formation in the unconscious mind (for Joyce discarded the notion that the mind's basic movements were primitive), he took settled words and images, them dismembered and re-constituted them.

These comments sum up what Joyce was trying to achieve in *Finnegans Wake*, but whether he succeeded is another matter. Many readers have wondered whether the effort required to understand the strange language in this book is worthwhile.

Ezra Pound and Harriet Shaw Weaver didn't care for it; neither did Stanislaus. When Stanislaus read extracts of 'Work in Progress' he wrote a long letter to his brother in August 1924 referring to the 'drivelling rigmarole' of a particular piece and saying that another section 'has certain characteristics of a beginning of something, is nebulous, chaotic but contains certain elements. That is absolutely all I can make of it. But it is unspeakably wearisome.'

When Pound received an episode in November 1926 he wrote to Joyce:

All I can do is to wish you every possible success. I will have another go at it, but up to present I make nothing of it whatever. Nothing so far as I make out, nothing short of divine vision or a new cure for the clapp can possibly be worth all the circumambient peripherization.

A little later he said:

Nothing would be worth ploughing through like this, except the Divine Vision – and I gather it's not that sort of thing.

Harriet Shaw Weaver wrote to Joyce half-apologetically but in some bewilderment about episodes received in 1926: 'But, dear sir, (I always seem to have a 'but') the worst of it is that without comprehensive key and glossary, such as you very kindly made out for me, the poor hapless reader loses a very great deal of your intention; flounders, helplessly, is in imminent danger, in fact, of being as totally lost to view as that illfated vegetation you mentioned.'

Joyce was upset by these criticisms but, with the encouragement of others, he continued his work on *Finnegans Wake*, even though his eyesight had greatly deteriorated, believing that the book would be understood in due course.

OTHER EVENTS

During the 1920s and 1930s, the Joyces spent most of their time in Paris but had holidays in different parts of France and in the south of England. In 1922 Nora, George and Lucia visited Nora's relations in Galway but didn't remain long there because the civil war between Government and Irregular forces had just broken out.

George worked for a bank in Paris for a while in 1923 but didn't like it and gave it up to take singing lessons in the Schola Cantorum, Paris.

During 1924 Joyce had two eye operations, the fifth and sixth so far, followed by further operations in 1925 and 1926. Despite this, he continued work on *Finnegans Wake*. His short book of poems, named *Pomes Penyeach*, was published by Shakespeare & Co. in July 1927. It made little impact. That same year Stanislaus married Nelly Lichtensteiger in Trieste; they had a son (James) born on 14 February 1943.

The French translation of *Ulysses* was published in February 1929.

In 1929 Stanislaus told his brother about an Irish-born tenor, John Sullivan, whom he had heard singing in Trieste and whom he had asked to call on Joyce when Sullivan was singing in Paris later that year. Sullivan had been born in Cork but came to live in France at the age of twelve, and was now a leading tenor in the French opera company. Joyce was enthralled with his voice and regarded him as the greatest tenor in the world. He met Sullivan several times and made great efforts to have his talents more widely recognised, so that he could be heard in London and New York. He was partially successful in this.

Nora had a hysterectomy operation in Paris in 1929. Cancer had been suspected but she made a complete recovery.

In 1930 Joyce met Paul Leon, who became his willing helper for many years. The Joyces and the Leons became close friends.

In April 1931 the Joyces moved to London and lived for some months in a flat at 28b Camden Grove, Kensington, so that Joyce could establish domicile in England and have his marital situation legally recognised, which meant going through a marriage ceremony in a registry office in London. In this way Joyce hoped to avoid possible future difficulties of inheritance for his family.

Joyce's father died in a Dublin hospital on 29 December 1931. Joyce was grief-stricken and had feelings of remorse for not having visited his father for many years. In a letter to Harriet Shaw Weaver he said: 'My father had an extraordinary affection for me. He was the silliest man I ever knew and yet cruelly shrewd. He thought and talked of me up to his last breath. I was very fond of him always, being a sinner myself, and even liked his faults.'

GEORGE AND LUCIA

In December 1930, George married Helen Kastor Fleischman, a wealthy divorced American woman ten years older than himself. Nora disliked the marriage at first, because of the age gap, but later became very friendly with Helen. This friendliness was endorsed when George and Helen had a son, Stephen, born on 15 February 1932, who, unknown to Joyce, was secretly baptised. Stephen turned out to be Joyce's only grandson. This marriage ended unsatisfactorily when Helen became mentally ill around 1938 and had to be kept in hospital for a while. (Helen's friends felt that George's lack of affection was the cause of the trouble; Joyce disputed this, and became estranged even with Paul Leon because he sympathised with Helen. They were reconciled later when the Germans occupied France.) Helen recovered later when she was brought home to America. George and Helen became divorced.

Lucia's mental condition continued to deteriorate. One of the symptoms of her illness was hostility towards her mother and an excessive preoccupation with her father. She ran away several times from home and from clinics. Joyce brought her from one specialist to another and spent a great deal of money on her treatment, but without success. He was reluctant to admit that she was mentally ill (with schizophrenia) and tried to maintain her at home, with the help of a nurse and his friends, but Lucia's behaviour was unpredictable. During 1931 she became passionately interested in Samuel Beckett, who often visited Joyce as a friend, but Beckett had no romantic interest in Lucia and made this clear to her. Her feelings were hurt and she told her mother, who urged Joyce to ostracise Beckett, which he did. This estrangement between Joyce and Beckett lasted about a year. Lucia became engaged to a brother-in-law of Paul Leon in 1932, but this came to nothing due to her condition. In February 1934 she struck her mother and was admitted to a clinic for a while. A few months later Joyce agreed to have her placed under the care of Dr Carl Jung, the famous psychotherapist, in Zurich, but this form of treatment was of no avail.

Harriet Shaw Weaver agreed to accept Lucia for a while in London but, despite her best efforts, Lucia proved to be too difficult. In 1935 Lucia went to stay with her aunt Eileen in Bray, County Wicklow, but she went missing for six days in Dublin until the police found her. Miss Weaver took her again for a while, and she was examined in St Andrew's Hospital, Nottingham, in December 1935. She was brought back to France in February 1936 and was admitted to a private mental home two months later, where she stayed until April 1951. Lucia was then transferred to St Andrew's Hospital, where she remained until her death on 12 December 1982, age 75.

WAR AGAIN

During the years 1938 and 1939 most people in France and Britain felt that war with Germany was almost inevitable, in view of the continuing territorial demands being made by Hitler. Joyce, who was relieved to have had *Finnegans Wake* published some months before war was declared, in September 1939, became extremely worried about the fate of Lucia in a war situation. In mid-September 1939 Lucia was transferred to a home at Pornichet, in Brittany, for safety.

In November Joyce telephoned Mrs Maria Jolas, who with her husband was a great friend of the Joyces, to ask whether she would look after Stephen in their house (then being used as a school) in the quiet village of St Gerand-le-Puy, near Vichy in southern France. Maria Jolas agreed and in fact invited the Joyces to spend Christmas with them. When they arrived on 24 December Joyce got severe stomach pains and had to go to bed. He hardly ate any Christmas dinner but drank white wine, and later became lively and even sang. Nora persuaded her husband to stay on in the village for safety. Joyce agreed, though he didn't like village life.

The war was relatively quiescent for several months, after Poland had been invaded and occupied by the Germans (and also by the Soviet Union) but this was the lull before the storm. German land and air forces invaded Denmark and Norway in April 1940 and invaded Belgium, the Netherlands and France in the following month. Belgium was overwhelmed and surrendered on 28 May. Paris was occupied by German forces on 14 June. (George had left Paris before its occupation and gone to join his parents.) The German army overran the area around St Gerand-le-Puy for a few days before retiring northwards to a line of demarcation around Vichy France, where a quisling French government was set up.

While awaiting news of developments Joyce spent time with Paul Leon (who had also taken refuge in the Vichy area) correcting misprints in *Finnegans Wake*. Beckett visited Joyce in April 1940. In September Paul

Leon went back to Paris and saved some of Joyce's papers and books in their vacant flat, which he handed to the Irish Embassy in Paris with instructions that they should be given to the National Library in Ireland and kept under seal for 50 years. Being a Jew, Leon had to be very cautious of the Germans, but despite this, he was arrested in 1941 and killed by the Nazis in 1942.

RETURN TO ZURICH

The question of the Joyces seeking asylum in neutral Switzerland now arose, as they were British citizens and liable to internment if arrested by the Germans. With the support of several friends in Switzerland, Joyce succeeded in obtaining a visa for the family, with the exception of Lucia, whose papers proved impossible to clear, to settle in Switzerland. It was also necessary to obtain permission to leave France, which he accomplished, although he failed to get permission for George. Nevertheless, George managed to get the four passports stamped and, on 14 December 1940, Joyce, Nora, George and Stephen arrived in Geneva. On 17 December they reached Zurich, where Joyce and Nora had stayed during the First World War. They spent Christmas with friends, and Joyce and George sang songs and played a record of John McCormack. But Joyce's health was deteriorating.

After dinner in a restaurant on Thursday, 9 January 1941, Joyce had another severe attack of stomach pains. George summoned a doctor who administered morphine to dull the pain, but as pain continued he was brought by ambulance to hospital. On Saturday morning an x-ray showed a perforated duodenal ulcer, for which surgical treatment was essential. Joyce demurred about undergoing an operation but when George assured him that the problem was not cancer he agreed to surgery. After the operation Joyce seemed stable, but he weakened on Sunday. Two Swiss soldiers donated blood for a transfusion but he went into a coma that afternoon. The hospital doctors advised Nora and George to go home and promised to call them immediately if there was any change in his condition. At 1 a.m. the following morning Joyce woke and asked the nurse to call his wife and son. They were summoned but Joyce died at 2.15 a.m., before Nora and George had arrived. The post-mortem report said the cause of death was 'perforated ulcer, generalised peritonitis'. A Catholic priest approached Nora about carrying out the last rites but she said: 'I couldn't do that to him.'

He was buried in Fluntern cemetery in Zurich. Harriet Shaw Weaver happened to hear of his death on the BBC radio news and, true to form, sent Joyce's quarterly allocation of £250 by telegram to Nora, who was thus able to meet the funeral expenses.

POSTSCRIPT

Nora, now a widow, decided to continue living in Zurich, with her son George and her grandson, Stephen. Her standard of living deteriorated, because of difficulties and delays in clearing Joyce's estate in England, and also due to foreign exchange control on money being sent abroad. Harriet Shaw Weaver, who was Joyce's literary executor, helped Nora financially until, in 1948, royalties from Joyce's published works began to mount and the Bank of England authorised payments to be made to her in Switzerland.

Stephen was placed in a Swiss boarding school until 1946, when he went to live and study in the United States, where his mother was living. During long school holidays he visited his grandmother in Zurich.

George had no occupation, apart from singing, and relied heavily on his mother. He became an alcoholic and suffered from migraine. He established a relationship with a German woman, a medical practitioner in Zurich, who was separated from her husband; they married in 1954. George died in 1976 in Germany, aged almost 71.

Suggestions were made to Nora that she might go to live in England, or Ireland, or Paris, but she was satisfied with Zurich, where she had made new friends. She did, in fact, visit Paris in 1948 and 1949 for a Joyce exhibition and for the sale of some of Joyce's manuscripts. In her last years she returned to the practice of the Catholic faith: she attended Mass regularly, went to Confession, and said the Rosary.

She suffered badly from arthritis and eventually had to enter a private clinic for long-term nursing care. Her heart became weak and she was given the last rites of the Catholic Church before she died on 10 April 1951. She was buried in Fluntern cemetery, but not in the same grave as her husband, because there was no space available. However, both their remains were moved to a permanent plot in 1966, and in 1981 a sculpture was erected at the grave depicting Joyce sitting crosslegged, smoking a cigarette.

BIBLIOGRAPHY

(1) Stanislaus Joyce, *My Brother's Keeper*. Faber & Faber, London, 1958.

(2) Kevin Sullivan, *Joyce among the Jesuits*. Columbia University Press, New York, 1958.

(3) Bruce Bradley, *James Joyce's Schooldays*. Gill & Macmillan, Dublin, 1982.

(4) Richard Ellmann, *James Joyce*. Oxford University Press, 1959 and 1982 (revised edition).

(5) Ulick O'Connor (ed.), *The Joyce We Knew*. Mercier Press, Cork, 1967.

(6) Thomas Merton, *Seven Storey Mountain*. Harcourt Brace Jovanovich, New York, 1948, and Sheldon Press, London, 1975.

(7) W.R. Rodgers (ed.), *Irish Literary Portraits*. British Broadcasting Corporation, London, 1972.

(8) William T. Noon, SJ, *Joyce and Aquinas*. Yale University
Press, 1957.

(9) Brenda Maddox, *Nora: a biography of Nora Joyce*. Hamish Hamilton, London, 1988.

(10) Willard Potts (ed.), *Portraits of the Artist in Exile*. University of Washington Press, Seattle, and Wolfhound Press, Dublin, 1979.

(11) Frank Budgen, *James Joyce and the Making of Ulysses*. Grayson & Grayson, London, 1934. Oxford University Press, 1972.

(12) William M. Chace (ed.), *Joyce: A Collection of Critical Essays*. Prentice-Hall, Englewood Cliffs, New Jersey, 1974.

(13) Harry Levin, *James Joyce: A Critical Introduction*. Faber & Faber, London, 1944.

(14) Peter Costello, *James Joyce*. Gill & Macmillan, Dublin, 1980.

(15) Peter Costello, *James Joyce: The Years of Growth 1882 – 1915*. Roberts Rinehart, Schull, Co. Cork, 1992.

JONATHAN SWIFT
(1667–1745)

Jonathan Swift, one of the greatest satirical writers in the English language, was also one of the earliest Anglo-Irish writers. In some respects he was as much an Englishman as an Irishman, and he often expressed regret at having been born in Ireland rather than in England, where his parents came from; but in later life he became more identified with Ireland.

Swift can be properly classified as a Dubliner: he was born in Dublin, received his university education in Trinity College, Dublin, and spent the last 30 years of his life in Dublin as Dean of St Patrick's Cathedral.

Swift's paternal grandfather, Thomas Swift (1595–1658), the Church of England vicar of Goodrich, Herefordshire, married Elizabeth Dryden from Northampton. In Swift's words, he had been 'persecuted and plundered two and fifty times by the barbarity of Cromwell's hellish crew' because of his loyalty to King Charles I, who was executed in 1649. Thomas died two years before the restoration of the monarchy in 1660, and by that time four of their six sons (they also had five daughters) had left England to seek their fortune in Ireland, where prospects for English settlers were promising.

Conditions in Ireland were unsettled after the Irish rebellion of 1641, which was followed by the ferocious military campaign of Oliver Cromwell in 1649–50. His military success led to an 'Act for the Settling of Ireland', under which the territory of Ireland was to be treated as confiscated property, to reward adventurers and soldiers. Those whose lands were confiscated, mainly Catholic landowners, were to be transferred to land west of the Shannon. The land confiscations were limited to some extent, however, when the monarchy was restored, and in 1662 an Act of Settlement tried to bring some order into the ownership of land. Some of the land was restored to Catholics, though not enough to undo the Cromwellian settlements.

The changes in the ownership of land gave rise to extra work for lawyers, and three of Thomas Swift's sons benefited from this. Godwin, the eldest son, had qualified as a barrister in England in 1660 and was called to the Irish Bar in 1663. Another son, William, became a solicitor in Dublin in 1661. A third son, Jonathan, got a position in the King's Inns in Dublin and became a solicitor too. Adam, the youngest son, did not become a lawyer, but was successful otherwise and eventually acquired an estate in County Down.

In 1664, Jonathan married Abigail Erick, whose parents had come from Leicestershire in 1634 and who had been born in Ireland in 1640. The newly married couple had two children, a girl named Jane, born in April 1666, and a boy, Jonathan (the subject of this chapter), born on 30 November 1667 in Hoey's Court near Dublin Castle, then a fashionable part of the city.

Shortly before Jonathan was born his father died, and thus Jonathan had a fatherless childhood. Furthermore, for much of his infancy he was looked after by a wet nurse, an Englishwoman who, when Jonathan was one year old, carried him with her when she had to return urgently to her parents' home in Cumberland. She had not consulted the baby's mother about this move and, when Mrs Swift learned of it, she advised the nurse to keep the baby in England until he was hardy enough for the return trip to Ireland. As a result, Jonathan spent the following two years or more in England, with his nurse.

His mother, now a widow with a young daughter, decided to return to the family home in Leicester, where she lived from then on. This arrangement meant that she became separated from Jonathan, and did not see him except when he visited her on his way to and from London in later years. Swift's biographer Irvin Ehrenpreis says: 'One is left with the impression that Mrs Swift had access to her son for the first year of his life, for a year or two before he entered school, and for short periods during infrequent visits afterwards.'[1] Not a great deal is known about Mrs Swift. She appears as a shadowy figure in the background of her son's life. But Swift had a high regard for his mother and, when she died in 1710, he wrote: 'If the way to Heaven be through piety, truth, justice and charity, she is there.'

This loss of his father and the absence of his mother for long periods must have retarded Swift's emotional development as a child and probably accounts for his rather caustic attitude towards humanity.

In an autobiographical fragment written by Swift in his seventies he made the following comment on his parents' marriage:

This marriage was on both sides very indiscreet, for his wife brought her husband little or no fortune, and his death happening so suddenly before he could make a sufficient establishment for his family; and his son (not then born) hath often been heard to say that he felt the consequences of that marriage not only through the whole course of his education, but during the greatest part of his life.[1]

His uncle Godwin agreed to assist in the rearing of young Jonathan, but as Godwin married four times and fathered eight children, it is unlikely that he had much time to spend with his young nephew. Nevertheless, Godwin seems to have paid for Jonathan's education in Kilkenny College, where he was a boarder from the age of six. But Swift resented having to depend on his uncle.

KILKENNY COLLEGE

Kilkenny College had been founded in the sixteenth century by the Earl of Ormond and was one of the best colleges in Ireland; many landed gentry sent their sons there to get a good academic and Protestant education. Two successive masters of the college during Swift's time were a Welshman (Edward Jones) and an Englishman (Henry Ryder), both of whom had been educated at Westminster School and Trinity College, Cambridge, before coming to Ireland. It seems clear, therefore, that the boys at Kilkenny College were educated in the same manner as the sons of the gentry in England. The students studied Latin, Greek, rhetoric, and Christian doctrine. There were prayers and scripture readings every day, and attendance at the Cathedral every Sunday.

Discipline was strict and the hours of study were long, but there were some compensations, if one can properly interpret the tone of a letter Swift wrote in middle age about the unreliability of memories of childhood:

> So I formerly used to envy my own happiness when I was a schoolboy, the delicious holidays, the Saturday afternoon, and the charming custards in a blind alley; I never considered the confinement ten hours a day to nouns and verbs, the terror of the rod, the bloody noses and broken shins.[2]

A near contemporary of Swift's in Kilkenny College was George Berkeley (1685–1753), the idealist philosopher – who became Dean of Derry and Bishop of Cloyne, County Cork – but he was a few years behind Swift in both Kilkenny and Trinity.

TRINITY COLLEGE

Swift became a boarder in Trinity College, Dublin, when he was fourteen years old. This is a young age for admission to a university college but many of the boys admitted that year were around sixteen years old, so Jonathan may not have felt too much out of place. Swift remained for about six years in Trinity, where there were then over 300 students.

One of the main functions of Trinity College was to train students for priesthood in the Church of Ireland, and many of its top personnel became bishops afterwards. Narcissus Marsh, for example, provost during 1679–83, became Bishop of Ferns and then, in turn, Archbishop of Cashel, Archbishop of Dublin and Archbishop of Armagh. Robert Huntingdon, provost during 1683–92, became a clergyman in England and ultimately Bishop of Raphoe. Swift's tutor in Trinity, Dr St George Ashe, was Professor of Mathematics and a Fellow of the Royal Society. He became provost during 1692–5 and then, in turn, Bishop of Cloyne, Bishop of Clogher and Bishop of Derry. Ashe was a lifelong friend of Swift.

In Trinity, Swift continued his study of Latin and Greek and became familiar with Aristotle's works and also with natural philosophy. He was not happy at Trinity, but in 1686 obtained a Bachelor of Arts degree, without distinction. This rankled. In later life he wrote that 'he was stopped of his degree for dullness and insufficiency, and at last hardly admitted in a manner little to his credit, which is called in that college *speciali gratia*. And this discreditable mark, as I am told, stands upon record in their college registry'.[2]

Ehrenpreis sums up Swift's studies in Trinity as follows:

> In other words, the young Swift did passably well in college, but not so well as the septuagenarian Swift could have wished. He excelled in those pursuits in which he was himself to be distinguished – language and literature; he did poorly in what he would always dislike – abstract philosophy and formal rhetoric.[1]

In 1689 he was still attending Trinity, preparing for an MA degree, when the conflict between William III and James II extended to Ireland, after James II had arrived there from France, where he had taken refuge. Trinity College suspended its sessions due to this upheaval, and Jonathan went to stay with his mother in Leicester.

MOOR PARK

Shortly afterwards Swift was fortunate enough to be taken on as secretary by a friend of the Swift family, Sir William Temple (1628–1699), a diplomat and a writer. Temple had lived for some years in Ireland and was a member of the Irish Parliament in 1661. His father had been Master of the Rolls in Ireland, and Temple himself had succeeded to that position, which was regarded as a sinecure. He became involved in English politics and was highly regarded by both King Charles II and by William III.

When Swift became employed by Temple, the latter had retired to a large house and estate called Moor Park on the outskirts of the town of Farnham in Surrey. (The house is still there.) Temple's main claim to fame was as the English diplomat who, in 1668, had successfully negotiated the short-lived Triple Alliance between England, Holland and

Sweden, which was aimed at curtailing the expansionist policies of France under King Louis XIV.

During his years at Moor Park, which lasted, with interruptions, until 1699, Swift helped to edit and publish some of Temple's writings (essays, memoirs, and letters), and this occupation no doubt enhanced his own literary skills and acquainted him with English politics.

At Moor Park, Swift met and took an interest in a young girl named Esther Johnson, the daughter of the housekeeper. Swift was 21 years old when they first met, and Esther was about six, but their friendship ripened over the years. He tried to inculcate in her a love of literature, and succeeded to the extent that he later wrote several poems to her, and also the famous letters which were subsequently collected and published under the title *Journal to Stella*. She achieved a niche in literary history under the nickname Stella, and played a very significant part in Swift's life, as will become clear later.

After the defeat of James II in 1690 Swift returned to Ireland, hoping to obtain better employment there, but as this was not forthcoming he returned to Moor Park at the end of 1691. He took his MA degree in Oxford in 1692 and continued working at Moor Park as Temple's assistant, which was interesting work as far as it went. Sir William valued his services but Swift wished for something more stable than the position of secretary to a retired elderly man, no matter how distinguished. He hoped and expected that Temple would utilise his contacts to get him a worthwhile appointment, but became disappointed at what appeared to be Temple's lack of effort on his behalf. Eventually Temple said he could get him a job as clerk in the office of the Master of the Rolls in Ireland, but Swift turned down the offer and told Temple that he proposed to go to Ireland to enter Holy Orders.

On his return to Ireland Swift made enquiries about becoming a clergyman in the Church of Ireland, for which he felt his Trinity College education and his MA degree in Oxford would qualify him, and discovered that, in order to proceed further, it would be necessary for him to obtain a certificate of his 'good life and behaviour' during the previous three years. Swift felt embarrassed at having to ask Sir William for such a testimonial, as he felt he had left Moor Park under a cloud, but he swallowed his pride and wrote a rather abject letter to Sir William, which Ehrenpreis quotes in full[1]:

May it please your honour,

That I might not continue by any means the many troubles I have given you, I have all this while avoided one, which I fear proves necessary at last. I have taken all due methods to be ordained, and one time of ordination is already elapsed since my arrival without effecting it. Two or three bishops, acquaintances of our family, have signified to me and them, that after so long a standing in the university, it is admired I have not entered upon something or other, above half the clergy in this town being my juniors, and that it being so many years since I left this kingdom, they could not admit me to the ministry without some certificate of my behaviour where I lived; and my Lord Archbishop of Dublin was pleased to say a good deal of this kind to me yesterday, concluding against all I had to answer, that he expected I should have a certificate from your honour of my conduct in your family.

The sense I am in, how low I am fallen in your honour's thoughts, has denied me assurance enough to beg this favour, till I find it impossible to avoid; and I entreat your honour to understand, that no person is admitted to a living here, without some knowledge of his abilities for it, which it being reckoned impossible to judge in those who are not ordained, the usual method is to admit men first to some small reader's place till by preaching upon occasions, they can value themselves for better preferment. This (without great friends) is so general, that if I were four-score years old I must go the same way, and should at that age be told, every one must have a beginning. I entreat that your honour will consider this, and will please to send me some certificate of my behaviour during almost three years in your family; wherein I shall stand in need of all your goodness to excuse my many weaknesses and follies and oversights, much more to say any thing to my advantage. The particulars expected of me are what relate to morals and learning, and the reasons of quitting your honour's family, that is, whether the last was occasioned by any ill actions. They are all entirely left to your honour's mercy, though in the first I think I cannot reproach myself any farther than for infirmities.

This is all I dare beg at present from your honour, under circumstances of life not worth your regard. What is left me to wish, next to the health and felicity of your honour and family, is that Heaven would one day allow me the opportunity to leave my acknowledgments at your foot for so many favours I have received, which, whatever effect they have had upon my fortune, shall never fail to have the greatest upon my mind, in approving myself, upon all occasions.

Your honour's most obedient and most dutiful servant,
J. Swift.

Sir William did not hold any grudge against him and furnished the necessary certificate without delay. Swift became a deacon in the Church of Ireland in October 1694, and was ordained as priest in Christ Church Cathedral, Dublin, in January 1695.

KILROOT

Swift's first appointment was to the parish of Kilroot in County Antrim; or rather to the union of three adjoining parishes: Kilroot, Templecorran, and Ballynure, not far from Carrickfergus, where William III had landed only five years earlier in his successful attempt to put an end to James II's claim to the kingdom of Ireland. Swift's parishes were rather run-down (the church building in Kilroot was in ruins) and the congregations were very small. The population of Antrim was predominantly Presbyterian, mainly descendants of families from Scotland who had arrived during the previous century as part of the plantation of Ulster. Swift was a strong upholder of the Church of Ireland and he disapproved of non-conformers of all kinds, particularly Presbyterians, whose religious ideas, he believed, tended to undermine the established church. It is not surprising, therefore, that he was not happy in Kilroot and left it after about a year, though he did not formally resign his appointment for another eighteen months, during which period he was granted leave of absence and returned to Moor Park at Sir William's request.

Though he disliked Kilroot, Swift had cause to remember it, for it was there that he experienced his first serious involvement with a young woman. She was Jane Waring, aged 21, the eldest of eight children of an archdeacon who had died three years earlier. Two of her cousins had met Swift in Trinity and this may have led to his meeting with Jane, whom he nicknamed 'Varina'. Their friendship became serious and he proposed marriage to her in a long and carefully phrased letter which, to modern minds, seems tortuous and business-like, certainly not amorous. This is an extract from that letter:

> Surely, Varina, you have but a very mean opinion of the joys that accompany a true, honourable, unlimited love; yet either nature and our ancestors have hugely deceived us, or else all other sublunary things are dross in comparison. Is it possible you cannot be yet insensible to the prospect of a rapture and delight so innocent and so exalted? Trust me, Varina. Heaven has given us nothing else worth the loss of a thought. Ambition, high appearance, friends and fortune, are all tasteless and insipid when they come in competition; yet millions of such glorious minutes are we perpetually losing, for ever losing, irrecoverably losing, to gratify empty forms and wrong notions, and affected coldnesses and peevish humour . . . I here solemnly protest, by all that can be witness to an oath, that if I leave this kingdom before you are mine, I will endure the utmost indignities of fortune rather than ever return again, though the king would send me back his deputy.[2]

Varina did not accept his proposal, mentioning her frail health and his low income. This was a devastating blow to Swift, and it rankled. A few years later, after Swift had left Kilroot, Varina let it be known that she had changed her mind about marriage, but in a cool reply he made it clear that the conditions that would surround their possible marriage were not acceptable to him. Varina, whose health was not very strong, never married and pre-deceased Swift by many years.

This encounter with Varina was the first example of his wary attitude towards women, some of whom nevertheless grew very fond of him, for he amused and entertained them. Whether he ever had intimate relations with any of them a matter of speculation, but certainly two women were to figure largely in his life, Stella and Vanessa.

It is worth mentioning here that Swift was popular not only with women but with men. He was well educated, witty, personable and of good appearance. Among his friends were the writers Addison, Steele, Congreve and Pope, and his voluminous correspondence shows that he was on good terms with many other persons. Unfortunately, from his twenties onwards he began to suffer from recurrent attacks of giddiness, vertigo and noises in his head, which he himself attributed to having eaten too many apples but which modern medicine says was Menière's disease. Bouts of this affliction upset him greatly in later years, when the noises in his head became worse.

Swift believed strongly in the virtues of regular exercise, which in his case consisted mainly of horse riding and walking. When confined to the house because of bad weather he would walk up and down the stairs instead.

MOOR PARK AGAIN

During Swift's last period at Moor Park (1696 – 1699) he wrote *The Battle of the Books* and part of *A Tale of a Tub*, though these works were not published until 1704, when they appeared in one volume, together with *The Mechanical Operation of the Spirit*. *The Battle of the Books* was a pamphlet which continued a controversy in which Temple had become involved, about the relative merits of ancient and modern writers (Temple favoured the ancients).

A Tale of a Tub is a much longer and more complicated work, and is regarded as an outstanding work of satire. The underlying story is supposed to be based on three magic coats which a man, just before his death, left to his three sons, Martin, Peter, and Jack. Martin represents the Church of England, Peter represents the Roman Catholic Church, and Jack represents the Dissenters. Swift puts forward the Church of England as the *via media* between the Catholic Church and the Calvinists, both of which he satirises and ridicules. But the book is not simply a satire on religious beliefs: it also mocks pretentiousness of all kinds. The satirical allusions in the book, though cleverly done, were not well received by the Establishment, and many commentators believe that this was the reason why Queen Anne would not approve of a church promotion for Swift in England.

Some critics maintained that the book was irreligious, and this so disappointed Swift that he added an 'Apology' to later editions of the *Tale*, explaining that the book was not a satire of true religion but of its abuses and corruption. In this 'Apology' he asked: 'Why should any clergyman of our church be angry to see the follies of fanaticism and superstition exposed, though in the most ridiculous manner; since that is perhaps the most probable way to cure them, or at least to hinder them from farther spreading?'

GOOD RESOLUTIONS

In 1699 Swift set down on paper for his own guidance a list of resolutions, which he called 'When I come to be old':

Not to marry a young woman.
Not to keep young company unless they really desire it.
Not to be peevish, or morose, or suspicious.
Not to scorn present ways, or wits, or fashions, or men, or war, etc.
Not to be fond of children, or let them come near me hardly.
Not to tell the same story over and over to the same people.
Not to be covetous.
Not to neglect decency, or cleanliness, for fear of falling into nastiness.
Not to be over severe with young people, but give allowance for their youthful follies and weaknesses.
Not to be influenced by, or give ear to knavish tattling servants or others.
Not to be too free of advice nor trouble any but those that desire it.
To desire some good friends to inform me which of these resolutions I break or neglect, & wherein; and reform accordingly.
Not to boast of my former beauty, or strength, or favour with ladies, etc.
Not to harken to flatteries, nor conceive I can be beloved by a young woman, *et eos qui hereditatem captant odisse ac vitare*.
Not to be positive or opiniative.
Not to set up for observing all these rules, for fear I should observe none.

[The sentence in Latin is 'To hate and avoid those who angle for an inheritance'.]

After Temple's death in January 1699 Swift returned to Dublin as chaplain to the Earl of Berkeley, one of the Lord Justices of Ireland, a position which brought him into contact with the powers that be in

Dublin Castle. A vacancy arose in the Deanship of Derry but Swift, to his annoyance, was not considered for it. Shortly afterwards, at the age of 32, he was made Vicar of Laracor in County Meath (actually of three parishes, Laracor, Agher and Rathbeggan).

VICAR OF LARACOR

Laracor is a village near the small town of Trim, County Meath, which Swift could reach in a few hours' ride from Dublin. From his comments in letters to Stella it is clear that he enjoyed the rural life of Laracor, and he held the appointment to the end of his days (in addition to becoming Dean of St Patrick's Cathedral). The parish church had been repaired some years earlier but there was no residence, until Swift built a modest parsonage later. He spent a fair share of his income on improving and extending the grounds at Laracor: he increased the size of the parish land from one acre to twenty acres; he planted willows, and laid a river walk.

His duties at Laracor were not onerous; most of the priestly duties seem to have been carried out by a curate who was paid a salary by Swift. The number of parishioners in Laracor was small, as most of the people in the area were Roman Catholics.

His appointment in September 1700, only a few months after being made Vicar of Laracor, as a prebendary of St Patrick's Cathedral turned out to be significant, as it involved him in the affairs of the cathedral as a member of its Chapter. This led, at an early stage, to his being nominated as spokesman for the Church of Ireland to travel to London to try to persuade Queen Anne and the government to restore the First Fruits to the Church of Ireland, which brought him into direct contact with the British Prime Minister.

In February 1702 Trinity College granted Swift the degree of Doctor of Divinity.

STELLA

In his will, Temple had bequeathed to Stella a lease of some land in Ireland, plus a lump sum on which Stella was able to live frugally in England. In 1701 Swift suggested to her that she and her friend and chaperone, Rebecca Dingley, should come to live in Ireland, where the cost of living was lower and interest on money higher. Stella agreed to move; she probably welcomed the chance to live near Swift. At that time she was twenty years old and Swift was 34. Miss Dingley was in her late thirties. For the rest of their lives the two maiden ladies lived in Dublin, except for a journey to England in 1708, at which time Swift was in London on church business and also writing political tracts.

There is no doubt that Stella and Swift were fond of each other, but Swift took great pains to make it clear to observers that their relationship was nothing more than friendship. He avoided being seen with Stella on her own and, when writing letters to her, as he did over a long period while he was in England, he always addressed them jointly to Stella and Miss Dingley.

A number of Swift's biographers have said that he secretly married Stella in 1716, on condition that they would continue to live apart, and there is some circumstantial evidence for this opinion. But other biographers say that there is no reliable evidence of their marriage, and that any evidence we have points the other way. It is argued, for example, that even after 1716 Stella, a God-fearing woman, signed herself as 'Spinster' in legal documents, including her will. There is the further puzzling aspect that, as there was no legal impediment to either of them getting married, it is difficult to understand why they should pretend to be unmarried if, in fact, they were married to each other. Why should Swift continue to pretend, over a prolonged period of years (from the date of their purported marriage in 1716 up to Stella's death in 1728, and from then until the end of his own life) that he was not married to Stella if, in fact, he was? What was to be gained by such a deception? And why would an independently minded woman like Stella carry out such a prolonged deception, apparently for no reason other than that Swift wished to keep their marriage secret?

Two of Swift's recent English biographers, J.A. Downie and David Nokes (see bibliography) hold different opinions on this question. Downie concludes his examination by saying: 'I can do no better than repeat John Lyon's [Swift's guardian during his later years] eminently sensible words: notwithstanding what has been said about it, there is no authority for it [the marriage] but a hearsay story, and that very ill-founded.'[3] Nokes says: 'My own view is that the balance of probabilities still favours the notion of the secret marriage in 1716. Apart from the weight of circumstantial evidence and hearsay reports, it seems to me to confirm, rather than contradict, the defensive network of reticences with which Swift surrounded this most private relationship.'[2]

His American biographer, Ehrenpreis, who probably researched Swift's life more thoroughly than anybody else, says that Swift 'evaded marriage' and adds the following comments:

> I do not believe that Swift ever went through a marriage ceremony with Esther Johnson, any more than that he ever had sexual relations with her. There is no way to prove either of these negatives, however. But

neither have we any document recording such a marriage. Besides, an unwitnessed ceremony would have been invalid. In documents sworn to by Esther Johnson, she described herself as a spinster; and of course she had nothing to gain from an unacknowledged, invalid marriage that left both of them living as celibate friends. I put great weight on the language of Swift's letters to Sheridan and Stopford on Stella's approaching death, and on the language of the prayers he wrote for her. In all of these he could have avoided the issue but chose words that specified their connection as merely one of friendship.[1]

Swift's marriage or non-marriage will continue to be a matter of contention and speculation as long as he is written about, for it is unlikely that definite proof one way or the other will now be found.

SWIFT IN LONDON

Swift visited London in 1701, 1702 and 1703, and during the years 1707 to 1714 spent most of his time there, firstly as an agent for the Church of Ireland seeking what has been called Queen Anne's Bounty, a concession by the Crown similar to what has been already conceded to the Church of England: remission of the First Fruits (the first year's revenues from benefices) which the Crown had taken over at the Reformation, before which they were paid to Rome; and secondly in writing political tracts on behalf of the English Tories, after he had become disenchanted with the Whigs. The First Fruits were eventually conceded to the Church of Ireland, though Swift was not given much of the credit for obtaining them. He felt annoyed at his efforts being ignored by the Irish bishops.

The letters he wrote from London to Stella and Miss Dingley during 1710–1713 were subsequently published under the title of *Journal to Stella*. It is not really a journal, though Swift himself mentioned in one of his letters (10 October 1710) that 'these letters of mine are a sort of journal, where matters open by degrees'. Swift would commence a letter on a given date and continue adding paragraphs to it during the following days, until he had used up the entire sheet of paper. Thus each letter covered a period of around ten to fourteen days. They were written to amuse and inform the two ladies in Dublin about Swift's activities in London – the people he met (including political figures), who he had dined with, the various items of gossip in London, and so on, and are an interesting commentary on daily life in London at the time.

VANESSA

Swift's long relationship with Stella is an interesting feature of his life,

indicating that despite his jaundiced view of humanity he was affectionate and understanding in his personal relations. However, around 1710
the picture became more complicated with the arrival on the scene of
another young woman named Hester Vanhomrigh, whom he met in
London and whom he subsequently nicknamed Vanessa. She was then
22 years old (seven years younger than Stella), and was the eldest of four
children. The Vanhomrigh family had come to London from Dublin,
where the father, a Dutchman, had been commissionary-general in the
Williamite army before his death in 1703. Mr Vanhomrigh had been a
well-known figure in Dublin and was Lord Mayor of the city for a while.
He left his family well provided for, but in 1707 Mrs Vanhomrigh decided
to transfer the family to London, where they rented rooms near St James's
Square, not far from where Swift had lodgings. It is probable that Swift
knew, or knew of, the Vanhomrigh family from his Dublin days, but he
certainly became a regular visitor to their London household from 1710
on, not only for meals but from an interest in the eldest daughter, Hester.
It is clear from the *Journal* that Stella became suspicious of his frequent
visits to the Vanhomrighs, but he reassured her by saying that it was Mrs
Vanhomrigh he visited, rather than the daughters. Vanessa was a strong-
minded young woman who eventually fell in love with Swift, though he
tried to keep her at arm's length. In 1713 he wrote a long poem for her
entertainment, *Cadenus and Vanessa*, not intended for publication, to try
to keep the relationship cool but friendly. He did not succeed in this
attempt and Vanessa's romantic interest in him continued unabated.
(The poem was published after Vanessa's death.)

When Swift returned to Ireland in 1714 he may have hoped that this
move would end the relationship with Vanessa. It did not, as Vanessa
came to live in Ireland soon afterwards. Mr Vanhomrigh had been a
wealthy man and had left a large house and estate at Celbridge, County
Kildare, which Vanessa now decided to occupy with her sister, who was
in poor health. She also rented lodgings in the centre of Dublin. During
the ensuing years Swift visited her (and her sister) in Dublin and in
Celbridge from time to time, but not as often as Vanessa wished. Many
of her letters contained entreaties to him to visit her more often. The
following correspondence between them, written towards the end of
1714, shows the state of Vanessa's mind and also Swift's guarded response to her approaches[4]:

(From Vanessa to Swift)
> You cannot but be sensible, at least in some degree, of the many
> uneasinesses I am slave to – a wretch of a brother, cunning executors
> and importunate creditors of my mother's – things I can no way avoid

being subject to at present, and weighty enough to sink greater spirits than mine without some support. Once I had a friend that would see me sometimes, and either commend what I did or advise me what to do, which banished all my uneasiness. But now, when my misfortunes are increased by being in a disagreeable place, amongst strange, prying, deceitful people, whose company is so far from an amusement that it is a very great punishment, you fly me, and give me no reason but that we are amongst fools and must submit. I am very well satisfied that we are amongst such, but know no reason for having my happiness sacrificed to their caprice. You once had a maxim, which was to act what was right and not mind what the world said. I wish you would keep to it now. Pray what can be wrong in seeing and advising an unhappy young woman? I can't imagine. You can't but know that your frowns make my life insupportable. You have taught me to distinguish, and then you leave me miserable. Now all I beg is that you will for once counterfeit (since you can't otherwise) that indulgent friend you once were till I get the better of these difficulties, for my sister's sake; for were not she involved (who I know is not so able to manage them as I am), I have a nobler soul then sit struggling with misfortunes, when at the end I can't promise myself any real happiness. Forgive me; and I beg you'd believe it is not in my power to avoid complaining as I do.

(From Swift to Vanessa)

I received your letter when some company was with me on Saturday night; and it put me in such confusion that I could not tell what to do. I here send you the paper you left me. This morning a woman who does business for me told me she heard I was in —- with one —-, naming you, and twenty particulars, that little master and I visited you, and that the Archbishop did so; and that you had an abundance of wit, etc. I ever feared the tattle of this nasty town, and told you so; and that was the reason why I said to you long ago that I would see you seldom when you were in Ireland. And I must beg you to be easy if for some time I visit you seldomer, and not in so particular a manner. I will see you at the latter end of the week if possible. These are accidents in life that are necessary and must be submitted to; and tattle, by the help of discretion, will wear off.

(From Vanessa to Swift)

Well, now I plainly see how great a regard you have for me. You bid me be easy, and you'd see me as often as you could. You had better said, as often as you could get the better of your inclinations so much, or as often as you remembered there was such a one in the world. If you continue to treat me as you do you will not be made uneasy by me long. 'Tis impossible to describe what I have suffered since I saw you last; I am sure I could have bore the rack much better than those killing, killing words of yours. Sometimes I have resolved to die without seeing you more; but those resolves, to your misfortune, did not last long. For there is something in human nature that prompts one so to find relief in this world, I must give way to it, and beg you'd see me and speak kindly to me; for I am sure you'd not condemn any one to suffer what

I have done, could you but know it. The reason I write to you is because I cannot tell it you, should I see you; for when I begin to complain, then you are angry, and there is something in your look so awful, that it strikes me dumb. Oh! that you may but have so much regard for me left, that this complaint may touch your soul with pity. I say as little as ever I can: did you but know what I thought, I am sure it would move you. Forgive me, and believe I cannot help telling you this, and live.

Many other letters between Swift and Vanessa are contained in Volume II of *The Correspondence of Jonathan Swift*, edited by Harold Williams (Oxford University Press, 1963). Swift seems to have found Vanessa to be an interesting and entertaining young woman while he was in London, but when she came to live near Dublin his interest in her cooled, though Vanessa did not fully realise this for some time.

DEATH OF VANESSA

Vanessa's health had not been good for a long period and in June 1723 she died, aged 35. Swift did not attend her funeral; he was, perhaps conveniently, out of town at the time.

In her will, made a month before she died, she left £3,000 (a considerable sum then) to George Berkeley, a complete stranger to her, but nothing to Jonathan Swift. (At that time Berkeley was trying to raise funds to build a Christian college in Bermuda, to serve as a base for the conversion of American Indians. It came to nothing.)

Swift was a sort of father-figure to Vanessa and Stella, both of whom were fatherless when he knew them, but Vanessa was clearly in love with him. Stella was very fond of him but seemed to be prepared to accept the arrangement whereby she was treated, in all public respects, as simply a good friend of Swift. For several years Vanessa and Stella were both living in the Dublin area, and he visited each of them, though trying to keep both ignorant of his contacts with the other.

DEATH OF STELLA

Stella died in January, 1728, aged 47, after an illness lasting several months. Swift wrote several prayers on her behalf during her last illness and these show his Christian piety, though it was a piety of a rather strict nature. The following is an extract from one of those prayers:

O Merciful Father, Who never afflicts Thy children but for their own good, and with justice, over which Thy mercy always prevails, either to turn them to repentance or to punish them in the present life, in order to reward them in a better; take pity, we beseech Thee, upon this Thy poor afflicted servant, languishing so long and so grievously under the weight of Thy hand. Give her strength, O Lord, to support her weakness, and patience to endure her pains, without repining at Thy correction. Forgive every rash and inconsiderate expression which her anguish may at any time force from her tongue, while her strength continues in an entire submission to Thy will.

Immediately following her death he wrote a glowing tribute to her as a friend and as a person, under the title of 'On the death of Mrs Johnson'. It runs to several pages of print but it is worthwhile quoting the first page of it here to give an insight into Swift's attitude towards Stella; it is also as an example of his style of writing on a serious subject:

This day, being Sunday, January 28th, 1727–8, about eight o'clock at night, a servant brought me a note with an account of the death of the truest, most virtuous, and valuable friend, that I or perhaps any other person ever was blessed with. She expired about six in the evening of this day; and as soon as I am left alone, which is about eleven at night, I resolve for my own satisfaction to say something of her life and character. She was born at Richmond, in Surrey, on the thirteenth day of March, in the year 1681. Her father was a younger brother of a good family in Nottinghamshire, her mother of a lower degree: and indeed she had little to boast of her birth. I knew her from six years old, and had some share in her education by directing what books she should read, and perpetually instructing her in the principles of honour and virtue; from which she never swerved in any one action or moment of her life. She was sickly from her childhood until about the age of fifteen; but then grew into perfect health, and was looked upon as one of the most beautiful, graceful, and agreeable young women in London, only a little too fat. Her hair was blacker than a raven, and every feature of her face in perfection. She lived generally in the country with a family, where she contracted an intimate friendship with another lady of more advanced years. I was then (to my mortification) settled in Ireland; and about a year after, going to visit my friends in England, I found she was a little uneasy about the death of a person on whom she had some dependance. Her fortune, at that time, was in all not above fifteen hundred pounds, the interest of which was but a scanty maintenance, in so dear a country, for one of her spirit. Upon this consideration, and indeed very much for my own satisfaction, who had few friends or acquaintance in Ireland, I prevailed with her and her dear friend and companion, the other lady, to draw what money they had into Ireland, a great part of their fortune being in annuities upon funds. Money was then at ten per cent in Ireland, besides the advantage of returning it, and all necessaries of life at half price. They complied with my advice, and soon after came over; but, I happening to continue some time longer in England, they were much discouraged to live in Dublin, where they were wholly strangers. She was at that time about nineteen years old, and her person was soon distinguished. But the adventure looked so like a frolic the censure held, for some time, as if there were a secret history in such a removal; which, however, soon blew off by her excellent conduct. She came over with her friend on the —- in the year 170-; and they both lived together until this day, when death removed her from us. For some years past, she had been visited with continual ill-health; and several times, within these two years, her life was despaired of. But, for this twelvemonth past, she never had a day's health; and, properly speaking, she hath been dying six months, but kept alive almost against nature by the generous kindness of two physicians and the care of her friends. Thus far I writ the same night between eleven and twelve.

In her will Stella left whatever remained of her money, after her mother and sister had died, to provide a stipend for a chaplain at Dr Steevens Hospital, which was under construction at the time of her death. She was buried in St Patrick's Cathedral.

ENGLISH POLITICS

Swift did not spend all or most of his time visiting or writing to his lady friends. He was occupied with his pastoral duties as a clergyman and also spent time writing political tracts, satirical works, verse and sermons.

By inclination Swift was a Whig in political affairs and a Tory in religious matters. He fully supported the 'Glorious Revolution of 1688' whereby King James II, a Catholic, was deposed and replaced by William of Orange, a Protestant (Calvinist by persuasion), who was married to the elder daughter of James II. This unseating of James II was mainly for the purpose of securing the Protestant succession to the English throne, but the terms of the settlement with William III emphasised the independence of Parliament and curbed the power of the monarch, thus bringing about a constitutional monarchy. On the other hand, Swift strongly supported the laws which debarred dissenters, particularly Presbyterians, from holding civil or military offices, and disagreed with the attempts by the Whigs to relax the legal restrictions on dissenters.

The Whig and Tory leaders alternated in office at the turn of the seventeenth century, and when Swift first raised the case for remission of the First Fruits for the Church of Ireland he received a cool reception from the Whig leader, Lord Godolphin, then Prime Minister, who hinted that the Church of Ireland should, as a *quid pro quo*, agree to the removal of the Test Act against dissenters. The Irish bishops would not agree to this. When the Tories succeeded in getting into power in 1710, Swift approached the Tory leader, Robert Harley, about remission of the First Fruits, and received a far more favourable reception. Swift came to know Harley well, and thought highly of him.

Harley had recognised Swift's literary talents and encouraged him to write tracts criticising the Whigs and the Duke of Marlborough, commander-in-chief of the allied forces, who was accused by the Tories of unnecessarily prolonging the war against France. Swift took on the mantle of political pamphleteer for the Tories and wrote a number of propagandist articles in the weekly Examiner. He concluded these attacks with his famous pamphlet, The Conduct of the Allies, in 1711. It was a great success and led to Marlborough's removal – though the Whigs reappointed him later.

DEAN OF ST PATRICK'S CATHEDRAL

When Swift became closely acquainted with Harley and other Tory leaders between 1710 and 1714, he expected that these contacts would eventually bring him the offer of a bishopric or at least a deanship in England, where he wished to remain, but his hopes were dashed on a number of occasions. One of the reasons for this was Queen Anne's lack of sympathy for Swift as the author of *A Tale of a Tub*, which she regarded as irreligious. This was a serious impediment, as church appointments had to be personally approved by the Queen. (Her husband, King William III, had died in 1702 as the result of a fall from his horse, so Anne wielded the powers of the monarch.)

Swift had made it quite plain to Harley that he was anxious to obtain a church appointment in England. For example, on 5 February 1712 he wrote to Harley, mentioning the availability of a deanship in Wells due to the death of the incumbent dean the previous day! Other vacancies for dean arose in Ely and Lichfield soon afterwards, but nothing materialised for Swift. He was greatly disappointed and began to think of a possible appointment in Ireland, perhaps even the deanship of St Patrick's Cathedral, where he was a prebend, if for some reason a vacancy should arise.

The Dean of St Patrick's at the time was John Stearne, who had been appointed in 1705 with the support of the cathedral Chapter, of which Swift was a member. Swift was very friendly with Stearne and had a high regard for him. It happened that the bishopric of Dromore became vacant and it occured to Swift to find out from Stearne whether he would be interested in that position. The response being favourable, Swift made representations to Harley and to the Duke of Ormond (who was then Lord Lieutenant for Ireland) on behalf of Stearne, and Stearne was, after some delays, appointed as Bishop of Dromore. The consequential vacancy for Dean of St Patrick's was filled by the appointment of Swift. It was the pivotal appointment of his life, as he never obtained a bishopric.

It is of particular interest to examine this episode in Swift's life through the letters he wrote from London to Stella in Dublin at the time. The letters concerned are printed near the end of *Journal to Stella,* and the following are some pertinent extracts.

A letter commencing on 25 January 1713 contains an entry dated 4 February which reads: 'I have named Dr Stearn to Lord Treasurer [Harley], Lord Bolingbroke and Duke of Ormond for a Bishopric, and I did it heartily; I know not what will come of it, but I tell you as a great secret that I have made D. Ormd promise me to recommend nobody till he tells me; and this for some reasons too long to mention.'

Another letter has the following revealing entry on 13 April:

This morning my friend, Mr Lewis, came to me and shewed me an Order for a warrant for the 3 vacant Deanearies, but none of them to me; this was what I always foresaw, and receive the notice of it better I believe than he expected. I bid Mr Lewis tell Lord Treasurer that I took nothing ill of him but his not giving me timely notice, as he promised to do, if he found the Queen would do nothing for me. At noon, Lord Treasurer, hearing I was in Mr Lewis's office, came to me and said many things too long to repeat. I told him I had nothing to do but go to Ireland immediately, for I could not with any reputation stay longer here, unless I have something honourable immediately given to me; we dined together at D. Ormds, he there told me he had stopped the warrants for the Deans, that what was done for me might be at the same time, and he hoped to compass it tonight; but I believe him not. I told the D. Ormd my intentions; he is content Stearn should be a Bishop, and I have St Patricks; but I believe nothing will come of it; for stay I will not; and so I believe for all who may see me in Dublin before April ends. I am less out of humour than you would imagine, and if it were not that impertinent people will condole with me, as they used to give me Joy, I would value it less: but I will avoid company and muster up my baggages and send them next Monday by the carrier to Chester, and come to see my willows against the expectation of all the world.

There are further references to the subject on 14, 15, 16 and 17 April, and the entry for 18 April reads:

This morning Mr Lewis sent me word that Lord Treasurer told him Queen would determine at noon. At 3 Lord Treasurer sent to me to come to his lodgings at St James's and told me the Queen was at last resolved that Dr Stearn should be Bishop Dromore and I Dean of St Patrick's; and that Stearns warrant should be drawn immediately. You know the Deanery is in the D. Ormonds gift, but this is concerted between the Queen, Lord Treasurer and D. Ormd, to make room for me. I do not know whether it will yet be done; some unlucky accident may yet come; neither can I feel joy at passing my days in Ireland: and I confess I thought the Ministry would not let me go; but perhaps they can't help it.

A hitch is mentioned on 19 April:

After dinner Mr Lewis sent me a note, that Queen stayed till she knew

whether Duke Ormd approved of Stearn for Bishop; I went this evening and found D. Ormd at the Cockpit, and told him, and desired he
would go to Queen and approve of Stearn. He made objections, desired
I would name any other Deanery, for he did not like Stearn, that Stearn
never went to see him, that he was influenced by Archbishop of Dublin
etc; so all is now broken again. I sent out for Lord Treasurer and told
him this. He says all will do well, but I value not what he says. This
suspense vexes me worse than anything else.

An entry for 20 April reads:

I went today by appointment to the Cockpit, to talk with D. Ormd; he
repeated the same proposal of any other Deanery etc. I desired he
would put me out of the case and do as he pleased; then with great
kindness he said he would consent, but would do it for no man alive
but me etc, and he will speak to the Queen today or tomorrow. So
perhaps something will come of it. I can't tell.

The following is entered for 21 April: 'D. Ormd has told Queen he is
satisfied that Stearn should be Bishop and she consents I shall be Dean,
and I suppose the warrants will be drawn in a day or two.'

The good news came on 23 April: 'This night the Queen has signed all
the warrants, among which Stearn is Bishop of Dromore and D. Ormd is
to send over an Order for making me Dean of St Patrick's. I have no doubt
of him at all.'

Landa says that Swift had a 'sincere belief that Stearne would make
an able bishop . . . Yet it is true that in serving Stearne, Swift was also
serving himself.'[6]

Swift was installed as Dean of St Patrick's in June 1713, but returned
to London in September and remained there until August 1714, when
Queen Anne died and George I of Hanover was proclaimed King of
England. The Tories fell from power and Swift returned to Dublin to fulfil
his duties as Dean.

For the rest of his life he remained in Ireland, except for occasional
visits to London to arrange for the publication of his writings. His last
visit to London was in 1727.

As Dean of St Patrick's, Swift had certain rights within the cathedral
which he jealously guarded, even against the Archbishop of Dublin. The
Archbishop during the period 1703–1729 was William King, with whom
Swift had a few tussles, but in later years they found common cause in
defending Irish interests against the English administration. Both objected
to English clergymen being appointed as bishops in Ireland.

An inkling of Swift's situation as Dean may be gained from a letter to
his friend, Alexander Pope, in June 1715:

I live in the corner of a vast unfurnished house; my family consists of
a steward, a groom, a helper in the stable, a footman, and an old maid,

who are all at board wages, and when I do not dine abroad, or make an entertainment (which last is very rare) I eat a mutton pie, and drink half a pint of wine; my amusements are defending my small dominions against the Archbishop, and endeavouring to reduce my rebellious choir.[3]

IRISH POLITICS

During the first few years after his return from London, Swift busied himself with his duties as Dean of St Patrick's and as Vicar of Laracor, and did not write very much. He became disillusioned with English politics when the Whigs got back into power under George I and took vengeful action against the former Tory leaders, some of whom were suspected of supporting the Stuart Pretender to the English throne. (For example, Harley was incarcerated in the Tower of London for two years.) Swift himself came under suspicion of being a Jacobite, but survived this danger. He kept out of politics, but could not ignore the poverty-stricken condition of the mass of the Irish people.

Eventually a dispute as to whether the Irish House of Lords had final jurisdiction on legal matters in Ireland awakened his interest Irish politics. The British Parliament decided to settle this question by passing an Act in 1720 (the Sixth of George I) 'for the better securing the dependency of the kingdom of Ireland on the crown of Great Britain', declaring that it had full authority to make laws binding the people and kingdom of Ireland. The British Parliament had long claimed to have such power, but formally incorporating the claim in an Act of Parliament aroused widespread opposition in Ireland. Swift joined in the chorus of dissent and published a pamphlet entitled *A Proposal for the Universal Use of Irish Manufacture, in Clothes and Furniture of Houses etc. utterly rejecting and renouncing everything wearable that comes from England*. The pamphlet, written in a sardonic vein, raised the possibility of the Irish House of Commons making a resolution against the wearing of any cloth or stuff which were not of the growth and manufacture of the kingdom of Ireland, asked: 'What if we should agree to make burying in woollen a fashion?', and said: 'Let a firm resolution be taken by male and female, never to appear with one single shred that comes from England; And let all the people say, AMEN.'

The pamphlet also made some other points:

I should be glad to learn among the divines, whether a law to bind men without their consent, be obligatory in foro conscientia; because I find Scripture, Sanderson and Suarez are wholly silent in the matter. The oracle of reason, the great law of nature, and general opinion of civilians, wherever they treat of limited governments, are indeed decisive enough ...

> I would now expostulate a little with our country landlords, who by unmeasurable screwing and racking their tenants all over the kingdom, have already reduced the miserable people to a worse condition than the peasants in France, or the vassals in Germany and Poland; so that the whole species of what we call substantial farmers will in a very few years be utterly at an end ...

> Whoever travels this country, and observes the face of nature or the faces and habits and dwellings of the natives, will hardly think himself in a land where either law, religion, or common humanity is professed ...

The pamphlet was published without the author's name, but the printer was prosecuted for publishing a scandalous and seditious work. The jury brought in a verdict of not guilty, but the Lord Chief Justice sent them back nine times to reconsider. The case against the printer was eventually dropped.

Another development soon afterwards increased Swift's new-found interest in Irish affairs: the 'Wood's Halfpence' controversy. In 1722 the British Crown granted a patent which would permit an Englishman, William Wood, to mint copper coins to a face value of £100,800 for use in Ireland. This was widely opposed in Ireland, not only by the Irish Commissioners of Revenue but by the Houses of Parliament. The fact that the patent had been granted to the King's long-term mistress, a German lady re-named the Duchess of Kendal who sold the patent to Mr Wood for £10,000, did not do anything for its acceptability in Ireland. This contentious proposal gave Swift a glorious opportunity of writing between February and October 1724 four devastating pamphlets deriding the scheme, pamphlets which became known as the Drapier's Letters, because they were supposedly written by M.B. Drapier.

The first letter was addressed to the shopkeepers, tradesmen, farmers and common-people of the Kingdom of Ireland 'concerning the Brass Half-pence coined by Mr Wood, with a design to have them pass in this Kingdom'. Swift tried to get the message across to the general public, particularly small tradesmen, that Wood's coinage would be made of base metal and would be intrinsically worth only one-twelfth of its face value. From this he argued that anybody selling goods and getting paid in the new coinage would lose money substantially. 'For example,' Swift wrote, 'if a hatter sells a dozen of hats for five shillings a-piece, which amounts to three pounds, and receives payment in Mr WOOD's coin, he really receives only the value of five shillings.' Swift then goes on to describe some far-fetched results that could come for using the coinage:

> The common weight of these HALFPENCE is between four and five to an ounce; suppose five, then three shillings and fourpence will weigh a pound, and consequently twenty shillings will weigh six pound butter weight. Now there are many hundred farmers who pay two

hundred pounds a year rent. Therefore when one of these farmers comes with his half-year's rent, which is one hundred pound, it will be at least six hundred pound weight, which is three horse load. If a squire has a mind to come to town to buy clothes and wine and spices for himself and family, or perhaps to pass the winter here; he must bring with him five or six horses loaden with sacks as the farmers bring their corn; and when his lady comes in her coach to our shops, it must be followed by a car loaden with Mr WOOD's money. And I hope we shall have the grace to take it for no more than it is worth.

Swift went on to argue that under the law of the land only gold and silver coins were proper currency, and that nobody could be compelled to accept these 'vile halfpence' of Mr Wood. 'Therefore my friends, stand to it one and all, refuse this filthy trash. It is no treason to rebel against Mr Wood.'

The feeling in Ireland against Wood's coinage was so widespread that the British government decided to back-pedal by reducing the total amount to be coined from £100,800 to £40,000. Swift rejected this in a further letter. A committee of the privy council in England then wrote a report setting out the precedents for the dependency of the government of Ireland. This too drew a retort from Swift. However, Swift's fourth Drapier Letter was the most effective broadside; it was a *tour de force* and is well worth reading in full. In the course of this letter he makes some pertinent comments on Irish people's rights to liberty and justice. The following are selected extracts from it:

Another slander spread by Wood and his emissaries is that by opposing him, we discover an inclination to 'shake off our dependence upon the crown of England'. Pray observe how important a person is this same William Wood, and how the public weal of two kingdoms is involved in his private interest. First, all those who refuse to take his coin are Papists, for he tells us that 'none but Papists are associated against him'. Secondly, they 'dispute the King's prerogative'. Thirdly, 'they are ripe for rebellion'. And fourthly, they are going to 'shake off their dependence upon the crown of England'. That is to say, 'they are going to choose another king'. For there can be no other meaning in this expression however some may pretend to strain it ... I have looked over all the English and Irish statutes without finding any law that makes Ireland depend upon England, any more than England does upon Ireland. We have indeed obliged ourselves to have the same king with them, and consequently they are obliged to have the same king with us ...

Let whoever think otherwise, I, M.B. Drapier, desire to be excepted, for I declare, next under God, I depend only on the King my sovereign, and on the laws of my own country; and I am so far from depending upon the people of England, that if they should ever rebel against my sovereign (which God forbid) I would be ready at the first command from His Majesty to take arms against them, as some of my countrymen did against theirs at Preston. [In 1715 a Jacobite rebel army surrendered there to loyalist forces which included troops from Ireland.]

'Tis true indeed, that within the memory of man, the Parliaments of England have sometimes assumed the power of binding this kingdom by laws enacted here, wherein they were at first openly opposed (as far as truth, reason and justice are capable of opposing) by the famous Mr Molineux, an English gentleman born here, as well as by several of the greatest patriots and best Whigs in England. But the love and torrent of power prevailed. Indeed the arguments on both sides were invincible. For in reason, all government without the consent of the governed is the very definition of slavery. But in fact, eleven men well armed will certainly subdue one single man in his shirt. But I have done. For those who have used power to cramp liberty have gone so far as to resent even the liberty of complaining, although a man upon the rack was never known to be refused the liberty of roaring as loud as he thought fit.

The printer of the fourth Letter was prosecuted but the jury refused to find a true bill. The British government eventually conceded defeat on this issue and the patent was withdrawn from Wood in September 1725. This result was widely acclaimed in Ireland, and Swift's popularity increased enormously. He came to be regarded as an Irish patriot, a defender of the civil rights of the Irish people (though Roman Catholics and Presbyterians may have had qualified views on that).

GULLIVER'S TRAVELS

Published in 1726, when Swift was 58 years old, Gulliver's Travels is probably Swift's most popular work. It is still reprinted regularly, often in an abbreviated form for children, but it was not written as a children's book. It is a sustained satirical attack on politicians, scientists, philosophers, military leaders and indeed human beings in general. It contains many sardonic comments. The following is a typical example, taken from Gulliver's visit to the kingdom of Luggnagg, where he was informed about those rare human beings, the Struldbruggs, who never die. Gulliver was entranced at the idea of such immortal humans, visualising the riches, knowledge and wisdom they could accummulate during perpetual life. His informant rapidly dispelled such illusions about the Struldbruggs, as follows:

He said they commonly acted like mortals, till about thirty years old, after which by degrees they grew melancholy and dejected, increasing in both till they came to fourscore. This he learned from their own confession; for otherwise there not being above two or three of that species born in an age, they were too few to form a general observation by. When they came to fourscore years, which is reckoned the extremity of living in this country, they had not only all the follies and infirmities of other old men, but many more which arose from the dreadful prospect of never dying. They were not only opinionative, peevish, covetous, morose, vain, talkative, but uncapable of friendship, and dead to all natural affection, which never descended below their grandchildren. Envy and impotent desires are their prevailing passions. But those objects against which their envy seems principally directed, are the vices of the younger sort, and the death of the old. By reflecting on the former, they find themselves cut off from all possibility of pleasure; and whenever they see a funeral, they lament and repine that others are gone to an harbour of rest, to which they themselves never can hope to arrive.

Gulliver adds mischievously:

If a Struldbrugg happen to marry one of his own kind, the marriage is dissolved of course by the courtesy of the kingdom, as soon as the younger of the two comes to be fourscore. For the law thinks it a reasonable indulgence, that those who are condemned without any fault of their own to a perpetual continuance in the world, should not have their misery doubled by the load of a wife.

In the Penguin edition of this book (1967) Michael Foot, one-time leader of the British Labour Party and an expert on Swift, said: 'No one can read *Gulliver's Travels* without at some point feeling a whip across his own back; no single sinner escapes. But it is arrogant, self-satisfied, savage, corrupt and corrupting power which comes off worst.'

George Orwell, himself a political writer of great merit, wrote a perceptive essay on *Gulliver's Travels* in which he said he would place it among the six books that should be preserved if all other books were to be destroyed. Despite his admiration for it as an imaginative literary work, Orwell is critical of Swift's underlying pessimism and his general disgust with human nature. He comments: 'But the most essential thing in Swift is his inability to believe that life – ordinary life on the solid earth, and not some rationalized, deodorized version of it – could be made worth living. Of course, no honest person claims that happiness is now a normal condition among adult human beings; but perhaps it could be made normal, and it is upon this question that all serious political controversy really turns.'[5]

A reader's evaluation of the merits of *Gulliver* will depend largely on the individual's own philosophical outlook. Some of the episodes in it may seem exaggerated but overall it is a thought-provoking satire on the frailties of human beings. In its denigration of human nature one suspects that Swift found it difficult to accept – or perhaps resented having to accept – the animal side of human nature. He seemed to find the bodily functions which mankind shares with the animals rather incongruous.

A MODEST PROPOSAL

In 1729 he published his *Modest Proposal for Preventing the Children of Poor People from being a burden to their Parents or the Country*. It is a savage satire and purports to advocate the mitigation of the widespread misery and poverty of Irish people by the selling off of a proportion of their infant children to be cooked as food for the more wealthy sector of society. He sets out six benefits that would result. The first is that 'it would greatly lessen the number of Papists, with whom we are yearly over-run, being the principal breeders of the nation as well as our most dangerous enemies, and who stay at home on purpose with a design to deliver the kingdom to the Pretender'. The sixth benefit is that it 'would be a great inducement to marriage, which all wise nations have either encouraged with rewards or enforced by laws and penalties. It would increase the care and tenderness of mothers toward their children, when they were sure of a settlement for life to the poor babes, provided in some sort by the public to their annual profit instead of expense'.

SWIFT'S VERSE

Swift is renowned as a writer of English prose, but he also wrote a considerable amount of verse. A good example is 'A Description of a City Shower', written in 1710:

> Careful observers may foretell the hour
> (By sure prognostics) when to dread a show'r:
> While rain depends, the pensive cat gives o'er
> Her frolics, and pursues her tail no more.
> Returning home at night, you'll find the sink
> Strike your offended sense with double stink.
> If you be wise, then go not far to dine:
> You'll spend in coach-hire more than save in wine.
> A coming show'r your shooting corns presage,
> Old a'ches throb, your hollow tooth will rage.
> Saunt'ring in coffeehouse is Dulman seen;
> He damns the climate, and complains of spleen.
>
> Meanwhile the South, rising with dabbled wings,
> A sable cloud athwart the welkin flings
> That swill'd more liquor that it could contain,
> And, like a drunkard, gives it up again.
> Brisk Susan whips her linen from the rope,
> While the first drizzling show'r is borne aslope;
> Such is that sprinkling which some careless quean
> Flirts on you from her mop, but not so clean:

You fly, invoke the gods; then turning, stop
To rail; she singing, still whirls on her mop.
Not yet the dust had shunn'd th'unequal strife,
But, aided by the wind, fought still for life,
And wafted with its foe by violent gust,
'Twas doubtful which was rain, and which was dust.
Ah! where must needy poet seek for aid,
When dust and rain at once his coat invade?
His only coat, where dust confus'd with rain
Roughen the nap, and leave a mingled stain.

Now in contiguous drops the flood comes down,
Threat'ning with deluge this devoted town.
To shops in crowds the daggled females fly,
Pretend to cheapen goods, but nothing buy.
The Templar spruce, while ev'ry spout's abroach,
Stays till 'tis fair, yet seems to call a coach.
The tuck'd-up sempstress walks with hasty strides,
While streams run down her oil'd umbrella's sides.
Here various kinds, by various fortunes led,
Commence acquaintance underneath a shed:
Triumphant Tories and desponding Whigs,
Forget their feuds, and join to save their wigs.
Box'd in a chair the beau impatient sits,
While spouts run clatt'ring o'er the roof by fits,
And ever and anon with frightful din
The leather sounds; he trembles from within.
So when Troy chairmen bore the wooden steed,
Pregnant with Greeks impatient to be freed
(Those bully Greeks, who, as the moderns do,
Instead of paying chairmen, run them thro'),
Laoco'n struck the outside with his spear,
And each imprison'd hero quaked with fear.

Now from all parts the swelling kennels flow,
And bear their trophies with them, as they go:
Filth of all hues and odours seem to tell
What street they sail'd from, by their sight and smell.
They, as each torrent drives with rapid force,
From Smithfield, or St'Pulchre's shape their course,
And in huge confluent join'd at Snow Hill ridge,
Fall from the Conduit prone to Holborn-bridge.
Sweepings from butchers' stalls, dung, guts, and blood,
Drown'd puppies, stinking sprats, all drench'd in mud
Dead cats, and turnip-tops, come tumbling down the flood.

This verse may not have lyrical beauty but it has descriptive realism, particularly the last eleven lines.

One of his most famous poems is 'Verses on the Death of Dr Swift', written in 1731. It is a long poem, but the following extracts are a good example of his later verse writing:

> The time is not remote, when I
> Must by the course of nature die:
> When I foresee, my special friends
> Will try to find their private ends.
> And tho' 'tis hardly understood
> Which way my death can do them good,
> Yet thus, methinks, I hear 'em speak:
> 'See, how the Dean begins to break!
> Poor gentleman, he droops apace,
> You plainly find it in his face:
> That old vertigo in his head
> Will never leave him, till he's dead:
> Besides, his memory decays,
> He recollects not what he says,
> He cannot call his friends to mind:
> Forgets the place where last he din'd:
> Plies you with stories o'er and o'er,
> He told them fifty times before.
> How does he fancy, we can sit
> To hear his out-of-fashion'd wit?
> But he takes up with younger folks,
> Who, for his wine, will bear his jokes.
> Faith, he must make his stories shorter,
> Or change his comrades once a quarter....
>
> 'Perhaps I may allow, the Dean
> Had too much satire in his vein,
> And seemed determin'd not to starve it,
> Because no age could more deserve it.
> Yet, malice never was his aim;
> He lash'd the vice, but spared the name.
> No individual could resent
> Where thousands equally were meant.
> His satire points at no defect,
> But what all mortals may correct;
> For he abhorr'd that senseless tribe
> Who call it humour when they jibe:
> He spar'd a hump, or crooked nose,
> Whose owners set not up for beaux,
> True genuine dullness moved his pity,
> Unless it offered to be witty.
> Those who their ignorance confess'd
> He ne'er offended with a jest;
> But laughed to hear an idiot quote
> A verse from Horace, learned by rote.
>
> 'He knew an hundred pleasant stories,

With all the turns of Whigs and Tories:
Was cheerful to his dying day,
And friends would let him have his way.
'He gave the little wealth he had,
To build a house for fools and mad:
To show, by one satiric touch,
No nation wanted it so much:
That kingdom he hath left his debtor,
I wish it soon may have a better.'

SWIFT'S RELIGIOUS OPINIONS

Some commentators have said that Swift's religious beliefs were not very deep and that he was more interested in his career as a churchman than in dedicating his life to the gospel of Jesus Christ. Swift's approach to the duties of a clergyman was rather mundane, and he seemed to be as much – if not more – interested in political matters as in Christian doctrine and theology.

Davis Noke has the following comments to make on Swift's religious belief[2]:

> Swift's deep aversion to public displays of faith is well known. His early biographers agree in presenting him as a man of great piety who nevertheless shunned all religious ostentation. 'During his residence in London ... he was seldom seen at church at the usual hours that pretenders to religion show themselves there'[Thomas Sheridan]. However commendable this dislike of display, it may have had deeper roots in doubt and confusion. The evidence suggests that Swift's ambivalence towards father-figures in his life extended also to God, and inhibited him from truly believing in the personal love, for him, of God the Father. His instinct for playing the hypocrite in reverse may well have been an attempt to project outwards a deep sense of hypocrisy that he felt within himself. We find the same tussle between conscience and conformity fought over again and again in his sermons. Where Hamm in Beckett's *Endgame* expresses the incoherent rage of a godfearing atheist, 'God ... the bastard! He doesn't exist!' Swift reveals the tormented pessimism of an orthodox clergyman who cannot really believe in God – certainly not in the loving God of the New Testament.

Nevertheless, his religious tracts and sermons indicate that he believed in the divinity of Jesus Christ and in the importance of living according to the teachings of Christ. Examples of his religious belief are the prayers he composed during Stella's last illness, one of which has already been quoted. However, there is a rather harsh tone about some of his sermons, particularly the sermon 'On the Causes of the Wretched Condition of Ireland'. It is more a tract than a sermon, and in it he enunciates his general views on poor people and beggars:

In most parts of this kingdom the natives are from their infancy so given up to idleness and sloth, that they often choose to beg or steal rather than support themselves with their own labour; they marry without the least view or thought of being able to make any provision for their families; and whereas in all industrious nations children are looked on as a help to their parents, with us, for want of being trained to work, they are an intolerable burden at home, and a grievous charge upon the public, as appears from the vast number of ragged and naked children in town and country, led about by strolling women, trained up in ignorance and all manner of vice ...

I shall now say something about that great number of poor who, under the name of common beggars, infest our streets, and fill our ears with their continual cries and craving importunity. This I shall venture to call an unnecessary evil, brought upon us for the gross neglect and want of proper management in those whose duty it is to prevent it. But before I proceed further, let me humbly presume to vindicate the justice and mercy of God and His dealings with mankind. Upon this particular He hath not dealt so hardly with His creatures as some would imagine, when they see so many miserable objects ready to perish for want: for it would infallibly be found, upon strict enquiry, that there is hardly one in twenty of those miserable objects who do not owe their present poverty to their own faults, to their present sloth and negligence, to their indiscreet marriage without the least prospect of supporting a family, to their foolish expensiveness, to their drunkenness, and other vices, by which they have squandered their gettings, and contracted diseases in their old age. And, to speak freely, is it any way reasonable or just, that those who have denied themselves many satisfactions and conveniences of life, from a principle of conscience, as well as prudence, that they might not be a burden to the public, should be charged with supporting others, who have brought themselves to less than a morsel of bread by their idleness, extravagance, and vice?

Even allowing for the abject poverty that was widespread in eighteenth-century Ireland, and the absence of social means adequate to relieve this burden of poverty (a workhouse was established in Dublin in 1704 but this catered for only a fraction of the very poor), it is evident that Swift had an unsympathetic and intolerant attitude towards the poor.

Lest we be regarded as too strict on Swift in this matter, however, it must be said that there is evidence in his personal dealings with people that he was a friendly and charitable man. He was popular among the ordinary people who lived in the vicinity of St Patrick's Cathedral, particulary among the weavers who were disemployed because of the restrictions on the export of wool from Ireland.

In a letter to his great friend, Alexander Pope (who, incidentally, was a Catholic) he wrote:

'I have ever hated all nations, professions and communities, and all my love is towards individuals ... but principally I hate and detest that animal called man, although I heartily love John, Thomas and so forth.'

RELIGIOUS TOLERATION

Swift was against religious toleration for citizens who were not members of the Established Church. As already mentioned, he opposed dissenters of all kinds, particularly Presbyterians, whose religious beliefs and practices he said were anti-monarchical and republican, as had been borne out by the overthrow and execution of King Charles I and the substitution of a Commonwealth for the monarchy.

Swift was strongly opposed to the Roman Catholic Church (which he referred to as Popery), but he regarded Presbyterianism as a greater threat to the Established Church, as he believed that the Penal Laws against Catholics had effectively removed the danger from that quarter. He made his views quite clear in the tracts he wrote on the need to continue in force the Sacramental Test against dissenters.

The Test Act had been introduced in England in 1673 and was brought into effect in Ireland in 1704 as part of additional legal restrictions 'to prevent the further growth of Popery'. The Test Act also applied to Presbyterians and deprived them of the right to hold any civil or military offices, unless they had recently received communion in accordance with the rites of the Established Church. In his first tract on this subject, *Letter concerning the Sacramental Test*, written in 1708, he incidentally made clear his views on Roman Catholics:

> We are told the Popish interest is here so formidable that all hands should be joined to keep it under; that the only names of distinction among us ought to be those of Protestant and Papist, and that this expedient is the only means to unite all Protestants upon one common bottom. All of which is nothing but misrepresentation and mistake. If we were under any real fear of the Papists in this kingdom it would be hard to think us so stupid not to be equally apprehensive with others, since we are likely to be the greatest and more immediate sufferers; but on the contrary, we look upon them to be altogether as inconsiderable as the women and children. Their lands are almost entirely taken from them, and they are rendered incapable of purchasing any more; and for the little that remains provision is being made by the late act against Popery that it will daily crumble away: To prevent which, some of the most considerable among them are already turned Protestants, and so in all probability will many more. Then the Popish priests are all registered, and without permission (which I hope will not be granted) they can have no successors; so that the Protestant Clergy will find it perhaps no difficult matter to bring great numbers over to the Church; and in the meantime the common people without leaders, without discipline, or natural courage, being little better than 'hewers of wood

and drawers of water' are out of all capacity of doing any mischief, if
they were ever so well inclined.

In 1731 and 1732 rumours began to circulate in Ireland that the government intended to remove the Test Act from Protestant dissenters, and
this motivated Swift to write further tracts on the subject. In 1732 he
published a tract called *The Advantages proposed by Repealing the Sacramental Test, impartially considered,* in which he put forward the thesis that 'in
whatever country that religion predominates there is one certain form of
worship and ceremony, which is looked upon as the Established; and
consequently only the priests of that particular form are maintained at
the public charge; and all civil employments are bestowed among those
who comply (at least outwardly) with the same Establishment'.

He followed this up in 1733 with the tract *The Presbyterian Plea of Merit
in Order, to take off the Test.* In this he set out to refute the arguments put
forward by Presbyterians that their claim was 'founded upon the services
they did towards the restoration of King Charles the Second, and at the
Revolution under the Prince of Orange'. He also questioned whether the
loyalty of Presbyterians could be relied upon if the Pretender landed an
army in northern Ireland. In the course of this tract he broke off to express
his views on Popery:

> As to Popery in general, which for a thousand years past hath been
> introducing and multiplying corruptions both in doctrine and disci-
> pline: I look upon it to be the most absurd system of Christianity
> professed by any nation. But I cannot apprehend this kingdom to be in
> much danger from it. The estates of Papists are very few; crumbling
> into small parcels, and daily diminishing. Their common people are
> sunk in poverty, ignorance, and cowardice, and of as little consequence
> as women and children. Their nobility and gentry are at least one-half
> ruined, banished, or converted: They all soundly feel the smart of what
> they suffered in the last Irish war. Some of them are already retired into
> foreign countries; others as I am told intend to follow them: and the
> rest, I believe, to a man, who still possess any lands, are absolutely
> determined never to hazard them again for the sake of establishing
> their superstition.

Later the same year he published another tract, *Reasons for repealing the
Sacramental Test in favour of Catholics,* in which he ironically put forward
arguments for freeing Catholics from the Test on lines similar to those
put forward on behalf of Presbyterians.

Because of strong opposition in the Irish Parliament to any repeal of
the Test Act, the government dropped the idea.

These tracts reveal Swift's prejudiced views towards Presbyterians
and Roman Catholics. He supported the Penal Laws against Roman
Catholics, most of which were enacted during his own adult life. He was
aware of, and criticised, the injustices suffered by Irish people under

English rule, but seemed to see no harm in laws aimed at strangling the Roman Catholic church and at impoverishing and degrading Roman Catholics. It is worth mentioning here, however, that such views were quite common among Church of Ireland clergy at that time, as is confirmed by Kenneth Milne, Principal of the Church of Ireland College of Education, in a recent short history of that church, where he says: 'While it is true that some Church of Ireland bishops and clergy spoke out against the harshness of the penal laws such men were few, and most churchmen had little fault to find with a position that gave them such ascendancy.'[7]

THE PENAL LAWS

The Penal Laws against Catholics were enacted by the Irish Parliament (in which there were no Catholics), with English approval, between 1691 and 1709, and their effect may be summarised as follows. Catholics could not become Members of Parliament or vote for a member of Parliament without taking an oath of allegiance and an abjuration against the doctrine of transubstantiation, together with a declaration that James III (the Pretender) had no right to the crown. They could not be appointed to any civil or military office without receiving holy communion according to the rites of the Church of Ireland and signing a declaration against transubstantiation. They were debarred from keeping a school and from sending their children abroad for education. They could not purchase any interest in land except for a lease not exceeding 31 years. If the eldest son of a Catholic landowner converted to the Established Church he became the owner of the property; otherwise, when the Catholic father died, the property was divided among the sons. Protestants and Catholics were forbidden to intermarry; a Protestant woman marrying a Catholic man forfeited her possessions, and a Protestant man marrying a Catholic woman was treated as a Catholic unless the woman conformed to the Established Church within a year. Catholic bishops and religious orders were banished from Ireland; if they returned they were liable to imprisonment and transportation, and if they returned again after transportation they were guilty of high treason. Catholic secular (parish) clergy were allowed to practise, but in 1709 they became registrable and had to remain in their county of registration.

The Penal Laws are now past history and were not always fully enforced, but they were unjust and indefensible, all the more so because they were directed against the majority of the population by an unrepresentative minority government. Fear of Irish support for the Jacobites, whose claim to the English throne was endorsed by Louis XIV of France, was undoubtedly a motivating factor behind the Penal Laws, but this scarcely justifies such a prolonged oppressive legal code.

With later growth in understanding and toleration the laws began to be relaxed in the 1770s, but it was not until 1829 that Catholics could be elected to Parliament.

Presbyterians also suffered civil and religious discrimination, but not to the same extent as Roman Catholics. The restrictions on Presbyterians began to be relaxed from 1719 onwards, under Indemnity Acts, though it was not until 1780 that the Test Act ceased to apply to them.

Though Swift's religious views were grossly intolerant of Presbyterianism and Catholicism, his writings on behalf of legislative independence and freedom of trade for Ireland were reformist and democratic. Apparently Swift did not see any inconsistency between his religious and social views. A modern observer may find this perplexing; so also, a century ago, did the Irish Protestant historian, W.E.H. Lecky, when he published his famous history of eighteenth-century Ireland[8], which contains the following comments on Swift:

> The patriotism of Swift himself was of a very mingled order. Though Irish by birth and education he always looked upon his country as a place of exile, and upon the great mass of its people with undisguised contempt. He had seen without a word of disapprobation the enactment of the most atrocious of the penal laws, which crushed the Catholics to the dust, and though declaring himself that there was no serious disloyalty among them, he looked forward with approval to the legal extirpation of their religion by the refusal of Government to permit any priest to celebrate its rites. If there was any hope of the Irish people maintaining their position in the face of English jealousy, it could only be by their union; but not content with cutting himself off from the Catholics by his approval of the penal laws, he allowed his passions as a Churchman to impel him to the bitterest animosity towards the Protestant nonconformists.

But further down the same page Lecky continues:

> Yet, in spite of all this, Ireland owes much to Swift. No one can study with impartiality his writings or his life without perceiving that, except in questions where ecclesiastical interests distorts his judgment, he was animated by a fierce and generous hatred of injustice, and by a very deep and real compassion for material suffering. Endowed by nature not only with literary talents of the highest order, but also with the commanding intellect of a statesman, accustomed to live in close intimacy with the governing classes of the Empire, he found himself in a country where all popular government was reduced to a system of jobbery, where the most momentous material and moral interests were deliberately crushed by a tyranny at once blind, brutal, and mean, where the people had lost

all spirit of self-reliance and liberty, and where public opinion was almost unknown.

Another highly respected Irish Protestant historian, J.C. Beckett, is also worth quoting on Swift's religious views:

> It remains only to ask why Swift should have resisted so fiercely claims that seem to most of us so reasonable, claims, moreover, that would appear to follow naturally from his own famous dictum: 'Government without the consent of the governed is the very definition of slavery.' Some would find the answer in a narrow-minded sectarianism; some say that he had learned to hate the presbyterians during his brief residence in County Antrim. But the truth is that Swift's reluctance to admit dissenters to any share of political power flows directly from his views on the church and its relations with the state. He quite sincerely regarded the Church of England, in its policy and doctrine (though not, of course, in its actual operation) as a model of apostolic purity. But this church had a dual existence. It was a divinely-instituted society, deriving its authority from Christ. It was also (as a result of an assumed contract) the official expression of the national religion; in this latter capacity it was subject to the supreme power of the state.[9]

LAST YEARS

In May 1740 Swift made his last will, in which he mentioned that he was of sound mind, although weak in body. But his mental and physical powers were deteriorating. In a note he wrote, in July of the same year, to Mrs Whiteway, a widowed cousin who visited him regularly, he said:

> I have been very miserable all night, and today extremely deaf and full of pain. I am so stupid and confounded that I cannot express the mortification I am under both in body and mind. All I can say is, that I am not in torture, but I daily and hourly expect it ... I am sure my days will be very few; few and miserable they must be.[2]

In May 1742, Swift was judged to be of such unsound mind and memory as to be incapable of transacting any business or managing his affairs. A committee of guardians was appointed to look after his interests.

He remained in the Deanery, where he was looked after by his servants, and Mrs Whiteway called to see him most days. His condition worsened and was described by Mrs Whiteway in a letter written towards the end of 1742:

> He walked ten hours a day, would not eat or drink if his servant stayed in the room. His meat was served up ready cut, and sometimes it would lie an hour on the table before he would touch it, and then eat it walking. About six weeks ago, in one night's time, his left eye swelled as large as an egg ... and many large boils appeared under his arms and body. The torture he was in is not to be described. Five persons could scarce hold him for a week, from tearing out his own eyes.[2]

However, Swift was not always in such a bad condition. He was not mad, but lacked normal mental powers. The end of his troubles came on 19 October 1745, when he died, aged 78. He was buried in St Patrick's where his epitaph, composed by himself in Latin, can still be read. A translation of this epitaph is:

> Here lies the body of Jonathan Swift, Doctor of Divinity and Dean of this Cathedral, where savage indignation can no more lacerate his heart. Go, traveller, and imitate if you can one who strove with all his might to champion liberty.

He left the bulk of his fortune to purchase land near Dr Steevens Hospital on which to build a hospital for idiots and lunatics. This project succeeded after his death, with the assistance of funds from Parliament and benefactors. The hospital (St Patrick's) was opened in 1757 and is still going strong.

BIBLIOGRAPHY

(1) Irvin Ehrenpreis, *Swift: The Man, his Works, and the Age*;
Three volumes, 1962, 1967 and 1983. Methuen, London.
(2) David Nokes, *Jonathan Swift: A Hypocrite Reversed*.
Oxford University Press, 1985.
(3) J.A. Downie, *Jonathan Swift: Political Writer*.
Routledge & Kegan Paul, London, 1984.
(4) A.M. Freeman (ed.), *Vanessa and Her Correspondence with Jonathan Swift*. Selwyn & Blount, London, 1921.
(5) George Orwell, *Collected Works*, Vol. II. Secker & Warburg, London, 1980.
(6) Louis A. Landa, *Swift and the Church of Ireland*. Oxford University Press, London, 1954.
(7) Kenneth Milne, *The Church of Ireland: A History*.
APCK Publication, year not given but apparently 1980.
(8) W.E.H. Lecky, *History of Ireland in the Eighteenth Century*.
London, 1892; reprinted 1972 by University of Chicago Press, London and Chicago.
(9) J.C. Beckett, *Confrontations: Studies in Irish History*.
Faber & Faber, London, 1972.
(10) The extracts from Swift's published works quoted in this chapter are taken from *The Oxford Authors: Jonathan Swift*, published by the Oxford University Press, 1984.
(11)The quotations from Swift's sermons and religious tracts are from Vol. IV of *Prose Works of Jonathan Swift*, edited by Temple Scott; George Bell, London, 1898.

WOLFE TONE
(1763 –1798)

Wolfe Tone's place in modern Irish history is assured because of the extent to which he dedicated the latter portion of his life to efforts to attain the independence of Ireland from British rule. In pursuance of this objective he went to France in 1796 to persuade the French revolutionary government to send a military expedition to Ireland to liberate the country. His efforts were successful, but the first French expedition, which reached Bantry Bay in 1796, was a failure due to a number of factors: inflexible instructions for the military commanders, indecision, bad weather, and bad luck. The second expedition, in 1798, comprised two small, separate French invasion forces: one with about 1,000 troops which landed at Killala, County Mayo, and had a limited success; and the second, with about 2,300 troops, which reached the coast of Donegal, where it was intercepted and defeated by a British naval force. Tone, an officer on board one of the latter French ships, was captured, tried and condemned to death.

Tone has been called the father of Irish republicanism, and every year representatives of Irish political parties, including the government of the day, attend at his grave in Bodenstown, County Kildare, to honour his memory. Extremist republican groups also visit his grave and claim to be Tone's true inheritors. But Tone's objective was to unite the whole people of Ireland – Protestant, Catholic and Dissenter – whereas the recent campaign of murders, kidnappings, car bombs, booby traps and wanton destruction of property carried out by the Provisional IRA in Northern Ireland resulted in increased dissension and bitterness among the people there.

In his memoirs, written while he was in France, Tone set out his republican philosophy in the following well-known passage:

> To subvert the tyranny of our execrable government, to break the connection with England, the never failing source of all our political evils, and to assert the independence of my country – these were my objects. To unite the whole people of Ireland, to abolish the memory of all past dissensions, and to substitute the common name of Irishmen, in the place of the denominations of Protestant, Catholic and Dissenter – these were my means.

~

Theobald Wolfe Tone was born in Dublin on 20 June 1763, the eldest son of Peter and Margaret Tone. At that time the family seems to have been living in St Bride Street, beside Dublin Castle, but soon afterwards moved to 44 Stafford Street (now Wolfe Tone Street), on the northern side of the river Liffey. It was a commodious house, for the Tones were prosperous middle-class people. Theobald was baptised in St Mary's Church, a stone's throw away.

Tone's ancestors came originally from France. After living in England for a while they settled in Ireland in the early part of the seventeenth century. Tone's grandfather was a farmer on 200 acres of freehold land near Clane, County Kildare. When he died in 1766, after a fall from a stack of corn, the farm went to his son Peter, who was a coachbuilder. Many years later, however, the ownership of the farm became the subject of litigation between Peter and his brother Jonathan; Peter lost the case and the legal costs impoverished him.

Tone's mother's maiden name was Lamport, and her father came from Drogheda. Like his father before him, Mr Lamport worked in merchant shipping. Margaret had been reared as a Catholic, but converted to the Church of Ireland in 1771, presumably so that all the the family would be members of the same church. This change does not seem to have caused any friction in the family.

Peter Tone's farm was situated on the estate of a family called Wolfe, who had a mansion at Blackhall, near Clane. The Tone family had regular contact with the Wolfes; in fact Margaret Lamport had, before her marriage, lived in the Wolfe mansion to assist Mrs Wolfe. When Peter and Margaret Tone had their first son they named him after the young squire of the estate, Theobald Wolfe.

Peter and Margaret Tone had sixteen children, but due to the ravages of tuberculosis only five of them survived into adult life. A brief look at the other four surviving children will help to put Theobald into perspective and show what an adventurous family the Tones were.

William, born 1764, ran away to London at the age of sixteen and joined the East India Company; he was killed in a war in India in 1802. Matthew, born 1771, went to America and the West Indies, and then to France, before he was 25, and joined the French army; he was with the French invasion force that landed in Ireland in 1798, and he was captured, court-martialled and hanged. Mary, born around 1774, accompanied Theobald when he went to the USA in 1795; on the return voyage she met a Swiss merchant whom she married in Hamburg; she died in Santo Domingo while still a fairly young woman. Arthur, born 1782, went to sea at twelve and became an officer in the Dutch navy, after which he went to America and joined the navy there; his further life story is unknown.

When he was about eight years of age Theobald began attending a small private school run by a man named Sisson Darling who, because Theobald was a bright pupil, recommended that he should go to a preparatory school in the hope of gaining entry to Trinity College, Dublin, which was within easy walking distance. For this purpose Theobold attended a school managed by a clergyman named William Craig in nearby Henry Street. However, he found school boring and, with a few other pupils, began to miss classes so that he could spend time sight-seeing in Dublin. He particularly liked watching military parades, then held fairly frequently in Dublin, particularly when the Lord Lieutenant was in residence in Dublin Castle.

At that time Dublin, with a population of about 150,000, was the second largest city in the British Isles and, during Tone's short life, was becoming very impressive due to the well-designed public buildings and squares recently built or under construction. Most of what is now known as Georgian Dublin was designed and constructed during the second half of the eighteenth century. Work on Merrion Square commenced in 1762 and continued into the 1780s. Fitzwilliam Square was developed around the same period. Mountjoy Square was built between 1782 and 1798. The Custom House was built between 1781 and 1791, and the Four Courts between 1786 and 1802. Gandon's extensions to Parliament House (now the Bank of Ireland) were carried out between 1782 and 1789. In other words, Tone had much to observe in Dublin during his school and college days.

While Theobald was still attending Mr Craig's school, his father's fortunes deteriorated and the family moved to the farm in County Kildare, though Theobald remained in lodgings in Dublin. Mr Craig eventually told Mr Tone about his son's absences from school. This led to a family row, during which Theobald said he wished to join the army. His father threatened to cut off his allowance and, with bad grace, Theobald went back to school and succeeded in entering Trinity College in February 1781, where his studies centred on the classics. He was not an assiduous student, but made an impression in the college Historical Society, where he got two medals for oratory and was elected Auditor during his final year.

At Trinity he took part in amateur dramatics and became infatuated with the beautiful young wife of a wealthy Galway landowner, Richard Martin, who later became known as 'Humanity Dick' because of his efforts to protect animals from cruelty. The Martins had a house in Kildare Street with a small theatre and this enabled them and Tone to share their mutual interest in amateur dramatics. As Mr Martin was often away on business, Tone and Mrs Martin became attracted to each other.

The affair lasted a couple of years but ended rather suddenly because of a strong disagreement between Tone and Mr Martin over a different matter. According to Tone's comments in his journal, the affair did not go beyond the bounds of propriety. Some years later, however, Mrs Martin became seriously involved with an Englishman, John Petrie, and was divorced by her husband. In his journal in later years Tone made the following interesting comments on his affair with Mrs Martin:

> I was the proudest man alive to have engaged the affections of a woman, whom even now I recognise to have had extraordinary merit, and who then appeared in my eyes more divine than human. In this intercourse of sentiment, which alternately pained and delighted me almost beyond bearing, we continued for about two years ... without however in a single instance overstepping the bounds of virtue, such was the purity of the extravagant affection I bore her ... The truth is I loved her with an affection of a seraphic nature; the profound respect I bore her, and my ignorance of the world, prevented my availing myself of opportunities which a man more trained than I was [Tone was 20 - 22 years old when he knew Mrs Martin], would not have let slip'.

Not long after this affair, and while still at Trinity, Tone met and fell in love with a fifteen-year-old girl named Matilda Witherington, who lived in Grafton Street (beside Trinity College) with her maternal grandfather, a clergyman named Fanning. The feeling was mutual and within a matter of months, in July 1785, they were married in St Ann's Church, Dawson Street. They spent their honeymoon in Maynooth and, when they returned to Dublin, Matilda's family accepted their marriage, though perhaps with some misgivings in view of their young ages and lack of financial resources.

Tone graduated from Trinity the following year and decided to study for the Bar, which entailed spending two years at the Middle Temple in London, from January 1787 to December 1788. During those two years he did not return home, presumably to avoid the 30-hour stagecoach journey from London to Liverpool, followed by a sea voyage to Dublin, and then back again to London.

He was often short of money while in London and had to borrow from his friends, some of whom were Trinity graduates like himself. In the meantime his wife and their first child (Maria) stayed with Tone's father in County Kildare. In all they had four children born in the years 1786 to 1793, but only one (William, born 1791) survived into full adult life; it was he who compiled and edited Tone's *Life*.

When Tone later became involved in political affairs he left much of the rearing of their children to his wife, but she seems to have accepted this task uncomplainingly, out of love for him and for them. Despite long separations, their marriage was a happy one.

Tone was a thin man of medium height, with sharp features and a sallow complexion. In other words, his appearance was not striking (in his journal, when describing his initial efforts to woo his future wife, he wrote modestly 'though certainly my appearance, neither then nor now, was much in my favour'), but he had animated features, with lively eyes, and both men and women were attracted by his engaging personality.

During his two years at Middle Temple he enjoyed, with some friends, the social life of London, including the company of the 'fair sex', as his journal indicates:

> At the age of 24, with a tolerable figure and address and in an idle and luxurious capital, it will not be supposed I was without adventures with the fair sex. The Englishmen neglect their wives exceedingly in many essential circumstances; I was totally disengaged, and did not fail to profit, as far as I could, of their neglect, and the Englishwomen are not naturally cruel. I formed in consequence several delightful connections in London, and as I was extremely discreet, I have the satisfaction to think that not one of those to whom I had the good fortune to render myself agreeable ever suffered the slightest blemish in her reputation on my account. I cherish yet the memory of one charming woman to whom I was extremely attached, and I am sure she still remembers me with a mutual regard.[2]

(These comments were not included in the published *Life* of Tone.[2] His son, as editor, explained in the preface: 'The only liberties which I have taken with the following memoirs, in preparing them for the press, were to suppress a few passages relative to family affairs, which concern nobody; and the account of some early amours, which my father, though a little wild in his youth, was too much of a gentleman to have allowed to appear, and which it would ill become his son to revive at this day').

TONE'S MEMOIRS

Our main source of information about Wolfe Tone is the *Life of Theobald Wolfe Tone*, compiled and edited by his son, William (1791–1828). It is made up largely of Tone's autobiographical writings and journals, supplemented by connecting narrative pieces, written by his son, covering the years 1793 to 1795 (for which period Tone's journals were lost in America), and an account of Tone's capture, trial and death. This *Life* was first published in Washington DC in 1826. It is out of print at present.

LONDON

While Tone was in London, ostensibly studying law, he was joined by his brother William, who had completed a term of eight years' service with the East India Company; when Tone returned to Dublin at the end of 1788, William went with him.

Tone was not a dedicated law student and instead began writing reviews and articles for periodicals. He also, with the help of two friends, wrote a romantic story called 'Belmont Castle', which was not a success. He became very interested in books about voyages of discovery, including Captain Cook's famous voyages in the Pacific, in the course of which Cook discovered the Sandwich Islands (now Hawaiian Islands) in 1778. The latter discovery was probably the origin for a rather strange memorandum which Tone wrote and handed into the Prime Minister's residence in Downing Street in August 1788, making a case for the establishment of a British colony on the Sandwich Islands, which could be used as a military base against Spain. When he received no reply within a fortnight, he wrote a lengthy letter to the Prime Minister (Pitt) explaining the benefits of the scheme, which, he added, he was prepared to administer if approved. There was no reply from Pitt. That this scheme was not simply a passing fancy of Tone's is borne out by the fact that he re submitted it in 1790 to the Duke of Richmond, Master of Ordnance, who replied saying it should be submitted to the Home Office. The Home Office turned it down.

After nearly two years at the Middle Temple, Tone returned to Dublin to try his hand at the Bar, with the assistance of a gift of £500 from his wife's grandfather, £100 of which he spent on the purchase of law books. With his wife and young daughter he settled in lodgings in Clarendon Street (where, incidentally, the first Catholic Church since the Reformation was allowed to be opened in Dublin, in 1793, as a result of relaxations of the Penal Laws).

He qualified as Bachelor of Law and became a member of the Bar on 4 May, 1789, having taken the oaths of allegiance and adjuration stipulated by the Penal laws, designed to keep Catholics out of the professions. He went on the Leinster Circuit but, as the Bar was overcrowded and there was a lot of favouritism in the allocation of briefs, Tone found time on his hands and began to write political pamphlets; he always had a greater interest in politics than the law. As the Whig party, in opposition, was more reformist than the Tories, his initial political interests were with the Whigs, but he soon found that their ideas were insufficiently radical for him.

IRISH POLITICS

In the eighteenth century Ireland was a separate kingdom with a separate Parliament, but giving allegiance to the English monarch. Despite some concessions granted by Britain in 1782, which theoretically gave legislative independence to the Irish Parliament, the Irish Administration was in the hands of the Lord Lieutenant, the king's representative in Ireland, who was appointed on the advice of the British government and, in effect, responsible to them. Tone was very scornful of this Irish Parliament, which was elected on a very limited suffrage: mainly landowners and men of substance. Catholics, who constituted about three-quarters of the total population of Ireland, were debarred from membership of the House, and were not even entitled to vote until 1793. Presbyterians were also discriminated against, in that they could not hold public or military office.

In his memoirs, Tone set out to give 'a rather rapid survey of the state of parties in Ireland, that is to say, of the members of the established religion, the Dissenters and the Catholics'. It is worthwhile quoting this 'rapid survey' at some length as it shows his political views at the time (1796):

> The first party, whom for distinction's sake I call the Protestants, though not above a tenth of the population, were in possession of the whole of the government, and of five-sixths of the landed property of the nation; they were, and had been for above a century, in the quiet enjoyment of the church, the law, the revenue, the army, the navy, the magistracy, the corporations– in a word, of the whole patronage of Ireland. With properties whose title was founded in massacre and plunder, and being, as it were, but a colony of foreign usurpers in the land, they saw no security for their persons and estates but in a close connexion with England, who profited of their fears; and, as the price of her protection, exacted the implicit surrender of the commerce and liberties of Ireland. Different events, particularly the Revolution in America, had enabled and emboldened the other two parties of whom I am about to speak, to hurry the Protestants into measures highly disagreeable to England and beneficial to their country; but in which, from accidental circumstances, they durst not refuse to concur. The spirit of the corps, however, remained unchanged, as they have manifested on every occasion since which chance has offered. This party, therefore, so powerful by their property and influence, were implicitly devoted to England, which they esteemed necessary for the security of their existence; they adopted, in consequence, the sentiments and the language of the British cabinet; they dreaded and abhorred the principles of the French Revolution, and were, in one word, an aristocracy in the fullest and most odious extent of the term.

The Dissenters, who formed the second party, were at least twice as numerous as the first. Like them, they were a colony of foreigners in their origin; but being mostly engaged in trade and manufactures, with few overgrown landed proprietors among them, they did not, like them, feel that a slavish dependence on England was essential to their very existence. Strong in their numbers and their courage, they felt that they were able to defend themselves, and they soon ceased to consider themselves as any other than Irishmen. It was the Dissenters who composed the flower of the famous volunteer army of 1782, which extorted from the English minister the restoration of what is affected to be called the constitution of Ireland; it was they who first promoted and continued the demand of a Parliamentary reform, in which, however, they were baffled by a superior address and chicanery of the aristocracy; and it was they finally who were the first to stand forward in the most decided and unqualified manner in support of the principles of the French Revolution.

The Catholics, who composed the third party, were above two-thirds of the nation, and formed, perhaps, a still greater proportion. They embraced the entire peasantry of three provinces, they constituted a considerable portion of the mercantile interest; but from the tyranny of the penal laws enacted at different periods against them, they possessed but a very small proportion of the landed property, perhaps not a fiftieth part of the whole. It is not my intention here to give a detail of that execrable and infamous code, framed with the heart and the malice of demons, to plunder, and degrade, and brutalize the Catholics. Suffice it to say, that there was no injustice, no disgrace, no disqualification, moral, political, or religious, civil or military, that was not heaped upon them; it is with difficulty that I restrain myself from entering into the abominable detail; but it is the less necessary, as it is to be found in many publications of the day. This horrible system, pursued for above a century with unrelenting acrimony and perseverance, had wrought its full effect, and had, in fact, reduced the great body of the Catholic peasantry of Ireland to a situation, morally and physically speaking, below that of the beasts of the field. The spirit of their few remaining gentry was broken, and their minds degraded; and it was only in a class of their merchants and traders, and a few members of the medical profession, who had smuggled an education in despite of the penal code, that any thing like political sensation existed. Such was pretty nearly the situation of the three great parties at the commencement of the French Revolution, and certainly a much more gloomy prospect could not well present itself to the eyes of any friend to liberty and his country. But as the luminary of truth and freedom in France advanced rapidly to its meridian splendour, the public mind in Ireland was proportionably illuminated; and to the honour of the Dissenters of Belfast be it said, they were the first to reduce to practice their newly received principles, and to show, by being just, that they were deserving to be free.[1]

There was a growing resentment among Catholics and Presbyterians at political and commercial power being largely in the hands of the Anglican ascendancy class. When the French Revolution got under way in June 1789, removing the privileges of the upper classes, and legislative authority became exercisable by a broadly based National Assembly, many people in Ireland, particularly northern Presbyterians (who had sympathised with Americans in their War of Independence against Britain), began to realise that radical political change towards a more democratic form of government was possible if sufficient pressure could be exerted on the administration. The formation of the Society of United Irishmen in October 1791, in which Tone took an active part, became part of this pressure.

Tone's first political pamphlet was *Review of the Conduct of Administration during the Last Session of Parliament*, which he wrote and published in Dublin in April 1790, signed 'An Independent Irish Whig'. Tone himself did not think highly of this pamphlet and described it in later years as 'barely above mediocrity, if it rose so high'. But it attracted the attention of the Northern Whig Club who reprinted it for use in electioneering.

Three months later, under the pseudonym 'Hibernicus', he wrote another pamphlet addressed to both Houses of the Irish Parliament, in which he queried why Ireland should become involved in a war between Great Britain and Spain simply because Britain proposed to do so to protect her own commercial interests. In this pamphlet, *Spanish War: An Enquiry how far Ireland is bound, of right, to Embark on the Impending Contest on the Side of Great Britain*, he argued that Ireland, as a separate kingdom with its own independent Parliament, was not bound to support a war declared by Great Britain.

> The King of Ireland may declare the war, but it is the Parliament only that can carry it on. If this be so, it follows very clearly that we are not, more than England, *ipso facto*, committed, merely by the declaration of war of our own King; and *a fortiori* much less are we committed by his declaration, as King of Great Britain, when our interest is endamaged, and the quarrel and the profit are merely and purely English ...
>
> We have no quarrel with Spain, no infraction of good faith, no national insult to complain of. No, but we have the resentments of a rapacious English East Indian monopolist to gratify, who, at the distance of half the globe, kindles the torch of war amidst the eternal snows of Nootka Sound [North America], and hurls it into the bosom of our commerce. The rising prosperity of Ireland is immolated on the altar of British pride and avarice; we are forced to combat without resentment in the quarrel of an alien, where victory is unprofitable and defeat is infamous.

Tone went on to deride the appeal for the good of the empire (which really meant England, he argued) and for the honour of the British flag (where is the national flag of Ireland? he asked); Ireland would continue to be denied trading rights.

AN ARGUMENT ON BEHALF OF THE CATHOLICS OF IRELAND

In August 1791 Tone published his most important pamphlet, *An Argument on Behalf of the Catholics of Ireland*, under the pseudonym 'A Northern Whig'. Tone said later, in his journal, that the pamphlet was 'addressed to the Dissenters' and that its object was 'to convince them that they and the Catholics had but one common interest, and one common enemy; that the depression and slavery of Ireland was produced and perpetuated by the divisions existing between them, and that consequently to assert the independence of their country, and their own individual liberties, it was necessary to forget all former feuds, to consolidate the entire strength of the whole nation, and to form for the future but one people'.

An Argument was written with an intense feeling of Irish nationhood; it appeals to the heart as well as to the head. It marks an important stage in the development of Tone's political philosophy as a radical nationalist, though as the pamphlet makes clear, he was then a monarchist, professing allegiance to the King of Ireland (not to the King of England, though both were the same person). The tract runs to about 24 pages and is too long to quote in full here. Nevertheless, for those anxious to follow the development of Tone's political ideas, it is worthwhile quoting long extracts from it, particularly as the pamphlet has been out of print for many years:

> Before I proceed to the object of this book, I think it necessary to acquaint the reader that I am a Protestant of the Church of Ireland, as by law established, and have again and again taken all the customary oaths by which we secure and appropriate to ourselves all degrees and professions, save one, to the utter exclusion of our Catholic Brethren. I am, therefore, no further interested in the event than as a mere lover of justice, and a steady detester of tyranny, whether exercised by one man or one million ...

> The misfortune of Ireland is that we have no National Government, in which we differ from England, and from all Europe ... What is our Government? It is a phenomenon in politics, contravening all received and established opinions: it is a Government derived from another country, whose interest, so far from being the same with that of the people, directly crosses it at right angles: does any man think that our rulers here recommend themselves to their creators in England, by promoting the interest of Ireland, when it can in the most remote

degree interfere with the commerce of Great Britain. But how is this foreign Government maintained? Look to your court calendar, to your pension list, to your concordatum, and you will find the answer written in letters of gold: this unnatural influence must be supported by profligate means, and hence corruption is the only medium of Government in Ireland. The people are utterly disregarded and defied: divided and distracted as they are, and distrustful of each other, they fall an easy prey to English rulers, or their Irish subalterns: the fear of danger is removed from Administration by our internal weakness, and the sense of shame speedily follows it: hence it is, that we see speculation protected, venality avowed, the peerage prostituted, the Commons corrupted. We see all this at the very hour when everywhere but in Ireland reform is going forward, and levelling ancient abuses in the dust. Why are these things so? Because Ireland is struck with a political paralysis that has withered her strength and crushed her spirit ...

The pride of the nation, the vanity of individuals concerned, the moderation of some honest men, the corruption of knaves, I know may be alarmed, when I assert that the Revolution of 1782 [Grattan's Parliament] was the most bungling, imperfect business that ever threw ridicule on a lofty epithet, by assuming it unworthily: it is not pleasant to any Irishman to make such a confession, but it cannot be helped if truth will have it so: it is much better that we should know and feel our real state than delude ourselves, or be gulled by our enemies with praises, which we do not deserve, or imaginary blessings which we do not enjoy ...

My argument is simply this: That Ireland, as deriving her Government from another country, requires a strength in the people which may enable them, if necessary, to counteract the influence of that Government, should it ever be, as it indisputably has been, exerted to thwart her prosperity: that this strength may be most constitutionally acquired, and safely and peaceably exerted, through the medium of a Parliamentary reform: and, finally, that no reform is honourable, practicable, efficacious, or just, which does not include, as a fundamental principle, the extension of elective franchise to the Roman Catholics, under modifications hereafter to be mentioned.

I beg I may not be misunderstood or misrepresented in my first position. When I talk of English influence being predominant in this country, I do not mean to derogate from the due exertion of his Majesty's prerogative: I owe him allegiance, and if occasion should require it, I would be ready, cheerfully, to spill my blood in his service; but the influence I mean is not as between the King and his subjects, in matter of prerogative, but as between the Government and people of England and the Government and people of Ireland, in matter of trade and commerce. I trust in God, we owe the English nation no allegiance; nor is it yet treason to assert, as I do, that she has acquired, and maintains, an unjustifiable and dangerous weight and influence over the councils of Ireland, whose interest, wherever it clashes, or appears to clash with hers, must immediately give way. Surely this is no question of loyalty. The King of England is King also of Ireland; he is, in theory, and, I trust, in practice, equally interested in the welfare of both countries; he cannot be offended that each of his Kingdoms should, by all honourable and just means, increase their own ability, to render him the service due to him; he cannot rejoice when he hears that his faithful Commons of Ireland, by their own law, exclude themselves from a commerce with half the known world, in complaisance to a monopolizing English company, though he may, as the common father of both his realms, rejoice when they vote £ 200,000 to secure the very commerce in which they can never bear a part ...

It is therefore extremely possible for the most truly loyal subject in this kingdom, deeply to regret, and conscientiously to oppose the domineering of English influence, without trenching, in the smallest degree, on the rational loyalty, so long and so justly the boast of Ireland. His loyalty is to the King of Ireland, not to the honourable United Company of Merchants, trading, where he must never trade, to the East Indies: nor is it to the clothiers in Yorkshire, nor the weavers of Manchester, nor yet to the constitutional reforming blacksmiths of Birmingham, that he owes allegiance. His first duty is to his country, his second to his King, and both are now, and by God's blessing will, I hope, remain united and inseparable ...

I fear I am wasting time in proving an axiom. Need more be said than that a nation governed by herself will pursue her interests more steadily, than if she were governed by another, whose interest might clash with hers? Is not this more applicable, if the governing nation has a means of perpetrating the mischief without much odium, by making the governed sacrifice her interests with her own hand? And can we deny that this is the case with Ireland? I may be told that we are not governed by England, and some proud and hot-brained Irishman will again throw across me the Revolution of 1782, wherein we 'gloriously asserted our claim to legislate externally, as well as internally, for ourselves.' And I will admit, that we did assert our claim, but I deny that we have availed ourselves of the exertion of the right. We are free in theory, we are slaves in fact ...

The question now resolves itself into this: Shall we be content to remain in our present oppressed and inglorious state, unknown and unheard-of in Europe, the prey of England, the laughing-stock of the knaves who plunder us? Or shall we temperately and constitutionally exert our power to procure a complete and radical emancipation to our country, by a reform in the representation of the people? If we choose the former, then are Irishmen formed of materials whose nature I cannot, and do not wish to understand. It is hopeless attempting to work on such spirits; but if they be of human feeling, if they partake of the common nature of man, if injustice and oppression have not extinguished every sentiment which raises us above the beasts that perish, and makes us feel that our existence is an emanation from the Divinity, then will I believe that my countrymen are not yet lost and buried in hopeless desperation; that, to rouse them to exertion, it is but necessary to point out their duty, to excite them to justice, to shew them what is just ...

But it will be said that the Catholics are ignorant, and therefore incapable of liberty ... If ignorance be their condemnation, what has made them ignorant? Not the hand of Nature: for I presume they are born with capacities pretty much like other men. It is the iniquitous and cruel injustice of Protestant bigotry that has made them ignorant; they are excluded by law from the possibility of education ...

But it is objected that certain tenets expressive of unconstitutional submission to their Holy Father, the Pope, in temporal as well as spiritual matters, are sufficient ground for excluding the Roman Catholics from their rights. 'If this were so, it were a grievous fault,' and, I may add, 'grievously has Ireland answered it.' But whatever truth there might have been in such an accusation in the dark ages of superstition, when, by the bye, Ireland did but share the blame with England and all Europe; yet now, in the days of illumination, at the close of the eighteenth century, such an opinion is too monstrous to obtain a moment's serious belief, unless with such as were determined to believe every thing which squared with their interested views. The best answer to such a calumny, if indeed it deserves any, is the conduct of the Catholics of England at this day, and their solemn declaration ... that neither the Pope and Cardinals, not even a General Council, have the smallest pretension to interfere between prince and subject, as to allegiance of temporal matters ...

Another argument that has been often successfully used is this: If the Catholics are admitted to franchise, they will get the upper hand, and attach themselves to France, for Ireland is unable to exist as an independent State! ... There is no one position, moral, physical, or political, that I hear with such extreme exacerbation of mind, as this which denies to my country the possibility of independent existence: It is not, however, my plan here to examine that question ... To the argument founded on this spiritless and pitiful position, time has given an answer, by bringing forth that stupendous event, the Revolution in France, an event which I do but name, for who is he that can praise it as it merits? Where is the dread now of absolute power, or the arbitrary nod of the monarch in France? Where is the intolerance of Popish bigotry? The rights of man are at least as well understood there as here, and somewhat better practised ...

I come now to a very serious argument. If you admit Catholics to vote, you must admit them to the House, and then you will have a Catholic Parliament. To this there are many answers: In the first place, it is incumbent on their opponents to show the mischief resulting from even a Catholic Parliament. There has been so bold a spirit, so guarded a wisdom, so pure a patriotism, exerted by a Parliament of Catholics in this kingdom, as the experience of modern Protestant Parliaments can give us no conception of. Have we ever read, or have we forgotten the manifesto of the Catholic Parliament held at Trim, in 1642? Let it be compared with our own declarations in 1782, and Catholics may well, with a generous confidence, stand the comparison ...

If, however, there be serious grounds for dreading a majority of Catholics, they may be removed by a very obvious mode; extend the elective franchise to such Catholics only as have a freehold of £10 by the year; and, on the other hand, strike off that disgrace to our Constitution and our country, the wretched tribe of forty shilling freeholders, whom we see driven to their octennial market, by their landlords, as much their property as the sheep or the bullocks which they brand with their names. Thus you will at one stroke purge yourselves of the gross and feculent mass which contaminates the Protestant interest, and restore their natural and just weight to the sound and respectable part of the Catholic community, without throwing into their hands so much power as might enable them to dictate the law; but I again and again protest, that I conceive there is not a shadow of ground for such apprehension; but other men may be more cautious than I, and I would wish to obviate and satisfy the apprehensions of the most timid.

For my own part, I see Protestantism is no guard against corruption; I see the most profligate venality, the most shameless and avowed prostitution of principle go forward, year after year, in assemblies, where no Catholic can by law appear: I see people plundered and despised, powerless and ridiculous, held in contempt and defiance, and, with such a prospect before my eyes, I for one, feel little dread at the thoughts of change, where no change can easily be for the worse. Religion has, at this day, little influence on politics; and when I contrast the national assembly of Frenchmen and Catholics, with other great bodies which I could name, I confess I feel little propensity to boast that I have the honour to be an Irishman and a Protestant ...

What answer could we make to the Catholics of Ireland, if they were to rise, and, with one voice, demand their rights as citizens and as men? What reply justifiable to God and to our conscience? None. We prate and babble, and write books, and publish them, filled with sentiments of freedom, and abhorrence of tyranny, and lofty praises of the Rights of Man! Yet we are content to hold three millions of our fellow creatures and fellow subjects in degradation and infamy and contempt, or, to sum up all in one word, in slavery.

The argument now stands thus: To oppose the unconstitutional weight of Government, subject as that Government is to the still more unconstitutional and unjust bias of English influence, it is absolutely necessary that the weight of the people's scale should be increased. This object can only be attained by a reform in Parliament, and no reform is practicable that shall not include the Catholics ...

If the whole body of the people unite with cordial sincerity, and demand a general reform in Parliament, which shall include restitution of the elective franchise to the Catholics, we shall then, and not otherwise, have an honest and independent representation of the people; we shall have a barrier of strength sufficient to defy the utmost efforts of the most profligate and powerful English Administration; we shall be enabled to avail ourselves of the infinite advantages with which Providence has endowed our country; corruption shall be annihilated, Government shall become honest perforce, and thereby recover at least some of that respectability which a long course of political depravity has exhausted. In a word, we shall recover our rank, and become a nation in something beside the name ...

But I will hope better things. The example of America, of Poland, and, above all, of France, cannot, on the minds of liberal men, but force conviction. In France, 200,000 Catholics deputed a Protestant, St Etienne, to the National Assembly as their representative, with orders to procure, what has since been accomplished, an abolition of all civil distinctions, which were founded merely on religious opinions. In America, the Catholic and Protestant sit equally in Congress, without any contention arising, other than who shall serve his country best: So may it be in Ireland! So will it be, if men are sincere in their wishes for her prosperity and future elevation. Let them but consider what union has done in small states, what discord in great ones. Let them look to their Government; let them look to their fellow slaves, who, by coali-tion with them, may rise to be their fellow-citizens, and form a new order in their society, a new era in their history. Let them once cry *Reform and the Catholics*, and Ireland is free, independent, and happy.

The pamphlet was a great success and sold 6,000 copies within a few months, followed by a further 10,000 copies printed by the Society of United Irishmen in 1792. It helped to influence both Presbyterians and Catholics towards support for parliamentary reform (though sectarian divisions recurred later).

A surprising feature of this trojan effort on behalf of Irish Catholics is that, when Tone wrote the pamphlet, he was not acquainted with even a single Catholic, a point specifically mentioned in his memoirs.

UNITED IRISHMEN

Tone first met Thomas Russell (born in County Cork) in Dublin in 1790, when Russell, then aged 23, was on half-pay from the British army, having served a term in India. He was a tall, dark, handsome man, and both Tone and Russell soon found that they had similar nationalist and reformist views. Russell became Tone's closest friend, and helped form the United Irishmen with him. Russell was imprisoned from 1796 to 1802 and took part in the abortive 1803 Rising, for which he was hanged for treason. He was such a remarkable person that it is worth quoting the comments Tone made about him in his journal while in France. Having mentioned the circumstance in which he met Russell as one of the most fortunate of his life, Tone went on:

There cannot be imagined a more perfect harmony, I may say identity, of sentiment, than exists between us; our regard for each other has never suffered a moment's relaxation from the hour of our first acquaintance, and I am sure it will continue to the end of our lives. I think the better of myself for being the object of the esteem of such a man as Russell ... and if I am ever inclined to murmur at the difficulties wherewith I have so long struggled, I think on the inestimable treasure I possess in the affection of my wife, and the friendship of Russell, and I acknowledge that all my labours and sufferings are overpaid. I may truly say that even at this hour, when I am separated from both of them, and uncertain whether I may ever be so happy as to see them again, there is no action of my life which has not a remote reference to their opinions, which I equally prize. When I think I have acted well, and that I am likely to succeed in the important business wherein I am engaged, I say often to myself: My dearest love and my friend Russell will be glad of this.

BELFAST

Tone visited Belfast for the first time in October 1791, at the invitation of a group of Presbyterians who had been impressed by his pamphlets and who wished to discuss with him the formation of a new radical organisation. The new organisation, which Tone, Russell, Samuel Neilson, and Henry Joy McCracken helped to form, was the Society of United Irishmen. Tone helped to draft its manifesto, aimed at achieving parliamentary reform for citizens of all denominations. A Dublin branch of the United Irishmen was founded the following month, with Napper Tandy as its secretary. (When Tandy went into hiding and was later imprisoned for a while, Tone acted as secretary to the Dublin branch.)

The Dublin branch decided that each member should make the following pledge, though Tone himself thought it might deter some potential recruits:

I,–, in the presence of God, do pledge myself to my country that I will use all my abilities and influence in the attainment of an adequate and impartial representation of the Irish nation in Parliament, and as a means of absolute and immediate necessity in the attainment of this chief good of Ireland, I will endeavour as much as lies in my ability, to forward a brotherhood of affection, an identity of interests, a communion of rights and a union of power among Irishmen of all religious persuasions, without which every reform must be partial, not national, inadequate to the wants, delusive to the wishes and insufficient for the freedom and happiness of this country.

This pledge makes it clear that, at that stage, the United Irishmen wished to achieve 'adequate and impartial representation' in a Parliament of Irish people 'of all religious persuasions', a perfectly valid political programme; but the government became fearful that the United Irishmen were adopting French revolutionary ideas. This fear intensified when the French assembly decided to execute King Louis XVI on 21 January 1793 and, eleven days later, France declared war on England. The danger of a French invasion of Ireland, as part of a military campaign against England, thus came into the reckoning. The British government adopted a dual policy to cope with the threatening situation – concessions to be granted to Catholics while pressure was being exerted on the United Irishmen.

The growth in the number of branches of United Irishmen, mainly in Ulster, began to worry the government to the extent that, in May 1794, they tried to suppress the organisation; but this attempt only drove it underground and it became a secret, revolutionary group. Though the aim of the movement was to attain civil rights for all, irrespective of religious belief, there were rumblings of discontent among the Presbyterians at the thought of Catholics being granted full civil rights. Bitterness between Catholics and Protestants in the north continued to show itself in sectarian strife, much to Tone's disappointment. This sectarian bitterness came to a head in September 1795 when a pitched battle took place between the Protestant 'Peep o' Day boys' and Catholic 'Defenders' at the Diamond in County Armagh. The Defenders were routed and that same evening the victorious Protestants founded the Orange Order to protect the interests of Protestants and to maintain the Protestant ascendancy. During the following few months Catholics in and around Armagh were persecuted to such an extent that thousands of them left the area to take refuge in Connacht.

In 1796 an Insurrection Act was passed which made it a capital offence to adminster any unlawful oath and which empowered the Lord Lieutenant and Privy Council to proclaim any district as 'disturbed'. In any district so proclaimed the magistrates were given extraordinary powers to search for arms and could, without trial, send suspected traitors and disorderly persons to serve in the British navy. It was largely the application of these harsh measures in the Wexford area that led to the partially successful uprising there during the 1798 Rebellion.

The above paragraphs describe the general political background to Tone's career in Ireland between 1791 and mid-1795, when he left for America, but we must now consider his own activities during those years.

There were about 400 members in the Dublin branch of the United Irishmen, largely Protestant professionals and businessmen, though only a minority attended the regular fortnightly meetings in Tailor's Hall. Tone found himself involved in arranging meetings. He also found that his contacts with the United Irishmen in Belfast were growing, and Belfast became almost a second home for him. From these contacts he developed a high regard for the Presbyterians in Belfast.

THE CATHOLIC COMMITTEE

A Committee to represent Irish Catholics had been in existence since 1756, but it was a rather conservative group, made up mainly of bishops and landed gentry. They had achieved a degree of success in persuading the government to remove some of the legal restrictions against Catholics, but when it became clear that reliance on respectful submissions was not gaining Catholics full civil and religious rights, a number of the more active members concluded that a vigorous approach was needed. This change in attitude arose when the Committee had an influx of middle-class, businesslike members, such as John Keogh, a successful Dublin silk merchant and landowner, who became one of the moving spirits of the organisation. Tone's writings had impressed leading members of the Committee, and when their agent, Richard Burke (only son of the famous Edmund Burke), was being paid off in 1792 Tone was invited to become assistant secretary to the Committee, and took up this post in July 1792, with a salary of £200 a year – which was very welcome, as he had a family to maintain. He praised his wife's support in the following terms:

> In these sentiments I was encouraged and confirmed by the incomparable spirit of my wife, to whose patient suffering under adversity – for we had often been reduced, and were now well accustomed to difficulties – I know not how to render justice. Women in general, I am sorry to say it, are mercenary, and especially if they have children, they are ready to make all sacrifices to their establishment. But my dearest love had bolder and juster views. On every occasion of my life I consulted her; we had no secrets, one from the other, and I unvaryingly found her think and act with energy and courage, combined with the greatest prudence and discretion. If ever I succeed in life, or arrive at anything like station or eminence, I shall consider it as due to her counsels and her example.

One of Tone's important tasks as secretary to the Catholic Committee was to arrange a national Catholic Convention, which was held in Tailors Hall, Dublin, on 3 December 1792. It was attended by 235 delegates, including the Archbishop of Dublin and the Bishop of Cork. The Convention passed two resolutions:

> 'That the Catholic peers, prelates and delegates, chosen by the people, are the only power competent to speak the sense of the Catholics of Ireland'; 'That a petition be presented to his Majesty stating our grievances and praying relief'.

The adoption of the second resolution was to make it clear that the Committee intended to appeal direct to King George III instead of to the Lord Lieutenant, as was customary. Five delegates were appointed to present the petition to the king and Tone went with them as their agent. They were received by the king in London on 2 January 1793 and, when the Lord Lieutenant opened the Irish Parliament eight days later, his speech contained the comment that 'His Majesty trusts that the situation of His Majesty's Catholic subjects will engage your serious attention and in the consideration of this subject relies on the wisdom and liberality of his Parliament'.

The petition to George III was successful; it resulted in the Relief Act of 1793 which gave Catholics the same voting rights as Protestants in parliamentary and local elections, removed the remaining restrictions on Catholics holding land, and opened most civil and military posts to them. But it did not remove the prohibition on Catholics becoming Members of Parliament; this was not achieved until 1829.

Tone himself was not satisfied with the results of the deputation, nor was Grattan, who wanted full Catholic emancipation; but the Catholic Committee were so satisfied that they voted 1,500 and a gold medal to Tone for his work and then dissolved the Committee.

Another concession worth mentioning was the passage of an Act in 1795 providing for the establishment of a national Catholic seminary in Maynooth, County Kildare (Maynooth College).

SUSPECTED TREASON

In April 1794 Tone unexpectedly found himself being seen as connected to an attempt by an agent of the French government to collect information. This information could have had more serious consequences for him, but nevertheless resulted in his opting for voluntary exile rather than risk a prosecution for aiding and abetting a spy. It happened as follows.

The French emissary was an Irish-born Church of England clergyman named William Jackson, who had had a rather chequered life as a womaniser and heavy drinker in England before going to France, where he became a supporter of the French cause. He approached the French Ministry of Foreign Affairs (where an Irishman named Nicholas Madgett was employed) and agreed to go to England and Ireland to assess opinion on the prospects of a French invasion. When he arrived in England in February 1794 he met a previous close friend of his named John Cockayne, a lawyer, to whom (presumably in confidence) he divulged his mission and who introduced him to a well-known Irish barrister, Leonard McNally, who had practised in London for a while but who was now in Dublin and a member of the United Irishmen. This seemed like a lucky break for Jackson, but unknown to him, Cockayne had informed Pitt, the Prime Minister, about Jackson's mission, and it had been agreed that Cockayne would accompany Jackson to Ireland and report back to Pitt about what was going on – in return for which he would be granted a pension.

Jackson met some of the United Irishmen, including Hamilton Rowan (who, though in Newgate prison, could receive visitors) and Tone. When Jackson told them that in England he had learned that the people would resist a French invasion, Tone said that public opinion in Ireland was different, because most people were dissatisfied with the government. Rowan asked Tone to prepare a memorandum outlining the situation in Ireland; Tone promptly provided him with a few pages. It commenced as follows:

> The situations of England and Ireland are fundamentally different in this: the Government of England is national, that of Ireland provincial. The interest of the first is the same with that of the people. Of the last, directly opposite. The people of Ireland are divided into three sects, the established Church, the Dissenters, and the Catholics. The first, infinitely the smallest portion, have engrossed, besides the whole Church patronage, all the profits and honours of the country, and a very great share of the landed property. They are, of course, all aristocrats, adverse to any change, and decidedly enemies to the French Revolution. The Dissenters, who are much more numerous, are the most enlightened body of the nation. They are devoted to liberty and, through all its changes, enthusiastically attached to the French Revolution. The Catholics, the great body of the nation, are in the lowest degree of ignorance and want; ready for any change because no change can make them worse; they have, within these two years, received a great degree of information, and manifested a proportional degree of discontent by various insurrections (they are known by the name of Defenders). There is no where a greater spirit of aristocracy than in all the privileged orders – the clergy and the gentry of Ireland, down to the very lowest; to countervail which there seems to be a spirit rising amongst the people which never appeared before, but which is spreading most rapidly, as will appear by the Defenders and other insurgents.

Tone went on to say that 'the great bulk of the people would probably throw off the yoke if they saw any force in the country sufficiently strong to resort to for defence', and that 'the Government of Ireland is to be looked upon as a government of force; the moment a superior force appears it would tumble at once as being neither founded in the interests nor in the affections of the people'.

Tone handed the memorandum to Rowan and intimated that it could be copied but the original should be burned. Rowan and Jackson were pleased with the memorandum, so pleased in fact that they suggested that Tone should go to France to explain the Irish situation there. The memorandum was amended by Rowan and it was this amended version that was found in Jackson's possession when he was arrested in his hotel room a few days later; a letter from Tone to Jackson cancelling a dinner appointment was also found in the room. (Cockayne had already given the government a copy of the memo.)

Tone and Rowan were now in a quandary but decided that, if questioned, they would tell the truth about the episode without giving names. Rowan succeeded in escaping from Newgate prison and made his way to France. Tone could possibly have fled also, but he decided to stay and take his chances, as he felt his part in the affair had not been a really serious one. Furthermore, he had some influential friends from his days at the Bar (including the then Attorney General, Arthur Wolfe, a cousin of the Theobald Wolfe after whom Tone had been named) and, after some parleying, a compromise was arrived at. It was agreed that he would not be charged or called as a witness against Jackson, but in return he would have to write a detailed description of what had happened and give an undertaking to leave Ireland. At that time the Castle authorities did not regard Tone as one of the main leaders of the United Irishmen, and they were satisfied with getting him out of the country.

Jackson's trial did not take place for nearly a year (23 April 1795) and in the meantime no further action was taken against Tone. He continued to go about his business as usual. Cockayne tried to avoid being called as a witness against Jackson, for fear of the consequences, but eventually agreed to do so, with great reluctance. Tone's name was mentioned during the trial but he was not called as a witness. The jury had no difficulty in reaching a verdict of guilty against Jackson but when he was brought back for sentencing it was noticed that his appearance was ghastly. He collapsed and died; it was determined later that he had taken poison, probably brought to him by his wife who had visited him that morning.

AMERICA

After many sad farewells to their friends in Dublin and Belfast, the Tone family (himself, his wife, three children and his sister) departed from Belfast on 13 June 1795 on the *Cincinnatus* and, after an adventurous voyage during which their ship was held up by British frigates and some of the crew and passengers were press-ganged into the navy (Tone himself was lucky to escape this misfortune due to the pleadings of his wife and sister), they landed in the port of Wilmington, Delaware, on 1 August. The following extract from Tone's journal about his last days in Ireland paints the picture well:

> Having paid all my debts and settled with everybody, I set off from Dublin for Belfast on 20th May 1795 with my wife, sister and three children, leaving, as may well be supposed, my father and mother in very sincere affliction. My whole property consisted in our clothes, my books, and about £700 in money and bills on Philadelphia. We kept our spirits admirably. The great attention manifested to us, the conviction that we were suffering in the best of causes, the hurry attending so great a change, and perhaps a little vanity in showing ourselves superior to fortune, supported us under what was certainly a trial of the severest kind. But if our friends in Dublin were kind and affectionate, those in Belfast, if possible, were still more so. During near a month that we remained there we were every day engaged by one or other; even those who scarcely knew me were eager to entertain us; parties and excursions were planned for our amusement; and certainly the whole of our deportment and reception at Belfast very little resembled those of a man who escaped with his life only by miracle, and who was driven into exile to avoid a more disgraceful fate. I remember particularly two days that we passed on the Cave Hill. On the first Russell, Neilson, Simms, McCracken, and one or two more of us, on the summit of McArt's fort took a solemn obligation – which I think I may say I have on my part endeavoured to fulfil – never to desist in our efforts until we had subverted the authority of England over our country and asserted her independence.

Tone did not waste time and about a week after his arrival in America proceeded to Philadelphia, where he met Dr Reynolds, one-time chairman of the Dublin United Irishmen, who had fled to America when Jackson was arrested, and also Hamilton Rowan, who had come via France. Rowan gave him a letter of introduction to the French minister (Adet) and Tone attended on Adet a few days later. Adet's English was not very good, nor was Tone's French, so they did not make much headway, but Adet asked him to submit a written memorial, which he did. Tone, when handing in the memorial, offered to go to France on the next available ship if this step would help to enable him to explain the Irish situation. Adet did not favour this early departure and assured Tone that his memorial would be transmitted to France without delay, with Adet's recommendation.

While awaiting developments Tone moved his family a couple of times before deciding to buy a farm of 180 acres, half of it under trees, outside Princeton, New Jersey, for a sum of £1,180. This deal had not been completed, however, before letters from Ireland reached Tone indicating 'that the state of the public mind in Ireland was advancing to republicanism faster than even I could believe', and which urged him to go to France as soon as possible to ask for their assistance. Having discussed the matter with his wife and sister, neither of whom raised objections, Tone contacted Adet and showed him the letters from Ireland. Adet's previously lukewarm attitude changed and he agreed to give Tone letters of recommendation to the French government and offered to pay the expenses of his journey to France (which Tone declined).

Tone decided to go to France at the earliest opportunity and asked his younger brother, Arthur, then aged thirteen (who had come to America around the same time) to return to Ireland to tell Neilson, Simms, and Russell in Belfast, and Keogh and McCormick in Dublin, that Tone would be going to France very soon. Arthur sailed from Philadelphia on 10 December 1795.

Tone meanwhile again met his Irish friends, including Napper Tandy, who had recently arrived in America from Hamburg, and made arrangements for his wife and children to remain in America. He sailed from New York on 1 January 1796, after only five months in America.

Before finishing this brief account of Tone's sojourn in America it may be of interest to quote an extract from one of the letters he wrote while there to Thomas Russell in Ireland, as it outlines his views on the different groups of people he had met:

In my first letter I wrote in terms of strong dislike, which I very sincerely feel to many points in the American character. I believe, however, I guarded it by observing I was but just arrived and that I spoke of the people of Philadelphia. They are the most disgusting race, eaten up with all the vices of commerce and that vilest of all pride, the pride of the purse. In the country parts of Pennsylvania the farmers are extremely ignorant and boorish – particularly the Germans and their descendants, who abound. There is something, too, in the Quaker manners extremely unfavourable to anything like polished society. But of all the people I have met the Irish are incontestably the most offensive. If you meet a confirmed blackguard, you may be sure he is Irish; you will of course observe I speak of the lower orders. They are as boorish and ignorant as the Germans, as uncivil and uncouth as the Quakers and, as they have ten times more animal spirits than both, they are much more actively troublesome. After all, I do not wonder at, nor am I angry with, them. They are corrupted by their own execrable Government at home; and when they land here and find themselves treated like human creatures – fed and clothed and paid for their labour, no longer flying from the sight of any fellow who is able to purchase a velvet collar to his coat – I do not wonder if the heads of the unfortunate devils are turned with such an unexpected change in their fortunes, and if their new-gotten liberty breaks out, as it too often does, into pettiness and insolence. For all this it is perhaps not fair to blame them; the fact is certain. In Jersey the manners of the people are extremely different; they seem lively and disengaged in comparison, and that among others was one reason which determined me to settle in this State. But if the manners of the Pennsylvanians be unpleasant their government is the best under heaven and their country thrives accordingly. You can have no idea, from anything you have ever seen or read or fancied, of the affluence and ease in which they universally live; and, as to the want of civility, they do not feel it.

After a voyage of exactly one month Tone landed in Le Havre, France, on 1 February 1796, where his destiny as an Irish republican patriot was to culminate within the remaining three years of his life.

FRANCE

Before Tone arrived in France their system of government had undergone a number of changes since the national assembly had seized power in 1789. In those intervening years there had been political upheavals, changes of government, confiscation of properties, efforts to suppress the Catholic church, mass executions, mob violence and a reign of terror, not to mention wars with several European states, some of which, including the war against Britain, were still in progress when Tone arrived.

At the end of 1795 a new constitution, of a more conservative form, had been brought into operation. Under it there were two legislative Chambers, elected by people with some property, and also a Directory of five persons, with executive powers. One-third of the members of the Chambers were to retire each year and be replaced by newly elected members. One member of the Directory was also to retire each year. This new system of government lasted only until the end of 1799, when Napoleon took over as First Consul. In effect, the Directory was the government of France, and Tone learned that the most effective way of doing business was to deal with the Directors as much as possible. In short, Tone pursued his efforts in France at a time of great political ferment. It is a tribute to his tenacity and patience that he succeeded so well in these circumstances.

Tone stayed in a hotel in Le Havre for eight days, during which he attended the theatre, on his own, almost every night, and enjoyed meals and wine at low prices, benefiting from the low exchange rate of the French franc; he had brought a fair amount of money with him. He was surprised to find how normal everything seemed to be, despite the revolution only a few years earlier. He mentioned in his journal that young French men were sober and decorous but that French women were ugly, and complimented the hotel staff on their civility and attentiveness.

During his stagecoach journey to Paris on 10 and 11 February, Tone noticed how prosperous and well cultivated the French countryside was – a feature that modern travellers also notice. In Paris he stayed for about two months in the expensive Hotel des Étrangers, rue Vivienne near the Palais Royal, previously the home and gardens of the Duc d'Orleans. He made the best of his situation by going to the opera, ballet or theatre fairly frequently and by enjoying good meals, usually accompanied by a bottle of burgundy.

On 15 February he got down to business and called on the American ambassador, James Monroe (later President of the USA), to whom he showed papers explaining the purpose of his mission. He then went to the Ministry of Foreign Affairs and handed Adet's coded letter of intro-duction to the Minister, Charles Delacroix. As the latter's knowledge of English was poor, he referred Tone to Nicholas Madgett, an Irishman working in the Ministry. Madgett welcomed Tone warmly and requested him to write down his ideas about conditions in Ireland and the prospects for a French invasion, which Madgett said he would translate into French for submission to the government. Tone wrote these memoranda within the following fortnight.

At a further meeting, Monroe advised him to seek a meeting with one of the Directors and suggested Carnot, who could speak English. On 24 February Tone succeeded in meeting Carnot and explained (in poor French, as Carnot insisted on speaking French) that Irish Catholics and Dissenters were anxious to achieve independence from England, were in sympathy with the French Republic and wished to encourage France to invade Ireland, with a large force if possible, so that British control of Ireland could be ended. Carnot listened attentively and promised to study the memoranda Tone was preparing. Carnot later passed Tone on to General Clarke of the War Office, whose forebears had come from Ireland after the Williamite wars. Clarke was interested but seemed to be out of touch with recent events in Ireland.

Months then passed during which Tone repeatedly called to the Ministry and the War Office, seeking news and emphasising the impor-tance of sending an adequate invasion force to ensure victory. He sug-gested 20,000 men for an invasion near Dublin, which he thought would achieve success fairly quickly. If such a large force were out of the question, he said that, in his opinion, the minimum number should be 5,000 men, with artillery, which should be landed in Ulster, where he thought they would attract many Irish supporters to help the cause. Tone stressed the importance of appointing a commander of repute in charge of the expedition.

He continued to attend the theatre and the opera, and visited the

Louvre (twice). He went to observe a sitting of the Lower Chamber (Council of Five Hundred) and found them disorderly and not well dressed. In May he sent a letter to his wife in America asking her to sell all his property, except his books, and to change the proceeds into gold and then come to France with the children. He learned later that the ship with this mail had been seized by the British, so that he had to send another letter to his wife.

Unknown to Tone, Lord Edward Fitzgerald and Arthur O'Connor, supporters of the United Irishmen, arrived in Hamburg in May or June with instructions to inform the French that the strength of the anti-government movement in Ireland was deteriorating because of arrests and imprisonments under the 1796 Insurrection Act, and that military support from France was an urgent necessity. They were informed that the Directory were aware of the situation in Ireland, from Tone and others, and that a positive decision had already been taken.

On 12 July, Tone was summoned to meet General Lazare Hoche, one of France's most able army generals. Hoche was five years younger than Tone, and a friendly relationship quickly developed between the two men. Hoche told Tone that he had read his memoranda about the situation in Ireland and wished to clarify some matters. He enquired whether, if a French force landed, there would be sufficient provisions for them, particularly bread. Tone assured him that bread, and cattle, were in good supply in Ireland. Hoche asked whether they would be able to form a provisional government, either of the Catholic committee or the chiefs of the Defenders. Tone's response was that if the invasion force was sufficiently strong there would be co-operation. Hoche asked if 10,000 men would be decisive. Tone's reply was that with a force of that size he had no doubt there would be sufficient support to form a provisional government. Hoche wondered whether the priests were likely to give trouble. Tone said he did not bank on their assistance but felt they would be unable to raise effectual opposition; discreetly handled, he thought the neutrality of the priests might be secured.

Another point raised by Hoche was the form of government to be adopted if the invasion succeeded. Tone replied: 'Most undoubtedly, a republic.'

At this point in the discussion, General Clarke entered the room and invited them to join Carnot and himself, and a few others, for dinner. After dinner, the French leaders conferred together in another room, and Clarke was able to inform Tone later that evening that 'everything was now settled'. Tone concluded his entry in the journal for that day as follows:

> This was a grand day; I dined with the president of the executive directory of France, beyond all comparison the most illustrious station

in Europe. I am very proud of it, because it has come fairly in the line of my duty, and I have made no unworthy sacrifices to obtain it. I like Carnot extremely, and Hoche, I think, yet better.

On 20 July 1796 Tone was commissioned into the French army as Chef de Brigade, with a promise by Hoche that he would be promoted to Adjutant-General later; the latter promotion was indeed granted when the invasion fleet was mounted at the end of that year. Tone was delighted at being a commissioned officer in the French army. It gave him a recognised military rank which, he hoped, would result in his being treated as a prisoner of war if he happened to be captured by the British; it would also enable him to participate directly in the invasion; and there was the further bonus that he would have an officer's salary. The latter consideration had become very important, because he was running out of funds.

On 16 September Tone received orders to go to Rennes, from where he reached the naval base at Brest on 1 November. At Brest he made efforts to attract recruits for the French navy from among the British prisoners of war held there. He succeeded in persuading about ten Englishmen and 50 Irishmen to join up.

While he was waiting to embark he wrote two letters to his wife who, he hoped, would by this time be on her way to France. Extracts from these letters show his genuine feelings of concern for his wife and children. In the first letter he said, *inter alia*:

> I presume you are by this on your passage to Havre, and I cannot express the unspeakable anxiety I feel for your safety and that of our dear little babies, exposed to all the inconveniences and perils of a winter passage. I trust in God you will get there safe and well and that by the time you receive this we shall have finished our business, in which case you and I will devote the remainder of our lives to each other, for I am truly weary of the perpetual separation that we have lived in, I may almost say, from the day of our marriage. The Government here has at length seriously taken up the affair of Ireland and, in consequence, shortly after my last letter to you I received orders to join General Hoche at Rennes, where he was quartered. After remaining at Rennes for nearly two months we set off for Brest in order to proceed to our destination, but great bodies move slow; it is only today that our preparations are completed and the day after tomorrow I expect to embark on board the Indomptable, of eighty guns. Our force will be of fifteen ships of the line and ten frigates and, I suppose, for I do not exactly know, of at least ten thousand of the best troops in France. If we arrive safe with that force I have not the least doubt of success, especially as Ireland is now wound up to the highest pitch of discontent ... I would not write thus to terrify you needlessly, but long before you receive my letter the affair will be over one way or the other – I hope happily for us, in which case I once more promise you never to quit

you again for any temptation of fame, honour, or interest. After all we have suffered a little tranquillity is now surely due to us.

In the second letter, written immediately before embarkation on 2 December, he wrote:

> I write in a state of the utmost anxiety and incertitude. If I remained in France and you were, with my babies, on the ocean, it would be full sufficient to keep me in continual uneasiness; or if you were here safe arrived and I was embarked, though my anxiety would be infinitely lessened, still I should have full sufficient to occupy me; but situated as we are I have both to encounter. Uncertain of your fate and that of our children, uncertain of my own, in which you and they are so deeply interested, I think it is hardly possible to conceive a more painful and anxious situation ... If we succeed in our enterprise I never will again hazard my happiness or yours for any imaginable temptation of honour or interest; if we fail, at least it is an honourable cause and on just principles; and in either case you shall not hear of my behaving in a manner to cause you or my children to blush for me. I have this moment received orders to embark in half an hour. I have of course no time to add more. I recommend you all to the protection of Heaven. God almighty forever bless and preserve you. *Adieu* my dearest life and soul. Kiss my darling babies for me ten thousand times and love me ever as I love you.

BANTRY BAY

Though they embarked on 2 December, the fleet of 43 ships, with almost 14,000 troops on board, did not sail until 15 December. For security purposes, it had been decided that the landing area in Ireland would not be revealed until after the ships had left Brest: it was to be Bantry Bay, which Hoche had chosen, rather than the areas suggested by Tone.

Admiral de Galles's instructions to the fleet were that, in the event of ships becoming separated, they should cruise for five days off Mizen Head, then a further three days off the mouth of the Shannon, and then, if no further instructions were received, they should return to Brest. These instructions, strictly interpreted, resulted in the collapse of the mission when one of the missing ships turned out to be the frigate *Fraternité*, on which were both Admiral de Galles, the naval commander, and General Hoche, the military commander. This misfortune proved to be catastrophic.

On board the *Indomptable* Tone kept a diary which clearly shows his changing moods of hope, worry, exasperation and dejection during the voyage. From the outset, when Admiral de Galles changed his orders at the last moment as to the channel the fleet should use for sailing out of Brest harbour to reach the high seas, things began to go wrong. Originally

de Galles had ordered the ships to use the southerly and rather dangerous Raz channel, to avoid being observed by the British fleet waiting
outside, but he changed his mind at a late stage and signalled that ships
should use the safer Iroise channel. Unfortunately, in the dusk a large
number of ships did not see the signals denoting this change of plan, with
the result that the fleet became split up after they emerged from Brest.
To make matters worse, on the way out one of the French ships, the
Seduisant, with 1,300 people on board (including 550 troops) struck a
rock; all but 45 perished.

Nevertheless, a total of 36 ships reached the Bantry Bay area on 21
December without encountering the British, and could have gone ahead
with the invasion during the following few days but for one missing vital
element – the frigate *Fraternité*, with General Hoche and Admiral de
Galles on board, was missing and unaccounted for. It was discovered
later that the *Fraternité* had been chased by the British and blown off
course by strong winds, and didn't arrive near the Irish coast until 30
December, by which time the ships that had succeeded in gathering at
Bantry Bay had turned towards home. Hoche had had a difficult voyage
and did not arrive back in France, at La Rochelle, until 12 January 1797.

Hoche's absence from the Bantry Bay area between 21 and 25 December turned out to be the crucial factor in the failure of the mission; the
commanders on the spot felt unable, because of their instructions, to
make a landing without the rest of the fleet. When the weather worsened
from 26 December onwards, several ships had to cut anchor and make
for the open sea, thus reducing the number of ships and troops available
for a landing; and, to make matters worse, these troops were without
horses and had little artillery.

Tone knew at an early stage that many of the French ships had been
lost or separated, but hoped that they would turn up in time to enable a
landing to be effected. On 22nd December he wrote in his diary: 'This
morning at eight we have neared Bantry Bay considerably, but the fleet
is terribly scattered. No news of the *Fraternité*; I believe it is the first
instance of an Admiral in a clean frigate, with moderate weather and
moonlight nights, parting company with his fleet. Captain Grammont,
our first lieutenant, told me his opinion is that she is either taken or lost,
and in either event it is a terrible blow to us. All rest now upon Grouchy
and I hope he may turn out well; he has a glorious game in his hands if
he has spirits and talent to play it. If he succeeds, it will immortalize him.'
(Grouchy, Hoche's second-in-command, and also Admiral Bouvet, were
on the *Immortalité*, which had reached Bantry Bay.)

On 24 December a deputation from Tone's ship went to the *Immortalité*
to try to persuade Grouchy to proceed with a landing even with the

depleted forces. Grouchy agreed, but during the following days the weather became so bad that a landing was impracticable. On 29 December the French fleet up-anchored and sailed for home. Tone's journal entry for that day was: 'At four this morning the commodore made the signal to steer for France; so there is an end of our expedition for the present; perhaps for ever. I spent all yesterday in my hammock, partly through sea-sickness, and much more through vexation. At ten we made prize of an unfortunate brig, bound from Lisbon to Cork, laden with salt, which we sank.' He arrived back in Brest on 1 January 1797.

Forty-three ships, with nearly 14,000 troops, had set out from Brest. By the end of the expedition eleven ships and 5,000 men had been lost.

It is difficult to assess whether a French invasion would have succeeded, even with the entire military force of nearly 14,000 men as planned. It might have done, as the number of British troops in the Cork area was not very large: about 3,000 men, which British General Dalrymple said could possibly be increased to 8,000 before the French, if they landed, could reach Cork. However, a French force of fewer than 9,000 men, with very little artillery, would hardly have succeeded, unless immediately supported by thousands of armed Irishmen. Such support was doubtful, as the local population did not seem to be particularly interested in helping the French ships which they could see off-shore and, besides, the United Irishmen were unaware that the French planned to land at Bantry Bay and had made no preparations for such a landing.

News of the French fleet's arrival off Bantry Bay on 21 December had reached the army commander in Cork within a matter of hours, by means of a messenger who had ridden from Bantry to Cork. The authorities in Dublin became aware of the invasion fleet on 24 December. The military commanders commenced preparations to resist the French and, as days went by without a landing, their preparedness for defence improved.

The Catholic Bishop of Cork issued a statement on 25 December urging his flock not to give any aid or comfort to the French invaders who, he said, had come only to plunder and destroy. The Bishop of Limerick issued a similar statement. When considering what these bishops said it should be borne in mind that they were conscious of the results of the French Revolution, including the confiscation and sale of all church property, the dissolution of religious orders, and the imprisonment, exile, execution or massacre of thousands of priests.

Though the invasion failed it highlighted one important point: that the French had been able to sail a fleet to the coast of Ireland and remain there for over a week despite the British navy. There were recriminations in England at the navy's failure to locate and defeat the French fleet. There were also recriminations in France at the failure to effect a landing. Admiral Bouvet was relieved of his command and his rank.

AFTER BANTRY BAY

When Tone reached Paris on 21 January 1797, feeling very dejected at the failure of the expedition, he found waiting for him a letter from his wife telling him that the family had reached Hamburg after a long and stormy sea voyage, which had left her very ill. This worried him, as did doubts about his future prospects. He had practically no money as the officers taking part in the expedition had not been paid before they left Brest. He wrote to his wife, advising her to remain in Hamburg, rather than risk a long journey in bad weather, until he found out what his future situation would be. He also wrote to Hoche, who had just been appointed commander of the Army of Sambre and Meuse (on the Rhine). Hoche responded in a friendly fashion and invited Tone to join his staff, an invitation which Tone readily accepted. On 31 January he wrote in his journal: 'I feel this moment like a man who is just awakening from a long terrible dream.'

Shortly afterwards he learned that he was being appointed to Hoche's headquarters at Cologne, to be in charge of the general's foreign correspondence, but it was not until 29 March that he received orders to go there. In the meantime he moved around Paris. On 3 March he was introduced to Thomas Paine, author of *The Rights of Man*, and liked him, though he added the comment: 'He drinks like a fish, a misfortune I have known to befall other celebrated patriots.'

He set out for Cologne on 29 March and then, with Hoche's consent, proceeded soon afterwards to Groningen, in Holland, to meet his wife and their three children (a girl and two boys) who were to arrive there from Hamburg. His journal contains interesting descriptions of the places visited. One particular entry, about a visit to a Catholic church, gives an inkling of his jaundiced view of the Catholic faith:

> There happened to be no one in the place but myself, and as I was gazing about I perceived the corner of a green silk curtain behind a thick iron lattice lifted up and someone behind it. I drew near in order to discover who it might be and it proved to be a nun, young, I am sure, and I believe handsome, for I saw only her mouth and chin, but a more beautiful mouth I never saw. We continued gazing on one another in this manner for five minutes, when a villainous, overgrown friar, entering to say his Mass, put her to rout. Poor soul, I pitied her from the very bottom of my heart and, laying aside all grosser considerations, should have rejoiced to have battered down the gates of the

convent and rescued her from her prison. These convents are most infernal institutions, but at the peace I trust the Republic will settle that business here, where, by the by, the people are dreadfully superstitious. All this last week we have had nothing but religious processions, particularly on the 14th, being Good Friday.

FAMILY REUNION

Tone's journal for 7 May records: 'At last this day, in the evening, as I was taking my usual walk along the canal, I have the unspeakable satisfaction to see my dearest love and our little babies, my sister and her husband, all arrive safe and well. It is impossible to describe the pleasure I felt.'

Some weeks later he arranged lodgings for his wife and children in Nanterre, on the outskirts of Paris, but he himself continued working for Hoche. He wrote to his wife from Hoche's headquarters:

Dear love – I look back on our last tour with the greatest delight. I never was, I think, so happy, and more happy I never can expect to be in future, whatever change for the better may take place, if any does take place, in our circumstances. It was delightful. I recall with pleasure every spot where we passed together. I never will forget it.

In Ireland the number of people joining the United Irishmen, particularly in the north, had increased after the Bantry Bay episode, and the government's clampdown was intensified. Martial law was imposed in Ulster, where the mouthpiece of the United Irishmen, the *Northern Star*, was suppressed. The dilemma facing the United Irish leaders was that if they started a rebellion before the French arrived they would be wiped out, but if French assistance did not arrive soon they would be disarmed and rounded up in the meantime. In view of this situation the United Irishmen sent Edward Lewins, a Catholic solicitor, as an envoy to France to explain the urgent need for French military intervention. Lewins arrived in France, via Hamburg, in May, and Tone vouched for his credentials. Lewins was now regarded in France as the official representative of the United Irishmen, though Tone's important role continued to be recognised in Paris

Lewins and Tone met Hoche to stress the need for another attempt to invade Ireland. Hoche accepted their case but explained that the mounting of another large force would take some months, as there were other demands on the French forces. (France was still at war with Austria, up to the peace treaty of Campo-Formio in October 1797, under which the defeated Austrian emperor had been forced to recognise the French annexation of the former Austrian Netherlands and the left bank of the

Rhine. There were also internal government upheavals in France at that time.)

THE BATAVIAN REPUBLIC

The French had absorbed Belgium and had annexed the Netherlands, the latter being termed the Batavian Republic. Hoche was able to inform Tone and Lewins that the Batavian (Dutch) authorities were in a position to send a sizeable invasion force to Ireland at an early date. The French supported this idea and indeed proposed to incorporate 5,000 elite French troops as part of the Dutch expedition. The Dutch commanders, General Daendels and Admiral Dewinter, were not in favour of mixing the troops, however, and, for this reason, Hoche arranged to visit the Hague, with Tone and Lewins, to discuss this problem with the Dutch. After discussion, Hoche agreed to an all-Dutch force, though he kept in mind the prospect that the French would send a supporting expedition from Brest.

At Hoche's request, Tone remained with the Dutch commanders to accompany them on their expedition. On 8 July 1797 he boarded the Admiral's ship, *Vryheid*, where he was welcomed by General Daendels and Admiral Dewinter. He was delighted to find that both were anxious to sail as soon as possible. But delays of one kind or another arose, much to Tone's annoyance and frustration. For a long period the delay was due to strong south-westerly winds which would help the English fleet awaiting off the coast of Holland, while hindering any attempt by the Dutch to sail out of their base.

Weeks went by, during which the Dutch commanders toyed with the idea of sending a small force to land in the south of England. Then a plan to invade Scotland from the North Sea, followed by an invasion of Ireland, entered their minds and was put on paper. General Daendels gave Tone a copy of a plan so that he could bring it to Hoche for approval. The proposal was that the Dutch fleet would sail northwards from their base, evading or breaking through the English fleet, and continue up the North Sea with the objective of landing a force of 15,000 troops in Scotland to capture Edinburgh and Glasgow. When this had been accomplished the Dutch would sail a fleet around the northern coast of Scotland, then south as far as the Clyde, where they would embark 5,000 troops and land them in northern Ireland. Tone was instructed to suggest to Hoche that the French might also send 15,000 troops to Scotland, making a total invading force of 30,000 men, which would be a serious threat to England.

Tone arrived at Hoche's headquarters on 13 September, where he was immediately struck by Hoche's obvious signs of ill health. In his journal he wrote: 'I should not be surprised, for my part, if, in three months, he were in rapid consumption. He is dreadfully altered and has a dry, hollow cough, that it is distressing to the last degree to hear.'

Nevertheless Hoche examined the new Batavian plan and turned it down as being unlikely to succeed. Tone made the following note in his journal:

> He [Hoche] shook his head at the idea of a second embarkation at the mouth of the Clyde, and observed that if we got safe into Scotland, the British would immediately detach a squadron of frigates into the Irish channel, which would arrive to a moral certainty before the Dutch frigates which were, according to the plan proposed, to go north about, and that they would thus cut us off all communication with Ireland.

A week later Hoche died, at the remarkably young age for a general of 29. His death was a great blow to Tone, not only because of his personal regard for Hoche, but because it meant that Tone's job in the army of Sambre et Meuse was now ended. He returned to Paris to make enquiries about his position.

Not long afterwards (on 11 October), the Dutch fleet sailed out of their base and was decisively defeated by the British navy at the battle of Camperdown. Tone noted: 'It was well I was not on board the *Vryheid*. If I had it would have been a pretty piece of business. I fancy I am not to be caught at sea by the English; for this is the second escape I have had; and by land I mock myself of them.'

NAPOLEON

In October 1797 Napoleon was appointed to command a new Army of England, which Tone took as a sign that the French were serious about an attack on England. This raised his hopes.

On 21 December Tone and Lewins were introduced to Napoleon, and Tone's journal contains the following comments:

> General Desaix brought Lewins and me this morning and introduced us to Bonaparte at his house in the rue Chantereine. He lives in the greatest simplicity; his house is small but neat and all the furniture and ornaments in the most classical taste. He is about five feet six inches high, slender and well-made, but stoops considerably; he looks at least ten years older than he is, owing to the great fatigues he underwent in his immortal campaign in Italy. His face is that of a profound thinker, but bears no marks of that great enthusiasm and unceasing activity by which he has been so much distinguished. It is rather, to my mind, the countenance of a mathematician than of a general. He has a fine eye and a great firmness about the mouth; he speaks low and hollow.

Tone met Napoleon briefly on two further occasions (to hand over papers about Ireland) and mentioned that his manner was cold, though perfectly civil, and that he spoke very little.

Tone's son, William, however, puts it differently: 'When my father was presented to him, and attached to his army as adjutant-general, he received him with cold civility, but entered into no communications. His plans were already formed. Ostensibly a great force was organised on the western coasts of France, under the name of the army of England; but the flower of the troops were successively withdrawn and marched to the Mediterranean.'[1]

A source of worry to Tone was that a large number of Irishmen had arrived in France, and sometimes gave conflicting opinions to the French authorities. In particular, Napper Tandy, who had arrived from America in June 1797, was critical of the status given to Tone and Lewins, as he regarded himself as the chief spokesman for Irish affairs in France. Tone's journal is critical of Tandy.

There were also differences within the United Irishmen movement at home: those in the north wished to stage an uprising without necessarily waiting for French assistance, whereas those in Dublin advised caution until French help arrived. It was eventually agreed that the insurrection would commence on 23 May 1798, with Lord Edward Fitzgerald as commander-in-chief. (Lord Edward had served for some years in the British army in north America.) But neither Tone nor the French government knew of the decision to start the insurrection on that date.

1798

On 25 March, Tone received letters appointing him as adjutant-general in the Army of England.

His journal entry for the following day is worth quoting in full, as it reveals an unusual degree of emotional upset brought on by news of the arrest of many of the leaders of the United Irishmen in Dublin:

> I see in the English papers of March 17th, from the Irish papers of the 13th, news of the most disastrous and afflicting kind, as well for me individually as for the country at large. The English government has arrested the whole committee of United Irishmen for the province of Leinster, including almost every man I know and esteem in the city of Dublin. Amongst them are Emmet, McNeven, Dr Sweetman, Bond, Jackson, and his son; warrants are likewise issued for the arrestation of Lord Edward Fitzgerald, McCormick and Sampson; who have not, however, yet been found. It is by far the most terrible blow which the cause of liberty in Ireland has yet sustained. I know not whether in the whole party it would be possible to replace the energy, talents, and

integrity, of which we are deprived by this most unfortunate of events. I have not received such a shock from all that has passed since I left Ireland. It is terrible to think of in every point of view. Government will move heaven and earth to destroy them. What a triumph at this moment for Fitzgibbon [Lord Chancellor]. These arrestations, following so close on that of O'Connor, give rise to very strong suspicions of treachery in my mind. I cannot bear to write or think longer on this dreadful event. Well, if our unfortunate country is doomed to sustain the unspeakable loss of so many brave and virtuous citizens, woe be to their tyrants if ever we reach our destination. I feel my mind growing every hour more and more savage. Measures appear to me now justified by necessity, which six months ago I would have regarded with horror. There is now no medium. Government has drawn the sword, and will not recede but to superior force – if ever that force arrives. But it does not signify threatening. Judge of my feelings as an individual, when Emmet and Russell are in prison, and in imminent peril of a violent and ignominious death. What revenge can satisfy me for the loss of the two men I most esteem on earth? Well, once more it does not signify threatening. If they are sacrificed, and I ever arrive, as I hope to do, in Ireland, it will not go well with their enemies. This blow has completely deranged me – I can scarce write connectedly.

Lord Edward Fitzgerald was captured on 19 May, after a struggle, and died from his wounds on 4 June, at the age of 35.

The government now knew that the United Irishmen had plans for an insurrection to take place soon, with the expected assistance of French forces, and at the end of March the Lord Lieutenant declared the whole country to be in a state of rebellion and directed the Commander-in-Chief General Gerard Lake, to take steps to quell it. This directive was carried out ruthlessly, and in numerous cases flogging, half-hanging and pitch-capping were used. Most of the arms held in reserve by the rebels were discovered and taken up.

In France, where Tone was not fully up-to-date about the deteriorating position in Ireland, he continued his contacts with the Directory to try to get immediate French support, but could get no definite commitment as to when they would supply arms and troops. This was largely due to a change of military strategy by the French government, based on Napoleon's advice. From his inspection of the French Channel ports in February 1798 Napoleon had concluded that the French navy was not capable of successfully conducting an invasion of England, and he advised the Directory in favour of an attack on Egypt, to interfere with English commerce. This plan was approved and Napoleon sailed for Egypt in May 1798, with a large French fleet transporting 40,000 troops. The troops were successfully landed but the French fleet was caught at anchor by the British navy, under Nelson, and was decisively defeated at the Battle of the Nile.

In the meanwhile, Tone attended to other aspects of his life. In January 1798 his brother Matthew arrived in Paris and succeeded in becoming a captain in the French army. Tone's youngest brother, Arthur, arrived in Hamburg shortly afterwards and became an officer in the Dutch navy.

Tone idled away his time during the following months, awaiting developments. He did, however, manage to visit his family in Paris periodically and was concerned about his children's education, in which music lessons featured. On 28 May he was ordered to Le Havre, as adjutant to the commanding general.

On 12 June he wrote to his wife: 'Judge what I feel at this moment when I reflect on the helpless situation I am in here, with my blood boiling within me and absolutely unable to make the smallest effort.' Reflecting on Lord Edward's capture and the arrest and the imprisonment of his colleagues, he began to show a wish for vengeance on those responsible. One journal entry reads: 'If the blood of this brave young man be shed by the hands of his enemies it will be no ordinary vengeance that will content the people, whenever the day of retribution arrives.' On 17 June he received news of the insurrection in the Dublin area which had taken place on 24 and 25 May.

The insurrection in Dublin, and isolated risings in parts of Leinster, were, however, largely ineffective and quickly suppressed. Only in County Wexford, from 26 May to 21 June, was there a successful rising, led by a Catholic priest, Fr John Murphy, whose people had been goaded into rebellion by the brutality of the government forces of militia and yeomanry. They were short of arms but used pikes effectively. Between 7 and 13 June there were also risings in counties Antrim and Down, but these did not last long. The leaders of the risings who were not executed were imprisoned or exiled.

The Directory, at last, initiated plans on 25 June for a landing in Ireland, not knowing that the rebellion had already been crushed, and expecting, from what they had been told by the United Irishmen, that when the French troops landed with arms they would receive wide support from the Irish people.

The Directory's plan was to send three relatively small expeditions, following close on each other, from three different ports, each under a different general. General Humbert sailed from La Rochelle on 6 August, with about 1,000 men. The second expedition, with nearly 2,300 men under General Hardy, had been ready to sail from Brest on 14 August but unfavourable winds and an accidental collision between two frigates caused delays, and they did not leave until 14 September. Tone was a member of this expedition and sailed with General Hardy on the flagship *Hoche*, which had 74 guns, 640 men and 24 officers. The proposed third expedition, under General Kilmaine, never sailed.

There was, however, a third separate sailing consisting of a single fast ship, the *Anacreon*, under Napper Tandy, who had been created a general by the French, with about 200 men on board, mainly United Irishmen but also including 80 French officers. Its purpose was to carry arms for General Humbert and for the Irishmen who were expected to join him. It sailed from Dunkirk on 4 September, up along the east coast of England, around Scotland, and anchored at Arranmore island, off the coast of Donegal, on 16 September.

General Humbert's small force landed at Killala, County Mayo, on 22 August, defeated a much larger British force at Castlebar, and, with several hundred Irish recruits, marched at first north-eastwards and then south-eastwards in the direction of Dublin. At Ballinamuck, County Longford, they were met by a British force of nearly 20,000 men on 8 September and were decisively defeated. The Irish recruits were pursued and slaughtered in large numbers. Matthew Tone and Bartholomew Teeling, who were with Humbert's army, were court-martialled and hanged.

Having reconnoitred the area and heard of General Humbert's defeat, Napper Tandy decided there was nothing to be gained by remaining there and sailed for Norway, whence he made his way to Hamburg, where he was arrested on a British warrant.

In the meantime General Hardy's expedition took a circuitous route to avoid the British navy and reached the Donegal coast, near Lough Swilly (their destination) on 12 October. Here they were confronted by a British naval force with superior gun power and, after a few hours' battle, the French fleet of ten ships was defeated: only three of their ships were able to make their way back to France. On the *Hoche* about 200 men were killed or wounded, and the vessel was on the point of sinking when captured. Tone commanded one of the batteries and was not injured. The captured French officers were transferred to the British ship *Robuste*, which intended to sail to Portsmouth with the *Hoche* in tow, but pro-longed bad weather prevented this voyage and, instead, she entered Lough Swilly and landed at Buncrana. Tone, wearing the uniform of a French officer, was one of the first prisoners brought ashore on 3 November, and was recognised by Sir George Hill, MP for Londonderry. In fact, Tone made no effort to escape detection and greeted Hill, whom he knew from their days at the Bar. Hill wrote that day to Edward Cooke, the Under-Secretary at Dublin Castle: 'This morning some hundreds of the prisoners are just landed; the first man who stepped out of the boat habited as an officer was T.W. Tone; he recognised me and addressed me instantly with as much *sang froid* as you might expect from his character.'

Tone was brought the same day to Derry prison, where he was put in irons. He felt insulted at being treated as a common criminal and wrote a letter of protest to General Lord Cavan, who was in command at Buncrana, pointing out that he was an officer in the French army and claiming the rights and privileges of a prisoner of war. Cavan replied immediately:

> Sir,
>
> I have received your letter of this date from Derry Jail in which you inform me that you consider your being ordered into irons as an insult and degradation to the rank you hold in the Army of the French Republic; and that you protest in the most precise and strongest manner against such indignity. Had you been a native of France, or of any other country not belonging to the British Empire, indisputably it would be so; but the motive that directed me to give the order I did this morning for your being put in irons was that I looked upon you (and you have proved yourself) a traitor and rebel to your Sovereign and native country, and as such you shall be treated by me. I shall enforce the order I gave this morning, and I lament, as a man, the fate that awaits you. Every indulgence shall be granted you by me individually that is not inconsistent with my public duty.
>
> I am, Sir, your humble servant
> Cavan, Major-General

Tone then wrote to the Chief Secretary, Castlereagh, seeking to be treated as a prisoner of war. General Hardy also wrote to the Lord Lieutenant, Lord Cornwallis, pointing out that Tone was a French citizen, a member of the French army, and a prisoner of war, and therefore should be treated with consideration and respect, and not like a criminal. These representations were of no avail; he was to be treated as a traitor.

Tone was brought to Dublin under military escort and on 10 November was tried by military court in the Royal Barracks (Collins Barracks), where John Philpot Curran, KC (who defended many other United Irishmen) acted on his behalf. Tone was charged with treason and, though he did not like the allegation that he had acted 'traitorously', he pleaded guilty and asked the court's permission to explain his actions. After some reservations, and a caution, the court allowed him to make a statement, which he read out as follows:

> Mr President and Gentlemen of the Court-Martial. It is not my intention to give the Court any trouble. I admit the charge against me in the fullest extent; what I have done, I have done, and I am prepared to stand the consequences.
>
> The great object of my life has been the independence of my country; for that I have sacrificed everything that is most dear to man. Placed in an honourable poverty I have more than once rejected offers considerable to a man in my circumstances, where the condition expected was in opposition to my principles. For them I have braved difficulty and

danger. I have submitted to exile and the fire of the enemy; after an honourable combat that should have interested the feelings of a generous foe, I have been marched through the country in irons to the disgrace alone of whoever gave the order. I have devoted even my wife and my children; after that last effort it is little to say that I am ready to lay down my life.

Whatever I have said, written, or thought on the subject of Ireland I now reiterate: looking upon the connection with England to have been her bane I have endeavoured by every means in my power to break that connection. I have laboured in consequence to create a people in Ireland by raising three millions of my countrymen to the rank of citizens. [Here the court intervened to say that his remarks were becoming irrelevant and inflammatory; as a result, Tone did not read out a passage paying a warm tribute to the Catholics who had always supported him.] Having considered the resources of this country and satisfied that she was too weak to assert her liberty by her own proper means, I sought assistance where I thought assistance was to be found; I have been in consequence in France where without patron or protector, without art or intrigue, I have had the honour to be adopted as a citizen and advanced to a super rank in the armies of the Republic. I have in consequence faithfully discharged my duty as a soldier; I have had the confidence of the French Government, the approbation of my Generals and the esteem of my brave comrades. It is not the sentence of any court however I may personally respect the members who compose it that can destroy the consolation I feel from these considerations.

Such are my principles, such has been my conduct. If in consequence of the measures in which I have been engaged misfortunes have been brought upon this country, I heartily lament it, but let it be remembered that it is now nearly four years since I have quitted Ireland and consequently I have been personally concerned in none of them. If I am rightly informed very great atrocities have been committed on both sides, but that does not at all diminish my regret. For a fair and open war I was prepared; if that has degenerated into a system of assassination, massacre, and plunder I do again most sincerely lament it, and those few who know me personally will give me credit for the assertion.

I will not detain you longer. In this world success is everything. I have attempted to follow the same line in which Washington succeeded and Kosciusko failed. I have attempted to establish the independence of my country; I have failed in the attempt; my life is in consequence forfeited and I submit. The Court will do their duty and I shall endeavour to do mine.

[The text of Tone's speech as quoted above is taken from Elliott's biography[2]; it differs in certain respects from the text given in Tone's *Life*, for reasons which Elliott discusses.]

When asked whether he wished to say anything more, Tone requested the death of a soldier, by firing squad, not from personal feelings but out of respect to the uniform he wore and the brave army in which he had fought. He was told the Lord Lieutenant would make the final decision.

Tone knew he would be condemned to death (as his brother Matthew had been only a few weeks earlier), but he earnestly believed he should be shot and not hanged. While awaiting the judgement he wrote letters to his wife and some friends, but refused to see either friends or family relations. To his father he wrote as follows on 10 November:

Dear Sir,

I hope you will not be offended that I have positively declined seeing you since my arrival in this place; the fact is I had not the courage to support a meeting which could lead to nothing and would put us both to insupportable pain. I shall give order on the arrival of my effects to have them sent to you. What money I have (about £50) I will share between you and my wife. I beg my sincerest and most respectful duty to my mother.

Your affectionate son

T.W. Tone
Adjt. General

P.S. Nothing can exceed the attention I have received since my arrival in Dublin from Major Sandys, to whom I have been given in charge; he is so good as to promise me he will send my effects.

To his wife he wrote as follows on the same day:

Dearest Love,

The hour is at last come when we must part. As no words can express what I feel for you and our children I shall not attempt it; complaint of any kind would be beneath your courage or mine. Be assured I will die as I have lived, and that you will have no reason to blush for me.

I have written on your behalf to the French government, to the Minister of Marine, to General Kilmaine, and to Mr Shee; with the latter I wish you especially to advise. In Ireland I have written to your brother Harry and to those of my friends who are about to go into exile, and whom I am sure will not abandon you.

Adieu, dearest Love. I find it impossible to finish this letter. Give my love to Mary and above all things remember that you are now the only parent of our dearest children, and that the best proof you can give of your affection for me will be to preserve yourself for their education. God Almighty bless you all.

Yours ever

T.W. Tone

P.S. I think you have a friend in Wilson [a Scotsman named Thomas Wilson whom Mrs Tone had met on board ship when returning from America and who became a great friend and, much later, her second husband] who will not desert you.

On the evening of the following day, Sunday, 11 November, Tone learned that he was to be hanged publicly at Newgate prison at 1 p.m. on the following day. That night he cut his throat with a penknife, almost severing his windpipe, but he did not die immediately. Mac Dermott's aacount of Tone's death then reads:[3]

> A military surgeon was summoned – a young French émigré named Benjamin Lentaigne, who later left the army and built up a practice in Dublin, where he was much esteemed both for his skill and his benevolence. He closed the wound as best he could, ordered Tone's head to be kept in a particular position and forbade him to speak. He also advised that to move him would be fatal .... Tone lingered on for a week and died on the 19th November. Lentaigne used to tell how, noticing he was a Frenchman by his accent, Tone addressed him in French, saying, when he heard that he might recover, 'I am sorry to have been so bad an anatomist.' The gay courage of the remark gives it a ring of authenticity.

In the meantime his counsel, Curran, had applied for a writ of *habeas corpus*, on the grounds that, while the King's Bench was sitting, a court-martial had no jurisdiction over a person who was not a member of the Crown forces. The presiding judge, Arthur Wolfe, who knew Tone, agreed to issue a writ of *habeas corpus* and a sheriff was sent to the prison to call for the suspension of the execution. At the prison the provost-marshall told the sheriff he could act only on orders from Major Sandys, and Major Sandys said he must obey the Lord Lieutenant. When the sheriff reported this situation to the court he was instructed to take Tone, the provost-marshal and Major Sandys into custody. The sheriff failed to gain admission to the prison but was informed of Tone's attempted suicide and returned to the court with the surgeon who had attended Tone (Dr Lentaigne), who told the court of Tone's wound, which might or might not be mortal; only time would tell.

An inquest was held on 19 November, the day of Tone's death, and permission was given for the body to be released to his friends, on condition that there be no assembly of people and that the interment be private. The body was brought to 52 High Street, where many mourners called to pay their respects. A plaster cast was made of his face and he was buried quietly in the family plot at Bodenstown. His father was so distressed that he did not attend the funeral.

AFTERMATH

Matilda Tone was left a widow, in Paris, at the age of 28, with a daughter aged twelve and two sons aged seven and five. She got a few small grants from the French government, and in 1804 Napoleon procured for her a modest pension, which was increased in later years. Her daughter,

Maria, died of tuberculosis in 1803, as did the younger son, Francis, in 1806. The other son, William, contracted tuberculosis but survived, and was a student at a military academy in Paris until 1810, when he entered a French cavalry school.

Matilda made representations directly to Napoleon and also to Talleyrand, Foreign Minister, on behalf of her son, as a result of which his educational expenses were met by the government. William fought in Napoleon's campaigns but when the monarchy was restored to France in 1815 he resigned his commission and he and his mother decided to leave France. They applied for permission to return to Ireland but this was refused by the authorities in Dublin Castle. In 1816 Mrs Tone married Thomas Wilson, in Paris, and they spent a year in Edinburgh before going to live in America, near Washington DC. William also went to America, where he studied law and obtained a position in the American War Office. It was he who compiled and edited Tone's *Life*. He married Catherine Sampson, the daughter of a Dublin man, by whom he had a daughter, and died of tuberculosis in 1828, aged 38.

Matilda died in 1849, aged 80, much respected as the widow of Wolfe Tone. The French ambassador, and American and French generals, attended her funeral.

BIBLIOGRAPHY

(1) *The Life of Theobald Wolfe Tone, compiled and edited by his son William*. First published in Washington DC in 1826.

(2) Marianne Elliott, *Wolfe Tone: Prophet of Irish Independence*. Yale University Press, New Haven and London, 1989.

(3) Frank MacDermott, *Theobald Wolfe Tone and His Times*. Macmillan, 1939, and Anvil Books, Dublin, 1968. (This contains copious extracts from Tone's journals.)

(4) Henry Boylan, *Theobald Wolfe Tone*. Gill & Macmillan, 1981.

(5) Thomas Pakenham, *The Year of Liberty*. Hodder & Stoughton, 1969, and Granada, 1972. (This deals only incidentally with Wolfe Tone, but is an excellent account of the 1798 Rebellion.)

(6) J.C. Beckett, *The Making of Modern Ireland 1603 – 1923*. Faber & Faber, 1966 and 1981 (new edition). This provides a good historical background.

OSCAR WILDE
(1854–1900)

Wilde's claim to literary fame rests mainly on his four witty plays of upper-class English life: Lady Windermere's Fan, A Woman of No Importance, An Ideal Husband and The Importance of Being Earnest. His serious, semi-religious play, Salomé, derived from the Gospel story of the beheading of John the Baptist, is quite different from the others, but still entertains audiences. He wrote essays and poems and also one novel, The Picture of Dorian Gray, which is still in print. Wilde's fame turned to notoriety, however, when he was convicted of acts of gross indecency and imprisoned for two years, an experience that ruined his reputation and his career, and left him a broken man.

Wilde spent the first part of his life in Dublin (apart from his terms as a boarder in Portora Royal School, Enniskillen) living with his parents at 1 Merrion Square. He won a scholarship to Trinity College, Dublin, and then a scholarship to Magdalen College, Oxford, which he entered at the age of twenty. Thereafter he lived mainly in England. The last three and a half years of Wilde's life, after his release from prison in 1897, were spent on the continent, mostly in Paris, where he died on 30 November 1900, aged 46 years.

Oscar Wilde (whose full name, given by his devoted parents, was Oscar Fingal O'Flahertie Wills Wilde) was born on 16 October 1854 at 21 Westland Row, Dublin. His father, William Wilde, was a well-known eye and ear surgeon, who was knighted in 1864. His mother was Jane Francesca Wilde (*née* Elgee), an outspoken Irish nationalist. Sir William had been born in Castlerea, County Roscommon, where his father was a medical practitioner. He wrote two medical textbooks, *Epidemic Ophthalmia* (1851) and *Aural Surgery* (1853), but his interests were not confined to medicine; he collected and published Irish folklore and wrote a book about the Boyne and Blackwater rivers in 1849 and another about Lough Corrib and Lough Mask in 1867. He had a fishing lodge (Illaunroe) in Connemara from 1853 onwards and, in 1864, he acquired a two-storey house (Moytura) at the northern end of Lough Corrib. As a result of holidays spent in these two places, Oscar became familiar with the rugged and beautiful countryside of Connemara. Before he married, Sir William had fathered three children: a boy, whom he maintained and educated and who became an eye surgeon, and two girls who were adopted by his eldest brother, a clergyman. Lady Wilde did not seem to be worried by this situation.

Lady Wilde was born in Dublin, but her father, a solicitor, had come from County Wexford. She too had a literary bent and had published articles and poems infused with Irish nationalism under the pen name 'Speranza'. In other words, Oscar had highly talented parents.

The Wildes had three children: Willie, born in 1852, Oscar, born in 1854, and Isola, a girl, born in 1857. Isola, the darling of the family, contracted a fever when she was nine years old and died after a short illness. Oscar, who was very fond of her, later wrote the following poem in her memory:

> Tread lightly, she is near
> Under the snow,
> Speak gently, she can hear
> The lilies grow.
>
> All her bright golden hair
> Tarnished with rust,
> She that was young and fair
> Fallen to dust.
>
> Lily-like, white as snow,
> She hardly knew
> She was a woman, so
> Sweetly she grew.
>
> Coffin-board, heavy stone,
> Lie on her breast,
> I vex my heart alone,
> She is at rest.
>
> Peace, Peace, she cannot hear
> Lyre or sonnet,
> All my life's buried here,
> Heap earth upon it.

Shortly after Oscar's birth the family moved to a larger house at 1 Merrion Square, just around the corner from Westland Row. Sir William died in 1876 but his widow remained in Merrion Square until 1879, when she decided to move to London, where her two sons were living. While the family lived in Merrion Square they had a number of servants, including a German governess and a French maid. Lady Wilde held receptions on Saturday afternoons for writers, actors, painters, musicians and other members of the Dublin intelligentsia.

Merrion Square was (and still is) spacious, made up of a large enclosed park surrounded by tall Georgian houses. On the west side of the square was Leinster House, owned by the Duke of Leinster; it is now the seat of Dáil Éireann, the Irish Parliament. The houses in the square were then occupied by professional people, but are now for the most part used as offices. In January 1864 the National Gallery of Ireland was opened within the grounds of Leinster House, facing on to Merrion Square. Presumably Oscar, who was then nine years old, visited this new art gallery which was only about a hundred yards from his home. Among the paintings on display was 'The Beheading of John the Baptist', by Mattia Preti, which might have impressed him.

The Wildes were members of the Church of Ireland; indeed, Sir William's two brothers were priests in that church. Lady Wilde had also been reared in the Church of Ireland, but showed an interest in Catholicism. When the Wilde family were on holidays in the picturesque valley of Glencree, in County Wicklow, Lady Wilde brought the boys, who were then only a few years old, to see the Catholic chapel in Glencree Reformatory, and asked the chaplain, Father Fox, to baptise Willie and Oscar (even though they had already been baptised in the Church of Ireland). This he did. When Sir William was informed he did not object, commenting simply that he didn't care what the boys were so long as they became as good as their mother. Oscar was interested in the Catholic church from time to time throughout his adult life, but held back from conversion until the very end.

In his biography of Wilde[1] Richard Ellmann says: 'Roman Catholicism threads its way through all Wilde's activities.' Wilde's son, Vyvyan Holland, in his introduction to the *Complete Works of Oscar Wilde*[2] says: 'All his life, my father had an intense leaning towards religious mysticism and was strongly attracted to the Catholic Church, into which he was received on his death bed in 1900.'

The Wilde children had private tutors when they were young, and learned to speak German and French. When Oscar was ten he and his brother were sent to Portora Royal School, Enniskillen, County Fermanagh, which could be reached by train from Dublin. (Another famous Dubliner who attended Portora, many years later, was Samuel Beckett.) Willie was popular there but Oscar was rather bored with the place. He disliked games, mathematics and science, but became interested in Greek and Latin, where his phenomenal memory helped. He was especially interested in the Agamemnon of Aeschylus and could quote passages from it. When he was seventeen he won a scholarship to Trinity College, Dublin, where his brother Willie was already preparing to become a barrister.

He attended Trinity for three years and was popular because of his good nature and witty conversation. He came under the influence of John

Mahaffy, Professor of Ancient History, who was an outstanding Greek scholar. In later years Wilde said: 'I got my love of the Greek ideal and my intimate knowledge of the language from Mahaffy and Tyrell [Professor of Latin]. They were Trinity to me; Mahaffy was especially valuable to me at that time. Though not so good a scholar as Tyrell, he had been in Greece, had lived there and had saturated himself with Greek thought and Greek feeling. Besides, he deliberately took the artistic standpoint towards everything, which was coming more and more to be my standpoint. He was a delightful talker, too; a really good talker in a certain way – an artist in eloquent words and vivid pauses.' Ironically, whereas Tyrell signed a petition in 1896 for Wilde's release from prison, Mahaffy refused to do so and said that Wilde was the one blot on his tutorship.

An exact contemporary of Wilde's during his time in Trinity was Edward Carson, who became a famous lawyer and political figure, and who cross-examined Wilde in the latter's ill-judged prosecution of the Marquess of Queensberry for criminal libel. Carson was not as brilliant a student as Wilde but was earnest and industrious.

In 1873 Wilde won a Foundation Scholarship in classics, which entitled him to £20 a year and free rooms in Trinity. In 1874 he won the Berkeley Gold Medal for Greek, the highest classical award available, and also a scholarship to Magdalen College, Oxford, worth £95 a year for five years. He left Trinity without taking a degree, and entered Magdalen College in October 1874, aged twenty.

While awaiting entry to Oxford, Wilde spent time correcting the proofs of Mahaffay's book, Social Life in Greece. In the preface, Mahaffay thanked Wilde (and another student) for having made improvements and corrections throughout the text. The first edition contained a couple of passages on homosexual love, one of which described it as 'that strange and to us revolting perversion, which reached its climax in later times, and actually centred upon beautiful boys all the romantic affections which we naturally feel between opposite sexes, and opposite sexes alone'. Another passage commented that modern society was shocked by 'the peculiar delight and excitement felt by the Greeks in the society of handsome youths'.[9] These passages were deleted from subsequent editions of the book, because of adverse comments, but no doubt Wilde was well aware of what Mahaffay had in mind.

OXFORD

In Oxford, Wilde came under the influence of tutors whose main interest in life was the appreciation of art and beauty in all their forms. Two in particular appealed to him: John Ruskin (then aged 55), Slade Professor of Art and author of *The Stones of Venice*, and Walter Pater (aged 35), a Fellow of Brasenose College and author of *Studies in the History of the Renaissance*. Ruskin's and Pater's views on art did not coincide, but Wilde learned from each. Ruskin believed that beauty was always associated with the good, whereas Pater maintained that works of art need not necessarily be morally good. Pater, who tended to have an amoral outlook (he came under a cloud in 1875 for writing letters signed 'Yours lovingly' to a student who was sent down for 'keeping and reciting immoral poetry') propounded the notion of 'art for art's sake' and argued that the fulfilment of one's life depended on experiencing each moment of life to the full. Wilde attended Ruskin's lectures on Florentine art and met him many times afterwards. He did not meet Pater until his third year at Oxford but had been very impressed by his book about the Renaissance.

Wilde had already acquired artistic sensibilities in Trinity but his four years in Oxford greatly increased his interest in art, particularly poetry, painting and sculpture. He proclaimed aestheticism and took to wearing flamboyant clothes to demonstrate this.

Among his close friends at Oxford were William Ward, who became a distinguished lawyer, and David Hunter Blair, who became a Catholic convert in 1875 and later Abbot of a Benedictine monastery. (A number of Magdalen students converted to Roman Catholicism at that time, under the carried-over influence in Oxford of John Henry Newman, whom Wilde greatly admired.) Blair tried to persuade Wilde to become a Catholic, in view of his obvious interest in that church, but to no avail. However, the following incidents show Wilde's continuing interest in Catholicism. In November 1875 he attended the dedication by Cardinal Manning of the new church of St Aloysius, the first Roman Catholic church to be built in Oxford since the Reformation, and he went to listen to Cardinal Manning in London in July 1876. In April 1877 Blair and Wilde were received by the Pope in Rome. In April 1878 he met a priest in Brompton Oratory, London, to discuss his possible conversion, but this came to nothing. After Wilde's death, Blair wrote his memories of Wilde at Oxford[4]:

> I have a vivid recollection of him at our first meeting: the large features lit up by intelligence, sparkling eyes, and broad cheerful smile; altogether an attractive personality, enhanced by his extraordinary conversational abilities. One could not know him, even slightly, without realising that he had brilliant gifts, inherited from a father of exceptional mental powers, and a mother not less remarkable in a quite different way.

Blair referred to discussions in Wilde's rooms, after the other guests had dispersed, between himself, Ward and Wilde and commented:

> Oscar was always the protagonist in these midnight conversations, pouring out a flood of paradoxes, untenable propositions, quaint comments on men and things; and sometimes, like Silas Wegg, 'dropping into poetry', spouting yards of verse, either his own or that of other poets whom he favoured. We listened and applauded and protested against some of his preposterous theories. Our talk was quite unrestrained and ranged over a vast variety of topics. Wilde said not a few foolish and extravagant things; but Ward and I could both testify, and it pleases me to emphasise this, that never, in our long and intimate intercourse, did we hear a coarse or unseemly word fall from his lips.

In the summer of 1875 Wilde toured northern Italy with Mahaffy and another friend, William Goulding, visiting Genoa, Milan, Turin, Florence, Verona, Padua, Ravenna and Rome, a trip which brought him into direct touch with the paintings and sculptures of the Italian Renaissance.

In July 1876 he stayed for a while in his father's lodge in Connemara, with a close friend, Frank Miles, a budding painter, who afterwards shared a house with Wilde in London. In the following month he corrected the proofs of *Rambles and Studies in Greece*, another book by Mahaffy, in the professor's house at Howth, just north of Dublin.

In April 1877, Ward and Blair decided to make a trip to Rome and invited Wilde to accompany them. Wilde wished to go but was short of money. Blair promised that when he was passing through Monte Carlo he would place a bet of two pounds on Wilde's behalf in the casino. Soon afterwards Wilde received £60, said to be the winnings, which enabled him to make the trip. However, he was also anxious to accompany Mahaffy and two other young men, William Goulding and George Macmillan (of the publishing firm), on a tour of Greece at around the same time. He contrived to join both parties and enjoyed the sights of Greece and the visit to Rome. Blair, who had become a Catholic in Rome two years earlier, had arranged for them to be received privately by the Pope (Pius IX). This meeting greatly impressed Wilde, who thereupon wrote a sonnet about it. But Blair became annoyed when, a few hours later, Wilde entered the Protestant cemetery nearby and prostrated himself before Keats's grave, about which he wrote another poem.

As a result of these trips, Wilde overstretched the mid-term break by three weeks and was rusticated when he returned to Magdalen. He lost not only tuition but the use of rooms in college until the end of the following term. This annoyed Wilde, but he used some of the spare time visiting London, where he stayed with Frank Miles. He was invited to attend the private session of the opening of a new art gallery, the Grosvenor Gallery, which was attended by Gladstone, Ruskin and Henry

James. He wrote an article about the new gallery for the *Dublin University Magazine*, and this was his first published piece of prose.

In his last year at Oxford, Wilde competed for, and won, the coveted Newdigate Prize for poetry. He was, perhaps, a bit lucky insofar as the subject set by the examiners was 'Ravenna', which he had visited during his first trip to Italy. Overall he did exceptionally well at Oxford and was awarded a double first in the finals in 1878. He could not afford to stay on at Oxford to become a Fellow and, instead, decided to become an art critic and a poet.

FINANCIAL PROBLEMS

While Wilde was at Oxford his father died, in April 1876, leaving heavy mortgages on his properties, to the disappointment of his wife and sons. Willie inherited 1 Merrion Square and Moytura (with their mortgages), subject to an annuity of £200 a year payable to Mrs Wilde from the rents of the Moytura property. Oscar inherited his father's four houses in Esplanade Terrace, Bray, which were also mortgaged. As a result, Oscar's inheritance was much smaller than he had expected, and he had to turn his mind to earning a living – or to marrying a rich heiress, as his mother had suggested.

The year 1877 was an eventful one for Wilde. He sold the houses in Bray for £3,000, but a legal dispute arose when he and his agent unwittingly agreed to sell them to two different purchasers. This led to a court case and he regarded himself as lucky when the court found in his favour.

On 9th June 1877, Wilde attended a dinner given by his step-brother, Henry Wilson. Henry became ill that evening and, despite efforts by a number of his medical friends, he died on 13 June. Henry, who was senior surgeon at St Mark's Ophthalmic Hospital, was unmarried, but his will was another disappointment to Oscar. A letter to a friend at the time explains why:

> My brother [Willie] and I were always supposed to be his heirs but his will was an unpleasant surprise, like most wills. He leaves my father's hospital about £8,000, my brother £2,000 and me £100, on condition of my being a Protestant. He was, poor fellow, bigotedly intolerant of the Catholics and seeing me 'on the brink' struck me out of his will. It is a terrible disappointment to me; you see I suffer a good deal from my Romish leanings, in pocket and mind.
>
> My father had given him a share in my fishing lodge in Connemara, which of course ought to have reverted to me on his death; well, even this I lose 'if I become a Roman Catholic for five years', which is very infamous. Fancy a man going before 'God and Eternal Silences' with his wretched Protestant prejudices and bigotry clinging still to him.[9]

FLORENCE BALCOMBE

Wilde's first romantic interest was a pretty young woman named Florence Balcome, three years younger than himself, who lived at 1 Marino Crescent, Clontarf, Dublin, one of the daughters of a retired English lieutenant-colonel. Wilde first met her in August 1875, when she was seventeen. A couple of weeks later he escorted her to an afternoon service in St Patrick's Cathedral, and that Christmas he gave her a small gold cross with their names linked. In September 1876, he sent her a watercolour he had painted of Moytura House. They became fond of each other but it seems that Wilde wooed her in a half-hearted manner, probably because he was still a college student with only moderate means.

At 15 Marino Crescent lived an ex-Trinity student named Bram Stoker, who was seven years older than Wilde and, at that time, a civil servant. He later achieved fame as the author of *Dracula*, published in 1897. Stoker was also fond of Florence, and when Wilde heard, from another source, that Florence had accepted Stoker's proposal of marriage, he was extremely upset. He sent her a letter of farewell which contained an unusual request:

Dear Florrie,
As I shall be going back to England, probably for good, in a few days, I should like to bring with me the little gold cross I gave you one Christmas morning long ago.

I need hardly say that I would not ask it from you if it was anything you valued, but worthless though the trinket be, to me it serves as a memory of two sweet years – the sweetest of all the years of my youth – and I should like to have it always with me. If you care to give it to me yourself I could meet you any time on Wednesday, or you might hand it to Phil, whom I am going to meet that afternoon.

Though you have not thought it worth while to let me know of your marriage, still I cannot leave Ireland without sending you my wishes that you may be happy; whatever happens I at least cannot be indifferent to your welfare: the currents of our lives flowed too long beside one another for that.

We stand apart now, but the little cross will serve to remind me of the bygone days, and though we shall never meet again, after I leave Ireland, still I shall always remember you at prayer.
Adieu and God bless you.[9]

Florence's marriage to Bram Stoker took place in Dublin on 4 December 1878. Florence was interested in the theatre and this may have been a factor in her choice of husband. Some time earlier Stoker had arranged an Irish tour for the English actor Henry Irving, and he subsequently became manager of the Lyceum Theatre in London. Florence made her stage debut in London in 1881. Wilde and Florence became friendly again. In 1888 he sent her a copy of *The Happy Prince and Other Tales*, and a few years later a copy of *Salomé*.

LONDON

When Willie sold the house in Merrion Square early in 1879, he and his mother went to live in London, where Oscar was already staying in rooms at 13 Salisbury Street, off the Strand, with his friend Frank Miles, who sketched portraits. Willie was inclined to be indolent but achieved some success in journalism, while Oscar supplemented his inheritance by writing poems and art critiques. To economise, Miles and Wilde moved to cheaper quarters in 3 Tite Street, Chelsea. (Wilde lived in Tite Street until his court conviction in 1895, though he moved from No. 3 to No. 16 after his marriage in 1884.)

Wilde's interest in the theatre led to meetings with Lily Langtry, a well-known actress. Miles made drawings of her and Wilde wrote poems for her; he also advised her on clothes and brought her to lectures. Later Wilde met, and fawned upon, two other famous actresses, Ellen Terry and Sarah Bernhardt.

In 1878 Wilde contracted syphilis from a female prostitute. At that time the usual treatment for syphilis was the use of mercury, which blackened Wilde's teeth. Because of this disfigurement he did his best to conceal his teeth when speaking.

In 1880 he wrote his first play, *Vera*, sub-titled *The Nihilists*, a political drama set in Russia. It did not attract a producer until Tsar Alexander II was assassinated in March 1881, at which stage an actress named Mrs Bernard Beere agreed to produce it with herself in the leading role. But the proposed first performance in December 1881 was cancelled, apparently for diplomatic reasons. The play was subsequently produced in August 1883, in New York, where it received mixed reviews and was withdrawn after a week. The New York Tribune referred to it as a 'foolish, highly peppered story of love, intrigue and politics.' It was tried in Detroit a few months later but did not catch on.

AMERICA

Because of his appearance and manner, as an apostle of aestheticism, the magazine *Punch* began to publish satirical drawings of Wilde in 1880. Gilbert and Sullivan wrote an operetta, *Patience*, a parody on the more pompous forms of aestheticism, which went down well in London and New York. When the producer, Richard D'Oyly Carte, was in New York it was suggested to him that if Wilde, a walking example of aestheticism, could be persuaded to give readings or talks in America, these might increase the public's interest in *Patience*, and incidentally make extra money for Mr D'Oyly Carte. He sent a cablegram to Wilde enquiring whether he would consider an offer to give fifty readings in America. Wilde replied: 'Yes, if offer good.' The arrangement agreed on was that D'Oyly Carte would pay for Wilde's expenses and would share equally the net profits. Wilde arrived in New York on 2 January 1882 and when asked by the customs officer whether he had anything to declare made the famous reply: 'Nothing but my genius.'

Wilde spent most of 1882 in America delivering lectures in 70 different cities and towns throughout the USA and Canada. His topics included 'The English Renaissance in Art', 'House Decoration', 'Dress Reform', 'Art and the Handicraftsman' and 'The Irish Poets of '48'. He was welcomed with enthusiasm by American women, but the men were not keen on his ostentatious manner and attire. In a few places, such as Boston and Rochester, he was mocked or heckled by university students. His first lecture, to a full house, was in New York on 9 January. An American woman made a note of his appearance:

> Costume – A dark purple sack coat, and knee-breeches; black hose, low shoes with bright buckles; coat lined with lavender satin, a frill of rich lace at the wrists and for tie-ends over a low turn-down collar, hair long, and parted in the middle, or all combed over. Enter with a circular cavalier pose now and then, the head inclining toward the strong foot, and keep a general appearance of repose. This disciple of true art speaks very deliberately and ... the closing inflection of a sentence or period is ever upward.

Wilde was over six feet tall and rather heavily built. His modulated voice, with a carefully cultivated Oxford accent, and his flamboyant attire, added to his impressive appearance. He spoke of the importance of beautifying the outward aspects of life, which he said would help to beautify one's inner life. Under the new English Renaissance, he said, there would be a sort of new birth of the spirit of man, leading to a more gracious and comely way of life, a passion for physical beauty, a search for new subjects of poetry, new forms of art, new intellectual and imaginative enjoyments. He commended the Pre-Raphaelites who, he said, were in reaction against empty conventional workmanship. It was the capacity to render rather than the capacity to feel which brought true art into being, and once in being, art conferred upon life a value it had not had beforehand. He ended his lecture by saying: 'We spend our days looking for the secret of life. Well, the secret of life is art.'

His next lecture was in Philadelphia and he arranged to call on the American poet, Walt Whitman, then 63, who lived in Camden, New Jersey. Wilde admired Whitman's verse very much and the two men got on well together, though Whitman was more down-to-earth in his artistic views. Wilde also met the novelist Henry James in Washington, but they didn't take to each other. He visited Longfellow in his home in Boston; the poet was in failing health and died two months afterwards.

In addition to New York, Philadephia and Washington, Wilde spoke in many other towns throughout the USA and Canada, including Baltimore, Boston, Rochester, Buffalo, Chicago, Cleveland, Indianapolis, St Louis, Minneapolis, San Francisco, Kansas, Denver, Colorado Springs, Montreal, Ottawa, Quebec, Toronto, Cincinnati, Memphis, New Orleans, Atlanta, Charleston, Atlantic City, Providence, Halifax, and St John. Such a prodigious lecture tour was physically demanding but he made no complaints and, as a fee was charged for each lecture, he made several thousand dollars from the venture. He ceased lecturing in October 1882 but did not leave America until 27 December. In the meantime he pursued his theatrical interests, welcoming Lily Langtry on her arrival in America, and discussing with Mary Anderson, an American actress, the possibility of her producing a new play he was then writing called *The Duchess of Padua*. She agreed to pay him £1,000 on account, with a further £4,000 to come if and when she accepted the completed version.

On his return to England he discarded the velvet jacket and knee-breeches and, for a few weeks, entertained parties in London by telling of his impressions of America. Two of his witticisms were: 'When good Americans die, they go to Paris; when bad Americans die they stay in America'; and: 'Of course, if one had enough money to go to America one would not go.' He then went to Paris for over two months, during which time he met many famous writers and painters, including Victor Hugo, Paul Verlaine, Degas and Pissarro. He also met a young Englishman, 21-year-old Robert Sherard, who at first did not take to Wilde, perhaps because of his perplexing witticisms, as seen for example in the following incident. Shortly after their first meeting Sherard called to Wilde's suite of rooms in a Paris hotel, overlooking the Seine, and praised the view from the window. Wilde replied: 'Oh, that is altogether immaterial, except to the innkeeper, who of course charges it in the bill. A gentleman never looks out of the window.'[1] Sherard and Wilde soon became close friends and, in due course, Sherard wrote three books about Wilde.

While in Paris, Wilde completed *The Duchess of Padua* and sent it to Mary Anderson, hopeful that she would produce it. *The Duchess* is a story of revenge mixed with passion. Guido Ferranti, son of the former Duke of Padua, has threatened to kill the murderer of his father, not knowing that the murderer is the present Duke. Guido's feelings become uncertain and when the opportunity to assassinate the Duke arises, he finds he cannot go ahead with it. However, the Duke's wife, believing that Guido wishes to kill her domineering husband because of his love for her, decides to do the killing herself. This deed horrifies Guido and he tells her that he no longer loves her. She seeks revenge by denouncing him as the murderer of her husband. As a result he is tried and executed. Mary Anderson felt that the play would not suit her and turned it down. In January 1891 the play was staged in New York for three weeks, under the title *Guido Ferranti*. It was not a success.

When he returned to London after spending his earnings from the American tour, Wilde was so short of money that he pawned the Berkeley gold medal which Trinity had awarded him. He paid a short visit to America to attend the rehearsals of *Vera* in New York but this was of little avail because, as already mentioned, the play was a flop.

He asked Colonel Morse, who had managed the American tour on behalf of D'Oyly Carte, to arrange a series of lectures for him in England and Scotland, and this was done for the following autumn and winter. One of his most popular lectures was called 'Personal Impressions of America'. This is an example.

When he referred to his visit to the mining town of Leadville in the Rocky Mountains, where the men wore red shirts, corduroy trousers and high boots, he described them as the only well-dressed men he had seen in America, and went on:

> I spoke to them of the early Florentines, and they slept as though no crime had ever stained the ravines of their mountain home. I described to them the pictures of Botticelli and the name, which seemed to them like a new drink, roused them from their dreams. I read them passages from the autobiography of Benvenuto Cellini, and they seemed much delighted. I was reproved by my hearers for not having brought him with me. I explained that he had been dead for some little time, which elicited the enquiry, 'Who shot him?' I had almost won them to reverence for what is beautiful in art when unluckily I described one of Whistler's 'nocturnes in blue and gold'. Then they leapt to their feet and swore that such things should not be. Some of the younger ones pulled out their revolvers and left to see if Whistler was prowling about the saloons. Had he been there, so bitter was their feeling that I fear he would have been killed. [The painter Whistler and Wilde were at loggerheads at that time, perhaps because Whistler, a well-known raconteur and wit, did not like being supplanted by an artistic wit twenty years his junior.]

CONSTANCE LLOYD

During Wilde's lecture tour in Britain he met, at a reception given by Lady Wilde in London, an attractive young woman named Constance Mary Lloyd, three years younger than himself. She had been born in London, the only daughter of an Irish-born barrister, Horatio Lloyd, who had studied at Cambridge and Lincoln's Inn but who had died in 1874 at the age of forty six. Her mother was Adelaide Atkinson, whose parents were still living at Ely Place, Dublin, a few minutes' walk from 1 Merrion Square. Thus Constance's maternal grandparents knew the Wildes well.

Constance's mother had married a second time and Constance went to live with her grandfather, John Horatio Lloyd, QC, and her aunt Emily, at their house in Lancaster Gate, London. (Incidentally, John Horatio Lloyd's mother was a Miss Holland, whose surname comes into the story later.) Constance was a tallish woman, with good features and chestnut hair. She was well educated, could read French and Italian, was a good pianist, and had an interest in the arts.

Wilde spent about a week lecturing in Dublin in November 1883 and met Constance a few times. It became known within their immediate circle that an engagement was likely. On Sunday, 25 November, he proposed to Constance in her grandparents' house at 1 Ely Place, and was accepted without hesitation. Constance immediately wrote to her brother Otho: 'Prepare yourself for an astounding piece of news. I am engaged to Oscar Wilde and perfectly and insanely happy.' Lady Wilde was delighted at the news, and wrote to Oscar:

> What lovely vistas of speculation open out. What will you do in life? Where live? Meantime you must go on with your work. I enclose another offer for lectures. I would like you to have a small house in London and live the literary life and teach Constance to correct proofs and eventually go into Parliament. May the Divine Intelligence that rules the world, give you happiness and peace and joy in your beloved.

They were married on 29 May 1884 in St James's Church, Sussex Gardens, London. (A few weeks after the wedding Constance's grandfather died and left her a share of his estate worth about £900 a year. This inheritance turned out to be a fortunate income for her after Wilde's bankruptcy.)

Wilde had decided that they would live at 16 (now 34) Tite Street, a five-storey house, including a basement, with two rooms on each floor, and a small garden at the back, which he had extensively (and expensively) redecorated. To defray the cost of redecoration Constance obtained an advance of £5,000 from her grandfather's estate, but even this wasn't enough; so they started their married life in debt. As a declared

183

expert on 'The House Beautiful', Wilde devoted great care and attention to the decoration of the new home, and employed an architect for the purpose.

The redecoration was colourful, to say the least. In Oscar's study on the ground floor the walls were painted pale primrose and the woodwork red. The colour scheme of the dining room at the back of the house was white, blending with pale blue and yellow; the carpet and dining-room chairs were white, the walls white picked out with blue, and the furniture yellow. In the drawing room on the first floor the ceiling had been designed by Whistler and incorporated peacocks' feathers. The walls were hung with etchings, plus a full-length painting of Wilde by an American admirer. A grand piano stood in one corner of the room and the chairs were of bamboo, painted black and white.

Marital relations between Oscar and Constance seem to have been satisfactory for the first few years. On the financial side, Constance's inheritance was useful, but Oscar did not have a steady income from his writings, and his lecturing had ended. During the following few years he applied for the position of Schools Inspector on three occasions, without success. In 1885 he became a book reviewer for the *Pall Mall Gazette* and a drama critic for the *Dramatic Review*. These jobs helped to meet domestic bills, which were increased by the birth of their first son, Cyril, on 5 June 1885, and a second son, Vyvyan, on 5 November 1886. Two children within two-and-a-half years of marriage seem to indicate a normal sexual relationship. However, within a few years of marriage Oscar lost interest in his wife, slept separately from her and was often absent from home.

ROBERT ROSS

In 1886 Wilde met Robert Ross, then aged seventeen, for the first time, and they became close friends. Ross's grandfather had been governor general of Canada, and his father had been an attorney in Canada until his early death in 1871, when Ross was less than two years old. Mrs Ross and her children moved to London and Ross succeeded in entering King's College, Cambridge, in October 1888. He left Cambridge after a year, for health reasons, and went to work as a journalist for the *Scots Observer* in Edinburgh. He returned to London after a short period and renewed his friendship with Wilde. Early in 1893 he became acquainted with Wilde's other close friend, Alfred Douglas, who was about one year younger than Ross. Wilde was more attracted to Douglas than Ross and this seems to have led to jealousy between the two young men.

In later years Ross and Douglas became bitter enemies and were involved in court cases against each other, mainly because of Douglas's efforts to disparage Wilde's reputation after his death. Ross turned out to be a sincere and loyal friend to Wilde, and became his literary executor.

WILDE'S LITERARY WORK

In 1887 Wilde was appointed editor of a monthly magazine called *The Lady's World* which, after a few months, he enlarged and called *The Woman's World*. The magazine prospered, but after two years as editor he found the daily attendance at the office too boring, so he resigned. The magazine lasted only a further year.

During the following few years, Wilde got down to creative writing. In 1887 he wrote four short stories: 'Lord Arthur Savile's Crime', 'The Canterville Ghost', 'The Sphinx without a Secret' and 'A Model Millionaire', which were published in one volume in 1891. He wrote five fairy stories which were published as *The Happy Prince and Other Tales* in 1888. In 1891 he published four short stories under the title *A House of Pomegranates*, an essay entitled 'The Soul of Man under Socialism', and his only novel, *The Picture of Dorian Gray*, which had originally appeared in shorter form in Lippincott's magazine the previous year. He also wrote, for magazines, four critical essays ('The Decay of Lying', 'Pen, Pencil and Poison', 'The Critic as Artist' and 'The Truth of Masks') which were reprinted in book form under the title *Intentions*.

His short stories were well received, while his critical essays were met with a mixture of annoyance and praise. *The Picture of Dorian Gray* was widely criticised in the press as being immoral and decadent.

THE PICTURE OF DORIAN GRAY

This novel can be considered in different ways: as a colourfully written melodrama with witticisms added, or as an examination of aestheticism and the philosophy of living life solely for pleasure.

There are three main characters in it, only one of whom (Dorian Gray) comes to life. The other two are Lord Henry Wotton, a cynical, egotistical man-of-the-world, and Basil Hallward, an artist, whose painting of Dorian as a beautiful young man leads to disaster.

Dorian, when viewing the completed portrait, reflects on the fact that the painting will continue to show him as a young man, whereas his own appearance will deteriorate with age. He wishes that it could be otherwise: that he could retain his good looks while the painting showed deterioration. He gets more than he bargained for when the portrait begins to show not only deterioration due to age but also deterioration due to his selfish and sinful life. He hides the portrait in a locked room so that nobody will see the changes in it.

When Basil Hallward insists on seeing the painting again, Dorian loses control and fatally stabs the painter. He persuades a friend, who is under some obligation to him, to get rid of the body. The friend subsequently commits suicide. Other tragedies occur, and Dorian becomes obsessed with the repulsive portrait. He decides eventually to destroy the painting, with the same knife he had used to murder Basil Hallward. The last words of the novel are:

> When they entered they found, hanging upon the wall, a splendid portrait of their master as they had last seen him, in all the wonder of his exquisite youth and beauty. Lying on the floor was a dead man, in evening dress, with a knife in his heart. He was withered, wrinkled, and loathsome of visage. It was not till they had examined the rings that they recognised who it was.

Hesketh Pearson said of this novel:

> The book is a strange concoction. It is, one may say, the most lifelike thing he ever produced, but it is utterly unlike life; in other words, it contains a full-length portrait of himself as a talker in the character of Lord Henry Wotton, with many of his most searching comments on life, side by side with a complete revelation of his emotional unreality in portraying human nature and the morbid strain in him which eventually wrecked his life.[7]

Richard Ellmann's comments are more analytical:

> Both in its magazine form, and in its form as a separate novel, *Dorian Gray* has faults. Parts of it are wooden, padded, self-indulgent. No one could mistake it for a workmanlike job: our hacks can do that for us. But its continual fascination teaches us to judge it by new standards. Wilde made it elegantly casual, as if writing a novel wre a diversion rather than 'a painful duty' (as he characterized Henry James's manner). The underlying legend, of trying to elicit more from life than life can give, arouses deep and criminal yearnings. These contrast with the polish of English civilization at its verbal peak, and create a tension beyond what the plot appears to hold. Wilde put into the book a negative version of what he had been brooding about for fourteen years and, under a veil, what he had been doing sexually for four. He could have taken a positive view of reconsidered aestheticism, as he would in 'The Critic as Artist', and 'The Soul of Man under Socialism', as he had already done in 'The Decay of Lying'. Instead, *Dorian Gray* is the aesthetic novel *par excellence*, not in espousing the doctrine, but in exhibiting its dangers.[1]

PLAYWRIGHT

During the period 1891–95 Wilde achieved outstanding success as a playwright with *Lady Windermere's Fan*, *A Woman of No Importance*, *An Ideal Husband* and *The Importance of Being Earnest*. He also wrote a completely different type of play, *Salomé*, based loosely on the New Testament account of the beheading of John the Baptist at the request of Herod's step-daughter. It is a play that still charms audiences.

Lady Windermere's Fan was first performed in the St James's Theatre, London, in February 1892 and was an instant success. Wilde earned £7,000 in royalties from its first production. He described it as 'one of those modern drawing-room plays with pink lampshades'. The story is a melodramatic one, but with elegant dialogue. It revolves around Lady Windermere who, due to a mishap, finds herself in a compromising situation, from which she is saved by Mrs Erlynne, a woman who had erred in the past and who, unknown to Lady Windermere, is really her mother. Mrs Erlynne saves her daughter's reputation, at the expense of her own, by pretending that she owns the fan which Lady Windermere had carelessly dropped in Lady Darlington's rooms late at night. However, the amusing dialogue ranges far beyond this theme.

Wilde was in Paris towards the end of 1891, and it was there that he wrote most of *Salomé*, in French, with two or three of his French friends helping to polish the language. He showed it to Sarah Bernhardt who agreed to act the main part in a London production, but because it depicted Biblical characters, the Lord Chamberlain refused to grant a licence for its public performance in England. As a result, the first performance of *Salomé* did not take place until February 1896, in Paris.

Wilde was so annoyed at the Lord Chamberlain's decision that he threatened to renounce his British citizenship and become a French citizen. He changed his mind, however, and wrote *A Woman of No Importance*, which was performed in the Haymarket Theatre in April 1893. It was a great success. The first Act is sheer comedy and is really a conversation piece on the frailties of men and women. But mid-way through the second Act, a sombre note appears when Mrs Arbuthnot arrives on the scene. It transpires that when she was a young woman, she fell in love with a young man named George Harford (now Lord Illingworth, the main character in the play), who refused to marry her when she was expecting his child. She left him and reared the child (a boy named Gerald) herself. Now, twenty years later, Gerald is about to be taken on by Lord Illingworth as his Secretary. When Mrs Arbuthnot discovers that Lord Illingworth is none other than the cad, George Harford, she pleads with her son not to work for him. A crisis arises when

Gerald discovers the truth, but no reconciliation is arrived at. Despite this sombre theme, Wilde maintains a mixture of comedy and pathos.

The following are examples of Lord Illingworth's paradoxes:

> Men marry because they are tired; women because they are curious. Both are disappointed ... One should always be in love. That is the reason one should never marry ... When one is in love one begins by deceiving oneself. And one ends by deceiving others. That is what the world calls a romance. But a really *grande passion* is comparatively rare nowadays. It is the privilege of people who have nothing to do.

Next was *An Ideal Husband*, performed in the Haymarket in January 1895, and also a success. It is a dramatic but witty comedy, with a number of important characters, including Sir Robert Chiltern, a Government minister, his wife, Lord Goring, and a dubious woman named Mrs Cheveley, who has acquired an incriminating letter written by Sir Robert, which enables her to try to blackmail him on a matter of Government policy. Mrs Cheveley is shown up by Lord Goring, who knows she is a thief, and the Chilterns find that they can look forward to a more hopeful future.

Bernard Shaw, then a theatre critic, reviewed the play in the *Saturday Review* and said:

> Mr Oscar Wilde's new play at the Haymarket is a dangerous subject, because he has the property of making his critics dull. They laugh angrily at his epigrams, like a child who is coaxed into being amused in the very act of setting up a yell of rage and agony. They protest that the trick is obvious, and that such epigrams can be turned out by the score by anyone light-minded enough to condescend to such frivolity. As far as I can ascertain, I am the only person in London who cannot sit down and write an Oscar Wilde play at will. The fact that his plays, though apparently lucrative, remain unique under these circumstances, says much for the self-denial of our scribes. In a certain sense Mr Wilde is to me our only thorough playwright. He plays with everything: with wit, with philosophy, with drama, with actors and audience, with the whole theatre.

Next was Wilde's greatest and most popular play, *The Importance of Being Earnest*, which was performed in the St James's Theatre in February 1895. It was received with delight by the audience, who rose and cheered. The story revolves around two young men and two young women who are in love, but suffer from mistaken identities and other mishaps. The first young man is Jack Worthing, of uncertain origin, who inherited wealth from a benefactor and who was appointed as guardian of a young lady, now aged 18, named Cecily Cardew. Jack is in love with a young lady named Gwendolen Fairfax, a daughter of Lady Bracknell, a battleaxe who does not take kindly to Jack. The second young man is Algernon Moncrieff, Jack's friend, who falls in love with Cecily.

There are complications, of course, and true love does not run smoothly. For one thing, Jack goes by the name Jack in the country and by the name Ernest in town, because, as Cecily's guardian, he has to adopt a high moral tone in the country. Whereas in town, as Ernest, he feels free to indulge in a more lively style of life. To enable him to carry out this dual role, he pretends to have a younger brother in town named Ernest. Algernon, on the other hand, has invented 'an invaluable permanent invalid called Bunbury,' in order that he may be able to go down the country whenever he chooses.

Such a situation is bound to lead to confusion, and does, in a hilarious manner. For one thing, Gwendolen has fallen in love with Jack, believing his name is Ernest, and says she so loves the name Ernest that she could not marry a man with any other name. Lady Bracknell refuses her consent to Gwendolen marrying Jack because of Jack's dubious parentage. But all is sorted out in the end, to everybody's satisfaction.

There are two subsidiary characters who add greatly to the comic background: Cecily's governess, Miss Prism, and an unmarried clergyman, Rev. Canon Chasuble.

For those not familiar with the play, the following is the famous scene in Act One where Lady Bracknell is interviewing Jack Worthing about his proposal of marriage to her daughter.

Lady Bracknell first questions him about his financial position and then asks, 'Are your parents living?':

JACK: I have lost both my parents.

LADY BRACKNELL: Both? To lose one parent may be regarded as a misfortune ... to lose both seems like carelessness. Who was your father? He was evidently a man of some wealth. Was he born in what the Radical papers call the purple of commerce, or did he rise from the ranks of the aristocracy?

JACK: I am afraid I really don't know. The fact is, Lady Bracknell, I said I had lost my parents. It would be nearer the truth to say that my parents seemed to have lost me ... I don't actually know who I am by birth. I was ... well, I was found.

LADY BRACKNELL: Found!

JACK: The late Mr Thomas Cardew, an old gentleman of a very charitable and kindly disposition, found me, and gave me the name of Worthing, because he happened to have a first-class ticket for Worthing in his pocket at the time. Worthing is a place in Sussex. It is a seaside resort.

LADY BRACKNELL: Where did the charitable gentleman who had a first-class ticket for this seaside resort find you?

JACK (gravely): In a hand-bag.

LADY BRACKNELL: A hand-bag?

JACK (very seriously): Yes, Lady Bracknell. I was in a hand-bag – a somewhat large, black leather hand-bag, with handles to it – an ordinary hand-bag in fact.

LADY BRACKNELL: In what locality did this Mr James, or Thomas, Cardew come across this ordinary hand-bag?

JACK: In the cloak-room at Victoria Station. It was given to him in mistake for his own.

LADY BRACKNELL: The cloak-room at Victoria Station?

JACK: Yes. The Brighton line.

LADY BRACKNELL: The line is immaterial. Mr Worthing, I confess I feel somewhat bewildered by what you have just told me. To be born, or at any rate bred, in a hand-bag, whether it had handles or not, seems to me to display a contempt for the ordinary decencies of family life that reminds one of the worst excesses of the French Revolution. And I presume you know what that unfortunate movement led to? As for the particular locality in which the hand-bag was found, a cloak-room at a railway station might serve to conceal a social indiscretion – has probably, indeed, been used for that purpose before now – but it could hardly be regarded as an assured basis for a recognised position in good society.

JACK: May I ask you then what you would advise me to do? I need hardly say I would do anything in the world to ensure Gwendolyn's happiness.

LADY BRACKNELL: I would strongly advise you, Mr Worthing, to try to acquire some relations as soon as possible, and to make a definite effort to produce at any rate one parent, of either sex, before the season is quite over.

JACK: Well, I don't see how I could possibly manage to do that. I can produce the hand-bag at any moment. It is in my dressing-room at home. I really think that should satisfy you, Lady Bracknell.

LADY BRACKNELL: Me, sir! What has it to do with me? You can hardly imagine that I and Lord Bracknell would dream of allowing our only daughter – a girl brought up with the utmost care – to marry into a cloak-room, and form an alliance with a parcel. [Jack starts indignantly.] Kindly open the door for me, sir. You will of course understand that for the future there is to be no communication of any kind between you and Miss Fairfax.

Wilde had now reached the summit of his career, with *An Ideal Husband* and *The Importance of Being Earnest* being staged at the same time in London, and *An Ideal Husband* in New York. But storm clouds were gathering.

ALFRED DOUGLAS

While Wilde was achieving fame as a playwright another side of his life began to raise problems. This was his friendship – indeed, it became an obsession – with Lord Alfred Douglas. They first met in June 1891 when a mutual friend brought Douglas to Wilde's house in Tite Street. Douglas had recently read *Dorian Gray* and was very anxious to meet its author. He was then 21, good looking, a student at Oxford, with a talent for writing sonnets. His mother idolised him, but his eccentric and bullying father, the Marquess of Queensberry, had turned against his independently minded son; in fact, he had difficulties with each of his three sons, and also with his wife, who had divorced him after many years of marital difficulties when Queensberry had suggested that his mistress should come to live with them. The family had been broken up as a result of the father's offensive behaviour.

Wilde took a liking to Douglas because of his youth, his good looks, his interest in poetry, and his aristocratic background. They soon became intimate friends, though they often quarrelled, as Douglas was self-indulgent and had an unruly temper.

Rumours soon began circulating about their behaviour, and when Queensberry learned that Wilde and his son were often seen together he tried to put an end to their friendship by threatening to stop his son's allowance. On 1 April 1894 he wrote to him:

> Your intimacy with this man Wilde must either cease or I will disown you and stop all money supplies. I am not going to try and analyse this intimacy, and I make no charge; but to my mind to pose as a thing is as bad as to be it. With my own eyes I saw you both in the most loathsome and disgusting relationship as expressed by your manner and expression. Never in my experience have I seen such a sight as that in your horrible features. No wonder people are talking as they are. Also, I now hear on good authority, but this may be false, that his wife is petitioning to divorce him for sodomy and other crimes. Is this true, or do you not know of it. If I thought the actual thing was true, and it became public property, I should be quite justified in shooting him at sight.

His son replied by sending a telegram reading: WHAT A FUNNY LITTLE MAN YOU ARE. This, of course, incensed Queensberry further, and he wrote back: 'If I catch you again with that man I will make a public scandal in a way you little dream of; it is already a suppressed one.' Queensberry visited various restaurants and told the managers that he would thrash both Wilde and his son if he discovered them together on their premises.

Queensberry followed this up by a letter of complaint to the father of his divorced wife, in which he said: 'Your daughter is the person who is supporting my son to defy me ... Your daughter appears now to be encouraging them, although she can hardly intend this. I don't believe Wilde will now dare defy me. He plainly showed the white feather the other day when I tackled him – damned cur and coward of the Rosebery type. As for this so-called son of mine, he is no son of mine, and I will have nothing to do with him. He may starve as far as I am concerned after his behaviour to me.'

On one occasion, Queensberry, accompanied by a boxer, called to Wilde's house and threatened him. Douglas continued to provoke his father but Wilde became worried about Queensberry's vitriolic outbursts, particularly as Wilde himself was now in the public eye as a successful playwright. He consulted an experienced solicitor, Charles Humphreys, to find out whether Queensberry's letter about him and his wife was actionable; and he was advised not to take any action, but that he was entitled to an apology. Queensberry refused to apologise.

While *The Importance of Being Earnest* was in rehearsal, Wilde and Douglas went on holiday together to Algiers. This further incensed Queensberry and he booked a seat for the first night of the play, for the purpose of creating a scene. Wilde heard of his intention and told the management, who cancelled Queensberry's booking and issued instructions that he was not to be admitted to any part of the theatre. Thus balked, Queensberry left a bunch of carrots and turnips at the stage door.

Four days later Queensberry arrived at the Albemarle Club in Dovet Street, of which Wilde was a member, and left his card with the hall porter, to be handed to Wilde. On this card he had written:

To Oscar Wilde, posing as a somdomite[sic].

The hall porter put the card in an envelope addressed to 'Oscar Wilde Esq.' and placed it in the letter-rack in the hall. As he was out of town, Wilde did not collect the envelope with the card until ten days later. The card had been seen by nobody except the hall porter, who didn't understand it, and Wilde could easily have ignored it and torn it up. But he was upset at Queensberry's unrelenting attacks and wrote immediately to Ross and Douglas informing them of the card and asking them to call to see him urgently. The note to Ross read:

Dearest Bobbie – Since I saw you, something has happened. Bosie's father [Alfred Douglas was known as 'Bosie' to his friends] has left a card at my club with hideous words on it. I don't see anything now but a criminal prosecution. My whole life seems ruined by this man. The tower of ivory is assailed by the foul thing. On the sand is my life spilt. I don't know what to do. If you could come here at 11.30 please do so tonight. I mar your life by trespassing ever on your love and kindness. I have asked Bosie to come tomorrow.

It seems that Ross's view was that no action should be taken, but Wilde favoured getting a solicitor's opinion. The following day Wilde and Douglas went to see the well-known solicitor Charles Humphreys, who

Wolfe Tone in Irish Volunteer's uniform

Above: Wolfe Tone with his mother and brother, Matthew, from the original drawing of 1778

Left: William Tone, who edited his father's memoirs

Irish rebels charge the cannons of the British, New Ross 1798

The defeat of 1798 at Vinegar Hill

Wolfe Tone in French Army uniform, as he was when he was captured

Aspects of Tone's death mask

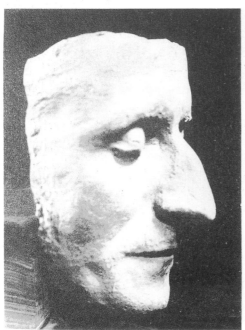

Oscar Wilde at the height of his fame, about 1894

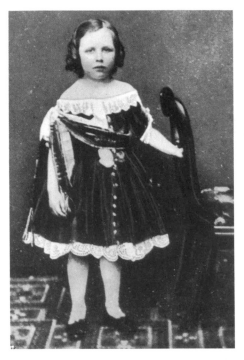

Above left: Oscar as a child

Above right: Oscar Wilde's birthplace in Westland Row (house to left of shop)

Left: The Wilde house in Merrion Square, where Oscar Wilde grew up

Lord Edward Carson from a portrait by Sir John Lavery (1856 - 1941)

Annette, Carson's first wife

Carson cross-examining Wilde at the
Old Bailey

Ulster arms: Carson addressing an anti-Home Rule meeting in September 1913

Ruby, Carson's second wife

'The Ulster King-at-Arms' by Bernard Partridge (*Punch* 1913)

September 1912: Ulster anti-Home Rule demonstration at South Derry – left to right H.J. Barrie MP, Sir Edward Carson, and F.E. Smith being cheered by the crowd on their arrival

Sir Edward Carson putting his name to the Ulster Solemn League and Covenant which was eventually signed by 100,000 Unionists in Ulster. On his left is Capt. James Craig, later Lord Craigavon, first Prime Minister of Northern Ireland

Memorial statue of Lord Carson in front of the parliament buildings at Stormont

said that Wilde would win a case for criminal libel if he was innocent of the imputation of sodomy. He asked Wilde whether there was any truth in the allegation and Wilde assured him that there was not. Douglas was strongly in favour of his father being prosecuted and, when Wilde said that he couldn't afford the cost of a legal action, Douglas replied that his mother and brother would meet the costs (which did not happen, a matter on which Wilde expands in *De Profundis*). Wilde then made the grave mistake of agreeing to prosecute Queensberry for an accusation which Wilde himself must have known could be substantiated. Mr Humphreys applied for a warrant for the arrest of Queensberry and the police arrested him the following morning, 2 March 1895. He was brought before the magistrate in Marlborough Street Police Court and, the following week, was sent for trial at the Old Bailey, on £500 bail and his own recognisance of £1,000.

THE COURT TRIALS

When Charles Humphreys approached Sir Edward Clarke, QC, to ask him to represent Wilde, Clarke told Wilde that he could accept the brief only if Wilde could assure him, 'on his honour as an English gentleman', that there was no foundation for the charges made against him. Wilde replied that the charges were false and groundless. This compounded the grave error he had made in similarly misleading his solicitor. Perhaps Wilde's denial was due to his own opinion, that there was nothing morally wrong with homosexual behaviour, but more likely it was due to his belief that the only evidence Queensberry had against him was a few of his letters to Douglas and some passages in *The Picture of Dorian Gray* which could possibly be interpreted as defending homosexual behaviour. If Clarke had known about Wilde's relationships with young men there is little doubt that he would have advised him to withdraw the prosecution rather than risk having his personal behaviour exposed in court, with the risk of being himself prosecuted.

While awaiting the commencement of the trial, Wilde and Douglas went to Monte Carlo on holiday, whereas Queensberry utilised the interval in hiring private detectives to search for evidence against Wilde. When Wilde returned to London and learned that Queensberry intended to justify the accusation of 'posing as a sodomite' and also to claim that the accusation had been made 'for the public benefit', he realised that the case was becoming far more serious than he had anticipated, but nevertheless he believed that he would succeed in the prosecution against Queensberry for criminal libel. He did not know until the court case was about to commence that private detectives working for Queensberry had traced a number of male prostitutes who had met Wilde in various hotels and houses, and who had agreed to be named in Queensberry's plea of justification.

An intriguing feature of the successful tracing of these men was that an actor named Charles Brookfield, who had a part in *An Ideal Husband*, then playing at the Haymarket Theatre, disliked Wilde so much that he assisted the search for evidence against him. He prevailed upon the commissionaire of the Haymarket to give Queensberry's solicitor the names of men who had tried to blackmail Wilde because of the suggestive wording of some of his letters to Douglas. (They had acquired these letters at an earlier stage, when Douglas had unintentionally left some in the pocket of an old suit which Douglas had given to an unemployed clerk named Alfred Wood, who became one of the witnesses against Wilde.) A copy of one of the letters had been sent to Mr Beerbohm Tree, the theatre manager, who handed it to Wilde with the comment that it could be misconstrued. Brookfield also put one of the private detectives in touch with a female prostitute who knew about Wilde's associations with young men. This prostitute gave the address of a Mr Alfred Taylor where, she said, the detective would find the evidence he needed. When the detective called to that address he found a box containing names and addresses of young male homosexuals and some papers linking Wilde with them. This enabled Queensberry's solicitor to contact them and to prepare a plea giving the names, dates and places of the alleged immoral acts with Wilde. Strangely enough, a number of them agreed to give evidence of their relations with Wilde, even though it seems they were not granted immunity in law.

Rumours that Queensberry had collected such information began to circulate and some of Wilde's friends advised him to drop the libel case and go abroad for a while, but Wilde refused to do so. Two days before the case opened he took a box for himself, his wife and Douglas in the St James's Theatre, where *The Importance of Being Earnest* was playing to full houses.

Charles Russell, solicitor for Queensberry, had prevailed upon Sir Edward Carson, QC (who at first declined the request) to defend Queensberry, and the case *Regina v. the Marquess of Queensberry* opened on 3 April 1895 in the Old Bailey, before Mr Justice Henn Collins and a jury. The transcript of this trial and of the two subsequent trials, edited with an introduction by H. Montgomery Hyde, is contained in his book *The Trials of Oscar Wilde*[5].

Hyde describes the opening of the trial in the following words[6]:

By the time the hands of the clock in the courtroom pointed to eleven o'clock, Sir Edward Clarke had begun his opening speech for the prosecution. Short, stout, and bewhiskered, he looked more like an old-fashioned parson than a successful Queen's Counsel. On this occasion he was at his best, although in its studied moderation his speech did not commend itself to Lord Alfred Douglas, who had been hoping for an all-out attack on his father. 'I never heard anything equal it in all my life,' said Carson afterwards to a friend in the House of Commons. 'Both matter and manner were superb.

[Wilde's biographer Ellmann did not agree with Carson's high opinion of Clarke's speech. His comments were: 'It was not a good performance. Most of it had been composed before he saw the Plea of Justification, and he merely inserted a reference to that at the beginning of his speech. It was no longer simply a matter of injured reputation.'[1]]

In his opening address on behalf of his client, Clarke pointed out that the words on the offending card were not a direct accusation that Wilde had committed a grave offence but that he had 'posed' as being such a person. He added that Queensberry's written plea of justification, which had been expanded from its original form, now included the names of certain persons with whom, it was alleged, Wilde had committed grave offences.

Clarke then went on to give details of Wilde's career and his friendship with Lord Alfred Douglas. He recounted the attempts made to blackmail Wilde over some of his letters to Douglas which had fallen into the wrong hands. He read out the text of one of these letters which, he commented, might 'appear extravagant to those in the habit of writing commercial correspondence', but made the point that Wilde was a poet and that this letter was really a 'prose sonnet'. Clarke went on to mention some of Wilde's writings, in particular *The Picture of Dorian Gray*, which he knew Carson would quote.

Wilde, as plaintiff for the prosecution, then entered the witness box, and acquitted himself well in answer to Clarke's various questions. When he finished just before lunch, Carson began his cross-examination with the following query:

CARSON: You stated that your age was thirty-nine. I think you are over forty. You were born on 16th October 1854 [holding up Wilde's birth certificate].

WILDE: I have no wish to pose as being young. I am thirty-nine or forty. You have my certificate and that settles the matter.

CARSON: But being born in 1854 makes you more than forty?

WILDE: Ah! Very well.

CARSON: What age is Lord Alfred Douglas?

WILDE: Lord Alfred Douglas is about twenty-four, and was between twenty and twenty-one years of age when I first knew him ....

Wilde, by stating that he was 39 years of age, when in fact he was 40, had given Carson an opportunity of catching him out in a lie or a pretence at the very beginning of his evidence. But Carson over-stated his correction when he said that Wilde was 'more than forty'. (Wilde and Carson were born in the year 1854, but Carson was eight months older than Wilde. Carson was born on 9 February and Wilde on 6 October. In other words, Carson was 41 years old at the date of the trial, whereas Wilde was 40. The question put to Wilde by Carson, 'But being born in 1854 makes you more than forty?' was true if applied to himself, but not to Wilde.) On the date of this cross-examination (3 April 1895) Wilde was exactly 40 years, five months and eighteen days old, i.e. still 40 years. But no doubt Carson was mainly interested in drawing the jury's attention to the disparity in the ages of Wilde and Douglas.

Wilde did not allow himself to be upset by this incident, and a few minutes later he was answering Carson's questions about *The Picture of Dorian Gray* in the following manner:

CARSON: This is in your introduction to *Dorian Gray*: 'There is no such thing as a moral or an immoral book. Books are well written or badly written.' That expresses your view?

WILDE: My view on art, yes.

CARSON: Then I take it that no matter how immoral a book may be, if it is well written it is, in your opinion, a good book?

WILDE: Yes, if it were well written so as to produce a sense of beauty, which is the highest sense of which a human being can be capable. If it were badly written it would produce a sense of disgust.

CARSON: Then a well-written book putting forward perverted moral views may be a good book?

WILDE: No work of art ever puts forward views. Views belong to people who are not artists.

CARSON: A perverted novel might be a good book?

WILDE: I don't know what you mean by a 'perverted' novel.

CARSON: Then I will suggest *Dorian Gray* as open to the interpretation of being such a novel?

WILDE: That could only be to brutes and illiterates. The views of Philistines on art are incalculably stupid.

CARSON: An illiterate person reading *Dorian Gray* might consider it such a novel?

WILDE: The views of illiterates on art are unaccountable. I am concerned only with my view of art. I don't care two pence what other people think of it.

CARSON: The majority of persons would come under your definition of Philistines and illiterates?

WILDE: I have found wonderful exceptions.

CARSON: Do you think that the majority of people live up to the position you are giving us?

WILDE: I am afraid they are not cultivated enough.

CARSON: Not cultivated enough to draw the distinction between a good book and a bad book?

WILDE: Certainly not.

CARSON: The affection and love of the artist of *Dorian Gray* might lead an ordinary individual to believe that it might have a certain tendency?

WILDE: I have no knowledge of the views of ordinary individuals.

CARSON: You did not prevent the ordinary individual from buying your book?

WILDE: I have never discouraged him.

When Carson turned to questioning him about various named young men to whom he had been introduced (usually by Alfred Taylor, who had rooms which Carson later referred to as 'a shameful den') the atmosphere in court changed, and Wilde's bantering replies did not prevent the truth from coming to light gradually. Carson questioned him closely about the age, social position, education, employment (if any) of these young men, and enquired how Wilde had met them, what interest he had in them, and why he had brought them to dinner, with wine and champagne, and then often spent the night with them in hotels, or sometimes in his own rooms, after which he usually gave them some money and often a gift of a silver cigarette case. Most of them were of humble origins and not well educated. When Carson put it to him that these lowly, uneducated young men were hardly of a type to attract the interest of a man of Wilde's social class and erudition, Wilde's reply was that he delighted in the society of people much younger than himself, that he liked those who might be called idle and careless, and that he recognised no social distinctions.

One incident in particular was damaging to Wilde. Carson asked him if he knew Walter Grainger, and Wilde said he did. 'How old is he?' enquired Carson. Wilde replied: 'He was about sixteen when I knew him. He was a servant at a certain house in High Street, Oxford, where Lord Alfred Douglas had rooms. I have stayed there several times. Grainger waited at table. I never dined with him.' The transcript then reads:

CARSON: Did you ever kiss him?

WILDE: Oh, dear no. He was a peculiarly plain boy. He was, unfortunately, extremely ugly. I pitied him for it.

CARSON: Was that the reason why you did not kiss him?

WILDE: Oh, Mr Carson, you are pertinently insolent.

CARSON: Did you say that in support of your statement that you never kissed him?

WILDE: No. It is a childish question.

CARSON: Did you ever put that forward as a reason why you never kissed the boy?

WILDE: Not at all.

CARSON: Why, sir, did you mention that this boy was extremely ugly?

WILDE: For this reason. If I were asked why I did not kiss a door-mat, I should say because I do not like to kiss door-mats. I do not know why I mentioned that he was ugly, except that I was stung by the insolent question you put to me and the way you have insulted me throughout this hearing. Am I to be cross-examined because I do not like it?

CARSON: Why did you mention his ugliness?

WILDE: It is ridiculous to imagine that any such thing could have occurred under any circumstances.

CARSON: Then why did you mention his ugliness?

WILDE: Perhaps you insulted me by an insulting question.

CARSON: Was that a reason why you should say the boy was ugly?

After some further exchanges, during which it was clear that Wilde had become unsettled by Carson's persistent questioning on this point, he agreed that he had given a flippant answer.

During Carson's concluding speech for the defence he referred to Alfred Taylor, 'a most notorious character – as the police will tell the court – who occupied rooms which were nothing more than a shameful den.' He went on: 'Taylor is really the pivot of the case for the simple reason that when the various witnesses for the defence are called and examined – as unfortunately will be necessary – as to the practices of Mr Oscar Wilde, it will be found that it was Taylor who introduced the young men to the prosecutor.'

On the third day Carson continued his speech, commenting on the reasons given by Wilde for befriending the various young men mentioned. At this stage, Sir Edward Clarke realised that Wilde's position was hopeless, and would become even more so if witnesses were called to describe what had happened between them and Wilde. He interposed and told the judge that the evidence given about Wilde's writings and his letters to Douglas was such that he could not resist a verdict of not guilty having reference to the word 'posing'. The judge accepted Clarke's request not to pursue the case further, but said that the verdict must be either 'guilty' or not guilty', without terms or limitations.

The jury, having received instructions from Justice Collins, found Queensberry not guilty; they also found that his plea of justification had been proven and that his statement was published for the public benefit.

In an attempt to exonerate himself Wilde despatched a letter to the *Evening News*:

Sir – It would have been impossible for me to have proved my case without putting Lord Alfred Douglas in the witness-box against his father. Lord Alfred Douglas was extremely anxious to get into the box, but I would not let him do so. Rather than put him into so painful a position, I decided to retire from the case, and to bear on my own shoulders whatever ignominy and shame might result from my prosecution of Lord Queensberry.

Wilde was urged by his friends to go abroad immediately, to escape possible criminal charges against himself, but he refused and went to the Cadogan Hotel, Sloane Street, where he had a room. Queensberry's solicitor immediately sent to the Director of Public Prosecutions copies of the witnesses' statements and of the shorthand notes of the trial. These were sufficient for a warrant for the arrest of Wilde to be issued that same evening, and Wilde was arrested by two police officers at 6.30 p.m. He was brought to Bow Street and charged with gross indecency under Section 11 of the Criminal Law Amendment Act, 1885, which made it a criminal offence for any man to commit or procure any act of gross indecency with another man, either in public or in private. On the following day Wilde was taken on remand to Holloway Gaol, without being allowed bail. In fact, Wilde was not allowed bail until after the end of this case, and was in custody for about a month.

While awaiting trial in the Old Bailey three weeks later, Wilde was declared a bankrupt, on the petition of the Marquess of Queensberry who claimed legal costs against him. As a result, Wilde and his wife suffered the indignity of having the contents of their house in Tite Street sold by public auction. Robert Ross collected many of Wilde's manuscripts before that happened, but many items were stolen.

His trial for acts of gross indecency commenced on 26 April and lasted five days. (Carson took no part in this trial or in the subsequent re-trial.) Alfred Taylor was also charged with acts of gross indecency and with conspiring with Wilde to procure the commission of acts of indecency. At the outset, Sir Edward Clarke (who had told Wilde he would accept no fees for representing him at this trial) objected to his client having to face charges of *conspiracy* to commit these acts, in addition to charges of committing them, as this would make for legal difficulties in calling him as a witness, but Justice Charles disagreed and the conspiracy charges remained.

As witnesses against Wilde the Crown called a number of young men together with some hotel staff and landladies, one of whom was the landlady of Taylor's rooms. The evidence and cross-examination of these witnesses lasted almost three days. On the morning of the fourth day, the counsel for the Crown (Charles Gill) informed the judge that, having re-examined the indictment, he had decided not to ask for a verdict on the conspiracy charges. This news greatly annoyed Clarke, who said that if the conspiracy charges had been withdrawn at the outset he would have applied to have Wilde and Taylor tried separately. After some wrangling on this point, Clarke made a long speech in Wilde's defence. One of the points he put forward in favour of Wilde's innocence was the fact that he had stayed in England to face the accusations, a thing he would hardly have done if he were guilty. 'Insane would hardly be the word for it', he said, 'if Mr Wilde really had been guilty and yet faced the investigation.'

Wilde gave evidence and was cross-examined by Mr Gill, firstly about his writings, his two letters to Douglas, and about two short poems written by Douglas. One of these poems was called 'Two Loves', the last line of which reads: 'I am the Love that dare not speak its name.' Mr Gill asked what this love was. Wilde replied:

> 'The Love that dare not speak its name' in this century is such a great affection of an elder for a younger man as there was between David and Jonathan, such as Plato made the very basis of his philosophy, and such as you find in the sonnets of Michelangelo and Shakespeare. It is that deep, spiritual affection that is as pure as it is perfect. It dictates and pervades great works of art like those of Shakespeare and Michelangelo, and those two letters of mine, such as they are. It is in this century misunderstood, so much misunderstood that it may be described as the 'Love that dare not speak its name', and on account of it I am placed where I am now. It is beautiful, it is fine, it is the noblest form of affection. There is nothing unnatural about it. It is intellectual, and it repeatedly exists between an elder and a younger man, where the elder has intellect and the younger has all the joy, hope, and glamour of life before him. That it should be so, the world does not understand. The world mocks at it and sometimes puts one in the pillory for it.

This reply led to a spontaneous burst of applause (and some hisses) from the public gallery. Mr Gill also questioned him about the various men Wilde had met.

Clarke made an excellent speech for the defence and pointed out weaknesses in the witnesses' statements. With regard to the three main witnesses who had said they were involved in acts of indecency with Wilde, Clarke said: 'These wretches who have come forward to admit their own disgrace are shameless creatures incapable of one manly thought or one manly action. They are without exception blackmailers ... I respectfully submit that no jury can find a man guilty on the evidence of these tainted witnesses. Those three witnesses, Charles Parker, Wood and Atkins, witnesses for the Crown, have admitted their participation in such practices as ought to disentitle their evidence to the slightest credence.' He ended by imploring the jury to let their judgement be affected only by those witnesses with regard to whom they could say, with a clear conscience, that, as honourable men, they were entitled to be guided by true and honest and honourable testimony.

After Mr Gill's closing speech, Justice Charles summed up the evidence for and against Wilde in a fair manner. He put four questions for the jury to answer, as follows:

1. Do you think that Wilde committed indecent acts with Edward Shelley and Alfred Wood and with a person or persons unknown at the Savoy Hotel, or with Charles Parker?

2. Did Taylor procure or attempt to procure the commission of these acts or any of them?

3. Did Wilde and Taylor or either of them attempt to get Atkins to commit indecencies?

4. Did Taylor commit indecent acts with Charles Parker or William Parker?

When the jury returned after nearly four hours' deliberation, the foreman informed the judge that they had reached a negative finding in regard to the third question but had been unable to reach agreement on the other three questions. In reply to the judge, the foreman said he feared there was no chance of the jury reaching agreement on these questions, even if they were to discuss the matter further. The accused were therefore found 'not guilty' on the count relating to Atkins and the judge said there would have to be a retrial on the other counts.

It was a great tribute to Clarke's advocacy that the jury had failed to agree on a verdict against Wilde. He applied for bail for Wilde and this was granted in the total sum of £5,000 – £2,500 on Wilde's own security and two sureties of £1,250 each. These two sureties were given by Queensberry's eldest surviving son, Lord Douglas of Hawick (which indicates the split in the family) and the other by a Church of England clergyman, the Revd Stewart Headlam, who sympathised with Wilde.

For the retrial, the prosecution was led by the Solicitor-General himself, Sir Frank Lockwood, QC, MP. Mr Gill became his junior.

Before the retrial commenced on 20 May some of Wilde's friends, and his wife, suggested that he should jump bail and go abroad, but he refused to run away. 'I could not bear life if I were to flee,' he said. 'I cannot see myself slinking about the continent, a fugitive from justice.' Besides, he still felt he had a chance of acquittal.

Clarke applied for separate trials for Wilde and Taylor, and this was granted. When Lockwood said he wished Taylor to be tried first Clarke objected, on the grounds that Wilde's name was first on the indictment and that the first count was against him, but the new judge (Justice Wills) ruled in favour of the Crown.

Taylor was tried and found guilty of indecent behaviour with Charles and William Parker, but not guilty of procuring. The judge decided to postpone sentencing him until Wilde's case had been heard. Wilde's retrial commenced on 22 May, before a new jury.

As it was a new trial, the prosecution had to go through the evidence again, though this time in a somewhat shortened form, because some of the earlier counts had been ruled out. The Crown witnesses for the charges of indecency were Charles Parker, Alfred Wood and Edward Shelley. Some staff members from the Savoy Hotel were also called to give corroborative evidence of Wilde having been seen with a young man there.

Shelley was called first and alleged that Wilde had made approaches to him, which he had resisted. However, under Clarke's cross-examination his evidence was shown to be contradictory in some respects; he also turned out to be a neurotic person, who admitted he had had mental problems. The judge eventually ruled out Shelley's evidence, because it had not been corroborated. This was an important gain for Wilde – or so it seemed at the time. Wood and Parker repeated their allegations of indecency with Wilde.

When Wilde entered the witness box he looked tired and haggard. He again denied all the accusations, and was cross-examined by Lockwood. The latter did not query Wilde about *The Picture of Dorian Gray*, but put questions about the wording of the two letters to Douglas. He asked Wilde why one of the letters commenced with the words 'My own Boy' and Wilde said it was because Douglas was so much younger than himself; 'the letter was a fantastic, extravagant way of writing to a young man' and 'it was like a little sonnet of Shakespeare'. He was asked to explain the phrases 'It is a marvel that those red rose-leaf lips of yours should have been made no less for music of song than for madness of kisses', 'Your slim gilt soul walks between passion and poetry', and 'Always, with undying love'. Wilde's explanation was that the letter was an attempt to write a prose poem in beautiful phraseology.

Wilde was cross-examined in detail about his meetings with the young men in question, and he was asked what sort of conversation he had with them, and what pleasure he could find in the society of young men much beneath him in social position. Wilde replied that he was enormously fond of praise and admiration, that he liked to be made much of by his social inferiors, that he made no social distinctions, and that he had read one of his plays to them.

In his closing speech, Clarke said:

Wood and Parker, in giving evidence, have established for themselves a sort of statute of limitations. In testifying on behalf of the Crown, they have secured immunity for past rogueries and indecencies. It is on the evidence of Parker and Wood that you are asked to condemn Wilde.

And Mr Wilde knew nothing of the characters of these men. They were introduced to him, and it was his love of admiration that caused him to be in their society. The positions should really be changed. It is these men who ought to be the accused, not the accusers.

During the course of his summing-up, Justice Wills mentioned Wilde's letters to Douglas and commented:

I may be dull myself, but speaking personally I cannot see the extreme beauty of the language said to be used. However, opinions may well differ on this point. But suppose that the letters are 'prose poems', suppose that they are things, of which the intellectual and literary value can only be appreciated by persons of high culture, are they thereby any the less poisonous for a young man? Is the language of those letters calculated to calm and keep down the passions which in a young man need no stimulus? It is strange that it should not occur to a gentleman capable of writing such letters that any young man, to whom they were addressed, must suffer in the estimation of everybody, if it were known.

As regards Wilde's friendship with the witnesses, the judge said:

Gentlemen, you have seen the Parkers, as you have seen Wood, and the same question must arise in your minds. Are these the kind of young men with whom you yourselves would care to sit down to dine? Are they the sort of persons you would expect to find in the company of men of education?

The jury deliberated for three hours and returned verdicts of guilty to the various charges of gross indecency with Charles Parker and Alfred Wood, and with another unknown male person.

Before pronouncing sentence the judge said he had no shadow of doubt about the guilty verdicts and that 'people who can do these things must be dead to all sense of shame'. He said it was the 'worst case' he had ever tried. Addressing the two defendants he said: 'That you, Taylor, kept a kind of male brothel it is impossible to doubt. And that you, Wilde, have been the centre of a circle of extensive corruption of the most hideous kind among young men, it is equally impossible to doubt.' He sentenced both Taylor and Wilde to two years' imprisonment with hard labour, the maximum sentence allowed by law for this offence. He added that in his judgement the sentence was totally inadequate for such a case.

Wilde was obviously shocked at the punishment but was not allowed to say anything before being taken away.

PRISON

At that time a sentence of two years with hard labour meant what it said – a full two years' imprisonment, without any remission for good behaviour, with some form of manual labour, depending on the prisoner's condition. Wilde was regarded as suitable for light manual labour.

He was first taken to Newgate prison, where the detention warrant was made out, then to Holloway prison, where his clothes were taken from him, his appearance and measurements were noted down (he was six feet tall and weighed almost fourteen stone), and he was fitted with a prison suit marked with large arrows. On 9 June he was transferred to Pentonville, a prison for convicted prisoners where conditions were very strict. He was kept in a cell, on his own, for most of the time, except for one hour's exercise each day, walking in single file without being allowed to speak to anybody. His cell was sparsely furnished, no personal belongings or photographs were allowed, and he had a plank bed with sheets, rugs and a cover, but no mattress (until this became earned by good behaviour). Food, ventilation and lighting were poor. For the first month his exercise consisted of walking on the treadmill for six hours a day. After one month he was put on manual work, sewing mailbags or picking oakum. The only books available were the Bible and *The Pilgrim's Progress*. No writing materials were allowed for the first three months, after which he could write one letter a month.Wilde later said that the three punishments allowed by law were Hunger, Insomnia and Disease (diarrhoea).

On 4 July he was transferred to Wandsworth prison, apparently as a result of representations on his behalf by R.B. Haldane (later Lord Haldane), a member of a Home Office committee then investigating prison conditions. Haldane had known Wilde and visited him in prison a few times; in fact, he was Wilde's first visitor, on 12 June 1895. Because of his official position, Haldane could get permission to visit Wilde periodically, but normally visitors were allowed for only 20 minutes once every three months, in the presence of a warder and separated from the visitor by wires.

After six months in Wandsworth, Wilde was transferred to Reading Gaol, where he remained until his release in May 1897. The governor of Reading, Colonel Isaacson, was an unfeeling martinet, but fortunately for Wilde he was replaced during the second year by Major Nelson, who was more understanding. Haldane succeeded in getting additional books for Wilde and also pen and ink. As regards writing paper, the arrangement was that Wilde could get one sheet at a time. When this was full, he handed it to the warder and got another sheet. In this way, during his last few months in prison, Wilde wrote the long and introspective letter to Douglas which was published after Wilde's death under the title *De Profundis*.

Constance visited him in September 1895 and he requested her forgiveness. At that stage she had been considering divorce but dropped the idea. When Lady Wilde died on 3 February 1896, Constance travelled all the way from Italy to tell Wilde of his mother's death. After this visit she wrote to her brother saying that Wilde was 'an absolute wreck compared with what he was'. The relations between Constance and Wilde became strained when difficulties arose regarding the amount of the allowance Wilde should receive from Constance. In February 1897, her solicitor visited Wilde to get him to sign a deed of separation from his wife, giving the custody of their children to Constance, and also agreeing to pay him an allowance of £150 a year on condition that he did not stay under the same roof as Douglas from then on. The loss of his two young sons was a great blow to Wilde but he signed the papers, as he knew he had wronged Constance.

WILDE'S SONS

Because of the notoriety attached to Wilde's conviction for acts of gross indecency, and the widespread publicity given to his transgressions, his wife decided to change her surname and that of her two sons to Holland, a name that had family connections with the Lloyds. (Constance's brother, two years older than her, had been baptised Otho Holland Lloyd.)

The boys were moved to Switzerland, then to Italy, then to a boarding school near Heidelberg in Germany. Vyvyan, the younger of the two, detested this school and was transferred to a Jesuit school in Monaco (which had been recommended to his mother by a friend, Princess Alice of Monaco), while his brother remained in Germany for another year. After their mother's death in April 1898, both boys were returned to England, where Vyvyan entered Hodder Place, a preparatory school attached to Stonyhurst (where he formally became a Roman Catholic) and then entered Stonyhurst itself. Cyril went to Radley school and then to the Royal Military Academy at Woolwich. Vyvyan's book, *Son of Oscar Wilde*[3], gives a vivid description of his early life under the strict supervision of his mother's relatives, who kept him completely in the dark about his father and his father's writings. As regards his early childhood, Vyvyan makes it clear that his father was a good and playful parent. He did not know the cause of his father's downfall until he was eighteen years of age, when an aunt in Lausanne told him. Afterwards, when he studied in Cambridge, he became familiar with his father's writings.

In his book, Vyvyan comments as follows on his father:

My feelings towards my father's memory have always of necessity been mixed ones. I think of my mother with deep affection and regret. I also have affectionate feelings towards my mother's family, who, however misguidedly, tried to construct a new life for my brother and myself on a foundation of sand. But I am also proud of my father and of his place in English literature, though, as I suppose the sons of all famous men must feel, it is embarrassing to bask in so much reflected glory.

I remember him as a smiling giant, always exquisitely dressed, who crawled about the nursery floor with us and lived in an aura of cigarette-smoke and eau-de-cologne. During his last years we were constantly in his thoughts; he was always asking Robert Ross to try and find out something about us, how we were and how we were getting on at school. And Ross told me that he wept bitter tears when he pondered on how he had failed us and himself and his ancestors.

Vyvyan Holland died in 1967, leaving a son, Merlin.

AFTER PRISON

Wilde was due to complete his prison sentence on 19 May 1897. On 18 May he was brought by train and cab to Pentonville prison, from which he was released at 6.15 a.m. on the following morning. He was met by two of his friends, More Adey and the Revd Stewart Headlam, who brought him by cab to Headlam's house, where he changed his clothes. His friends Mr and Mrs Leverson arrived to greet him, and Mrs Leverson recalled that he came into the drawing room apparently very relaxed and looking better than he had two years earlier. His comment to Mrs Leverson showed that he still retained his flair for witty remarks: 'How marvellous of you to know exactly the right hat to wear at seven o'clock in the morning to meet a friend who has been away. You can't have got up, you must have sat up.' He wrote a letter to the Jesuits at Farm Street requesting a six-months' retreat, and sent it by special messenger, who was told to wait for a reply. To Wilde's disappointment, the Jesuits replied that they could not take him in on the spur of the moment and that a year's preparation would be needed.

That same night he took the boat to Dieppe and was met by Ross, who had been informed by Wilde that he wished him to become his literary executor, and another friend, Reggie Turner. Wilde had with him the bundle of written pages containing his long letter to Douglas, which the prison authorites had not allowed him to send out beforehand. He handed the bundle to Ross, who had already been instructed by Wilde to have typed copies made, on good paper with a wide margin for corrections (from this, it seems that Wilde had intended revising the script, but this did not happen).

FINAL DAYS

In March 1898, Ross wrote to Constance pointing out that Wilde and Douglas were now living apart and enquiring whether the allowance to her husband might be restored. Constance agreed to resume paying £150 a year and added a codicil to her will so that this payment would be continued after her death, without conditions. This codicil proved to be of benefit to Wilde. Some years earlier Constance had injured her spine as a result of a fall down the stairs in their house in Tite Street. She underwent an operation but it was not very successful. She continued to suffer pain and, at times, could hardly walk. Early in April 1898 she underwent a second spinal operation which was also unsuccessful. She died on 7 April, aged 40, and was buried in Genoa. Constance, a good woman, was perhaps the most unfortunate victim of Wilde's downfall. As Ellmann says, Wilde's behaviour destroyed her.[1]

Douglas, who was then living in Paris, visited Wilde to offer his condolences on the death of Constance. Douglas returned to London in November 1898. In the following month, the writer Frank Harris offered to bring Wilde to the south of France for three months, hoping that this might encourage him to do some writing. Wilde and Harris stayed in a hotel at La Napoule, near Cannes, but Wilde wrote nothing, except letters.

While in La Napoule, Wilde met an English man, Harold Mellor, who invited him to come as his guest to Switzerland. On the way there Wilde made a detour to Genoa, to lay flowers on his wife's grave. The inscription on the headstone read: 'Constance Mary, daughter of Horace Lloyd, QC'. Wilde was very upset at the complete absence of his own name; it was as if he had never existed in Constance's life. [The words 'Wife of Oscar Wilde' were added later.]

After leaving Mellor, Wilde stayed for a while at Santa Margharita on the Italian coast, and wrote to Ross, complaining of boredom. Ross arrived in May, paid his debts, and brought him back to Paris, where he idled his time with little money. On another visit to Paris, Douglas invited him to dinner to celebrate the publication of a book of Douglas's poems. Later, Wilde bumped into Nellie Melba, the opera singer, and said to her: 'Madame Melba, you don't recognise me? I'm Oscar Wilde, and I am going to do a terrible thing. I'm going to ask you for money.' She gave him whatever she had in her purse.

After a trip to Palermo, Naples and Rome with Harold Mellor in April 1900, he returned to Paris and stayed at Hotel d'Alsace, which turned out to be his last place of abode. It was a small hotel but the proprietor tried to make Wilde as comfortable as possible.

Wilde's health began to deteriorate noticeably in 1900, and by September of that year he had to spend most of his time in his hotel room. The doctor attached to the British Embassy in Paris, Maurice a'Court Tucker, visited him many times, but his condition did not improve. His inner ear became extremely painful (he had injured it in a fall in prison) and Dr Tucker advised an operation. With money borrowed to pay the surgeon, he was operated on, in the hotel room, on 10 October. Ross arrived from London on 16 October (Wilde's 46th birthday) and, with Reggie Turner, helped in whatever way they could. The ear trouble developed into an abscess, and meningitis was suspected.

On 6 November, Ross wrote to Douglas telling him of Wilde's poor condition. (The Marquess of Queensberry had died on 31 January 1900, leaving Douglas with about £20,000.) Ross left on 12 November to visit his mother in the south of France, leaving Reggie Turner in charge. The two doctors wrote a report which said that on 25 November there were significant cerebral disturbances stemming from an old suppuration of the right ear, and that on the 27th the symptoms became much graver, and a diagnosis of encephalitic meningitis must be made.

When Ross returned on 29 November Wilde was in pain and could hardly speak. Ross, who was a Catholic convert, knew of Wilde's long-standing interest in the Catholic church but had doubted his sincerity. However, he had promised Wilde to summon a priest for him if he were dying, and went to the house of the Passionist Fathers in Paris, where he handed in a card which said: 'Can I see one of the fathers about a very urgent case or can I hear of a priest elsewhere who can talk English to administer last sacraments to a dying man.' As a result, an Irish Passionist priest, Fr Cuthbert Dunne, returned with Ross to Wilde's room. Fr Dunne spoke to the dying man to explain what was taking place. Wilde tried but failed to speak, but Fr Dunne was satisfied that Wilde was sufficiently conscious to know what was happening and that he was able to indicate consent. Fr Dunne's record of the occasion is quoted in Hyde's biography [6], as follows:

> He made brave efforts to speak, and would even continue for a time trying to talk, though he could not utter articulate words. Indeed I was fully satisfied that he understood me when I told him that I was about to receive him into the Catholic Church and give him the Last Sacraments. From the signs he gave as well as from his attempted words, I was satisfied as to his full consent. And when I repeated close to his ear the Holy Names, the Acts of Contrition, Faith, Hope and Charity, with acts of humble resignation to the Will of God he tried all through to say the words after me.

Wilde died at 2 p.m. on 30 November 1900. Douglas arrived on 2 December and was the chief mourner at the funeral, which he paid for.

Requiem Mass was said by Fr Dunne at St Germain-des-Prés and Wilde was buried on 3 December at Bagneux. In 1909 his remains were moved to Pére Lachaise, where a monument by Epstein was later erected. The inscription on the monument, taken from *The Ballad of Reading Gaol*, reads:

> And alien tears will fill for him
> Pity's long-broken urn,
> For his mourners will be outcast men,
> And outcasts always mourn.

EPILOGUE

When Wilde died in 1900 Richard Ross continued as his literary executor. By 1906 he had cleared off Wilde's debts and recovered the copyright of his writings, after which Wilde's two sons benefited from the royalties. One of the items that helped clear off the debts was Richard Strauss's opera Salomé, first performed in Germany in December 1905 and based on Wilde's play. (Wilde's plays were popular in Germany from an early date.)

When the abridged edition of *De Profundis* was published in England in 1905 it sold five editions within a year. This encouraged the publishers (Methuen) to go further, and they published a collected edition of Wilde's works in 1908.

As he grew older, Lord Alfred Douglas became even more argumentative and controversial, and he campaigned against the influence of Wilde, about whom he wrote three books. He became a Roman Catholic convert in 1911 (a move which Ross did not like) and died in 1945.

With the passage of time, the literary and dramatic value of Wilde's writings and plays proved themselves, and he is now recognised as one of the literary stars of the late nineteenth century. His plays continue to entertain the public, and the downfall which broke him is one of the great literary tragedies.

BIBLIOGRAPHY

(1) Richard Ellmann, *Oscar Wilde*. Hamish Hamilton, 1987.

(2) Vyvyan Holland (ed.), *Complete Works of Oscar Wilde* (in one volume). Collins, 1948 and 1966.

(3) Vyvyan Holland, *Son of Oscar Wilde*. Rupert Hart-Davis, London, 1954.

(4) Vyvyan Holland, *Oscar Wilde: A Pictorial Biography*. Thames & Hudson, London, 1960.

(5) H. Montgomery Hyde, *The Trials of Oscar Wilde*. Hodge, London, 1948.

(6) H. Montgomery Hyde, *Oscar Wilde: A Biography*. Methuen, 1976.

(7) Hesketh Pearson, *The Life of Oscar Wilde*. Methuen, 1946.

(8) Richard Pine, *Oscar Wilde*. Gill & Macmillan, Dublin, 1983.

(9) Davis Coakley, *Oscar Wilde: The Importance of Being Irish*. Town House, Dublin, 1994.

Edward Carson
(1854–1935)

Edward Carson was born and reared in Dublin, where he lived for most of the first 38 years of his life. Yet, because of his unwavering support for the Ulster Unionists in their prolonged efforts to defeat Home Rule for Ireland, his memory is honoured in Belfast (where he never lived, apart from periodic visits) rather than in Dublin. He consistently sought to preserve the union between Great Britain and Ireland that had existed since 1801, and became leader of the Irish Unionist Parliamentary Party from 1910 to 1921, in which year he became a Lord of Appeal in the House of Lords.

Carson did not wish to see Ireland partitioned, but when it became clear that Home Rule would be brought into operation by the British Parliament despite the opposition of the Irish Unionists, he fought at first for the exclusion of Ulster, and then for the exclusion of the six north eastern countries, in order that the predominantly Protestant and Unionist part of Ireland would remain within the United Kingdom.

When Northern Ireland was established in 1921 he told Sir James Craig, the first Prime Minister, that 'Ulster will always be my first love and my greatest memory'. When he died in England in 1935 his body was brought by warship to Belfast, for burial in St Anne's Cathedral.

In front of the parliament buildings at Stormont is a large bronze statue of Edward Carson, with right arm aloft as if in defiance. This is the memory of Carson that Ulster Unionists like to preserve.

Edward Carson was born on 9 February 1854 in 4 Harcourt Street, Dublin, and was baptised in St Peter's (Church of Ireland), Aungier Street. His paternal grandfather, William Carson, had come to Dublin from Scotland in 1815 and became a successful general merchant. William had three sons, two of whom attended Trinity College, Dublin and became clergymen in the Church of Ireland. The other son, Edward, became an architect and in 1851 married Isabella Lambert, whose father, Captain Peter Lambert, had an estate near Athenry in County Galway. Captain Lambert was descended from a Yorkshire man who had been a major-general in Oliver Cromwell's army, and the Lamberts had been in Ireland since the end of the seventeenth century.

Edward and Isabella Carson had two daughters and four sons; the second son was Edward, the subject of this biography. With the increase in the family, they moved to a larger house (No. 25) in Harcourt Street, where the father also had his architect's office.

Young Edward Carson first attended a school run by a Church of Ireland clergyman in Harcourt Street. When he was twelve years old he was sent, with two of his brothers, to Arlington House boarding school in the small town of Portarlington, County Laois (then called Queen's County). He was a tall, ungainly schoolboy and was not as robust as his brothers; he had trouble with his health throughout his life and was regarded as hypochondriac, but nevertheless lived to the age of 81. He was not an outstanding student, but made an impression in the school debating society.

Edward's father did not wish him to be an architect and advised him to become a barrister. In 1871 he passed the entrance examination for Trinity College, within easy walking distance of his home, where he studied the classics. He took part in boating, swimming and hurling. (Oscar Wilde entered Trinity College that same year, but they did not mix.) In his third year Carson joined the college Historical Society, the then auditor of which was Bram Stoker, who later achieved fame as the author of *Dracula*. The Society awarded Carson a silver medal for composition in 1876. In due course he obtained a pass arts degree. (In old age Carson said: 'I have no more pleasant recollection in my life than my career in Trinity College, and especially in the college Historical Society.')

Students for the Bar had to take an arts degree, followed by a year in Trinity law school and two years in King's Inns, on the north side of the city. Carson was called to the Bar in 1877 but, as it was then a requirement that every Irish graduate in law had to spend four terms 'eating dinners' in one of the English Inns of Court, he chose Middle Temple in London and, after completing these terms, returned to Dublin. The Bar library in the Four Courts was the centre of action and he made many friends there, including a number who afterwards, like himself, achieved high office.

Like many young barristers, Carson found it difficult to attract briefs at first, but he regularly attended the criminal court in Green Street and went on the Leinister Circuit. One of Carson's best friends, also a barrister, was James Shannon, who had been a boarder with him in Arlington House. They sometimes went yachting together in Dun Laoghaire (then called Kingstown) and it was here, in 1879, that Carson noticed an attractive, fair-haired young woman watching the boats. Shannon knew her and introduced Carson. She was Annette Kirwan, who lived in the area with her father, a retired police inspector. (Her mother had died while Annete was a young girl.) Carson fell in love with her and within a matter of months they began to talk of marriage. His income was small and Annette had no dowry, but they married on 19 December 1879 in

Monkstown parish church, with Shannon as best man. The couple spent their honeymoon in London.

A relative of Annette's allowed them to stay in his house in Herbert Place, off Baggot Street, but it was not long before they were able to rent their own house at 9 Herbert Place. Their first child, a boy (William Henry, known as Harry), was born there on 2 October 1880. Their first daughter, Aileen, was born on 13 November 1881, another girl (Gladys) was born at the end of 1885, and their second son, Walter, in 1890.

POLITICS

Tenant farmers in nineteenth-century Ireland had practically no legal rights against landlords, who could fix rents and evict tenants almost at will. The Land League, founded by Davitt in 1879 with Charles Stewart Parnell as its president, tried to remedy this situation, not always peacefully. The government tried to improve the situation by passing the Land Act of 1881, which set up the Land Commission to fix rents, but this did not solve the problem completely. Even with State assistance, few tenants could raise enough capital to purchase the land, and large numbers were outside the scope of the Act, so that acrimonious disputes between landlords and tenants continued. In October 1881 Parnell was imprisoned in Kilmainham for obstructing the law, leading to further civil strife when the Land League advised tenants to withhold rents until their grievances were settled. Parnell was released in April 1882 as a result of an understanding whereby the government would help tenants in arrears with their rent and Parnell would use his influence to calm the country and secure acceptance of the Land Act.

The Conservative and Liberal parties competed with each other for influence, but when the Irish Party increased its representation in Parliament in 1885 they found themselves holding the balance of power. This enabled Parnell to make a deal with whichever party would promise to improve conditions in Ireland. Both parties were prepared to do something for tenant farmers, but only the Liberals were prepared to countenance Home Rule for Ireland. Gladstone had become convinced that the most effective means of bringing peace and order to Ireland was to grant Home Rule. He introduced two Bills to provide a limited form of Home Rule, but neither was successful. The 1886 Bill was defeated in the House of Commons (because 93 dissident Liberals voted with the Conservatives against it) and the 1893 Bill, though passed by the Commons, was rejected by the House of Lords.

The Conservative and Unionist policy was to retain the union between Great Britain and Ireland, and they strongly opposed the Liberals' Home Rule Bills. The Conservatives nevertheless brought into effect Land Acts which improved the position of tenants, and it was the Conservative Land Act of 1903 (the Wyndham Act) which went a long way towards resolving the land problem, by encouraging landlords to sell entire estates and by enabling tenants to obtain long-term loans (repayable over 68 years at 3.25 per cent interest) to purchase their farms.

AT THE BAR

Civil unrest in Ireland gave rise to numerous court cases in which Carson often participated, so much so that by 1886 his income had improved to the extent that he was able to purchase a large Georgian house (No. 80) in Merrion Square, an area favoured by professional people. Soon afterwards he also bought a small house in Dalkey, where the family stayed during the summer months. He had become a respectable professional man, with family responsibilities.

HOME RULE

But all was not well in Ireland, where there were strongly felt divisions of opinion on political, religious and social issues. Several leading Conservatives let it be known that they would unreservedly support Ulster Unionists in their campaign against Home Rule. The best-known example of this was Lord Randolph Churchill's emotional speech to Orangemen in the Ulster Hall, Belfast, on 22 February 1886, when he told his audience:

> The Loyalists in Ulster should wait and watch – organise and prepare. Diligence and vigilance ought to be your watchword; so that the blow, if it does come, may not come upon you as a thief in the night and may not find you unready and taken by surprise ... If it should turn out that the Parliament of the United Kingdom was so recreant from all its high duties, and that the British nation was so apostate to tradition of honour and courage, as to hand over the Loyalists in Ireland to the domination of an Assembly in Dublin which must be to them a foreign and an alien assembly ... I do not hesitate to tell you most truly, that in that dark hour there will not be wanting to you those of position and influence in England who would be willing to cast in their lot with you and who, whatever the result, will share your fortunes and your fates.

A few weeks later he expressed similar views in a letter to a Liberal MP which received much publicity:

If political parties and political leaders should be so utterly lost to every feeling and dictate of honour and courage as to hand over coldly the lives and liberties of the Loyalists of Ireland to their hereditary and most bitter foes, make no doubt on this point – Ulster will not be a consenting party. Ulster at the proper moment will resort to the supreme arbitrament of force. Ulster will fight, Ulster will be right. Ulster will emerge from the struggle victorious, because all that Ulster represents to us Britons will command the sympathy and support of an enormous section of our British community, and also, I feel certain, will attract the admiration and approval of free and civilised nations.

These statements inevitably increased tension in Belfast, where Protestants were a sizeable majority, and it is not surprising that there were serious sectarian riots in Belfast in the summer of 1886, after the introduction of the Home Rule Bill in April of that year. Thirty-two people were killed and 442 arrested, and 377 police were injured.

Carson's had a keen interest in party politics. In the 1886 election, for example, he spoke in support of Sir Edward Sullivan, a Liberal-Unionist candidate for the St Stephen's Green division of Dublin.

CROWN PROSECUTOR

When the Conservatives were returned to power with an overall majority at the end of 1886, they decided to apply resolute government to Ireland and carried through the Criminal Law and Procedure Act of 1887, which gave additional legal powers to the Lord Lieutenant and to magistrates. The Lord Lieutenant could 'proclaim' an association as dangerous and suppress it. The government could also 'proclaim' a district, with the result that criminal trials could be moved to another district and heard before a special jury. Offences such as conspiracy, intimidation, unlawful assembly, and obstructing officers of the law became punishable on summary conviction before a resident magistrate, without a jury.

It was in this atmosphere that Carson's talents as a criminal lawyer became evident, and when the new Act was brought into operation he was appointed Crown Prosecutor, to assist the Irish Attorney-General.

The first prosecution under the same Act was conducted by Carson in Mitchelstown, County Cork, where the Irish Nationalist MP William O'Brien had set about applying the 'Plan of Campaign' to the estate of the Countess of Kingston, just outside the town. (The 'Plan of Campaign' was a scheme organised by the National League under which tenants on particular estates were encouraged to act as a body, to offer the landlord what the tenants regarded as fair rents, and, if these were refused, to pay the rents into a fund for the benefit of evicted tenants.)

O'Brien and another MP (John Mandeville) were charged with conspiracy and summoned to appear before the Resident Magistrate in Mitchelstown on 9 September 1887. To show their contempt for the charge, the two MPs held a public meeting in Mitchelstown on the same date, which was addressed by John Dillon, MP. A large crowd gathered and, when the police tired to force a way through for an official reporter to take a note of what Dillon was saying, the crowd became obstructive and began to stone the police. A riot followed and the police opened fire, killing two men.

While this meeting was taking place in the town square, Carson had obtained from the resident magistrate warrants for the arrest of the two accused, who had not presented themselves in court. O'Brien and Mandeville were duly arrested and confined in Cork jail, while awaiting trial in Mitchelstown two weeks later.

O'Brien's arrival for the trial was attended by a huge crowd, for he was one of the leading members of the Irish Party, a great orator, and editor of the weekly paper *United Ireland*.

Counsel for O'Brien was Tim Harrington, Nationalist MP and Secretary of the National League. When Carson proceeded with the case against O'Brien, and quoted from his speeches as reported by policemen who had taken notes, Harrington became involved in arguments with Carson, and eventually withdrew from the case and left the court. Next day O'Brien conducted his own defence, but the two accused were found guilty and sentenced to three months imprisonment. They immediately appealed and were released on bail. After various delays their appeal was heard and dismissed, and they served their prison sentences, though Mandeville died before completing his.

The post of Crown Prosecutor was a demanding and dangerous occupation, but Carson, who usually carried a revolver on these trips, carried out his duties without fear. He formed a high regard for Arthur Balfour, Chief Secretary for Ireland, because of his steadfastness in upholding the law. The feeling was mutual.

In June 1889 Carson was appointed a Queen's Counsel, becoming, at 35, the youngest QC in Ireland. The practical effect of this promotion was that Carson moved to the front benches in court and sat beside the Attorney-General, instead of behind him as he had previously done. He continued to be briefed for important prosecutions and became Senior Crown Prosecutor for Dublin City and County, in charge of all government work at Green Street courthouse.

BALFOUR

Arthur Balfour (1848–1930), Chief Secretary for Ireland from 1887 to 1891 and Prime Minister from 1902 to the end of 1905, had a great influence on Carson's career, particularly on his decision to enter politics by competing for one of the Trinity College parliamentary seats, and on Carson's decision to move to England with his wife and family.

In 1890 there were reports that the Irish Attorney-General, Serjeant Madden, one of the two MPs representing Trinity College, was likely to be appointed a judge in the near future, thus creating a parliamentary vacancy in Trinity. Balfour was anxious to have an Irish Law officer in Westminister and wrote to Carson on 12 May:

> Dear Mr Carson,
>
> I do not know that I have any right or title to interfere directly or indirectly in the question now pending with regard to the representation of Trinity College in the event of there being a vacancy, but if my opinion in the matter be desired I see no reason why you should not state that you have my good wishes for your success and that I regard your presence in the House of Commons in the event of the Attorney-General leaving it as not merely a matter of convenience to the Government but one little short of absolute necessity.
>
> There is no objection to your showing this to Dr Stubbs or any other leading member in the constituency should you think it advisable, but I feel so strongly that I have no title to express an opinion on the choice by the Constituency of their representative in Parliament that I should hesitate to publish it in any form or shape lest I should give rise to misconception.
>
> Yours very truly,
> Arthur James Balfour.

Balfour wrote in similar vein to another Trinity graduate, the Revd James Rountree, who was regarded as having influence among Trinity graduates in England.

An election did not occur for a further two years and, in the meantime, Carson discovered that not all Trinity staff looked with favour on his candidature, as the two Trinity seats had always been filled by Conservatives, whereas he was a Liberal Unionist. When a third candidate (a Conservative) was nominated, there had to be a contest.

Shortly before the general election of July 1892, the Government made a number of legal appointments as a result of which Carson became Solicitor-General for Ireland. (This appointment lasted only a few months, as the Conservatives went out of office after the election.)

MEMBER OF PARLIAMENT

Carson decided to go ahead with his application for a Trinity seat, and when the Provost sat in the Examination Hall on 4 July 1892 to receive nominations, Carson was nominated by the Revd Dr Stubbs, Senior Fellow of the College, and seconded by Richard Falkiner, QC, Recorder of Dublin. The other two candidates were the outgoing MP for Trinity, David Plunkett, QC, and Colnonel J. Lowry.

The graduates and students were addressed by the three candidates. Carson said: 'Sixteen years ago I left the University to engage in the great struggle of life in the noble profession which I adopted, and I have come back after that comparatively long period, having now the confidence of Mr Balfour and Her Majesty, and having had bestowed upon me the high honour of Solicitor-General for Ireland. I come here to ask you to elect me to Parliament, not because I want promotion but because I have got it.' After the nominations and speeches the Provost called for a vote by a show of hands but Colonel Lowry's proposer requested a poll to determine the result. This was granted and the poll showed that Plunkett received 2,188 votes, Carson 1,609 votes, and Lowry 897 votes.

Carson told the students: 'It may be that we will be upon the Opposition benches, or it may be that we will be upon the Government benches, but wherever we be we will have the one and the same duty to perform – the duty of preserving intact the Union between Great Britain and Ireland. For that we stand pledged. To that you stand pledged.' These remarks were loudly cheered.

Carson took the boat-train to London for the opening of the new Parliament on 4 August and sat with the Conservatives on the Front Bench.

Following the Queen's Speech, several members spoke on the controversial subject of Home Rule. One speech that impressed Carson was by Colonel Edward Saunderson, Unionist MP for North Armagh, who took the Liberals to task for their proposed new Home Rule Bill. Pointing at the benches opposite, he said: 'No man who comes over to Belfast will laugh at the Ulster Loyalists. I say that whether the House of Lords rejects this Bill or does not, we reject it; and that, although you may occupy the House of Commons in years to come with academic debates on the values of this Home Rule Bill, when all is said, and even if you pass this Bill, I say in the name of my people, we will reject it.' John Redmond, the new leader of the Irish Party, dismissed Colonel Saunderson's remarks as being exaggerated, but they made a profound impression on Carson.

With the help of the Irish Party, the Liberals' censure motion on the Conservative government was carried by 40 votes and Lord Salisbury resigned as Prime Minister. Gladstone, then aged 83, was elected Prime Minister for the fourth time. Henry Asquith became Home Secretary and John Morley became Chief Secretary for Ireland, a post he had also held some years earlier. The House adjourned to give the new government time to prepare its programme of business, and Carson went home to Dublin to prepare himself for a change of career.

The leader of the Conservatives within the House of Commons was Arthur Balfour, who wished to rely on Carson to brief him on Irish affairs. As this would entail regular attendances at Westminster, Carson made a decision that changed his whole life: he would bring his wife and children with him to London, where he would attend Parliament regularly and also practise at the English Bar.

LONDON

When he returned to London at the beginning of January 1893, Carson visited the Carlton Club, of which he had become a member, and was introduced to Charles Darling, QC. When Carson mentioned that he proposed to practise in England, Darling explained that the arrangements there were different to those in Dublin, where a desk in the Law Library was sufficient. In England a group of barristers joined together, in the same chambers, sharing a clerk who looked after the fees and kept the fees books. Carson was disappointed at this news and felt he would not get many briefs until he had become known. Darling assured him that his reputation as Crown Prosecutor in Ireland was well known in England, and invited Carson to share chambers with him.

Morley was now Chief Secretary for Ireland in Dublin Castle and lost little time in making changes. He repealed the provisions in the Criminal Law Amendment Act which had enabled magistrates to carry out special inquiries, and ordered the release of certain prisoners. He set up a Commission to consider the position of tenants who had been evicted for participating in the Plan of Campaign, and appointed Mr Justice Mathew as president of it. Justice Mathew was a Catholic, a known supporter of Home Rule and father-in-law of John Dillon, the Nationalist MP.

Carson received a brief to appear before the Evicted Tenants Commission in Dublin in November 1892, on behalf of Lord Clanricarde, reputed to be the most hated landlord in Ireland. The proceedings got off to a bad start. Justice Mathew noted that Lord Clanricarde was not present and commented that if his Lordship refused to attend he must be prepared for the inference that evidence was being deliberately withheld. Carson intervened immediately: 'I appear for him and I don't see why these observations should be made.' Justice Mathew then said that the press might have to be excluded, as both tenants and landlords wished the hearings to be in private. Carson intervened again to point out that, as far as landlords were concerned, this was not so.

The first witness called was John Roche, Nationalist MP for East Galway, who had organised the Plan of Campaign on the Clanricarde estate in County Galway. He made a long statement about the iniquities of the landlords and the misfortunes of the tenants. Carson stood up and asked leave to cross-examine Mr Roche. Justice Mathew demurred but, when Carson repeated his request, said he might do so after lunch. After lunch, however, Justice Mathew told Carson he could submit written questions which, if considered relevant, would be put to the witness by one of the Commissioners. Carson protested and was ordered to leave the room. Carson was furious and insisted on his right to cross-examine unless every Commissioner ordered him to withdraw. Justice Mathew replied that the Commissioners had come to the unanimous conclusion that they would not hear him.

Carson responded very deliberately:

'My Lord. If I am not at liberty to cross-examine, I say the whole thing is a farce and a sham. I willingly withdraw from it. I will not prostitute my position by remaining any longer as an advocate before an English judge.'

'I am not sitting as a judge, 'remarked Justice Mathew.

'Any fool could see that,' Carson muttered under his breath.

'Your observations are disgraceful, 'said Justice Mathew, who had heard the remark.

A counsel for another landlord supported Carson's request, but he too was refused. Carson then threw his papers on the table and left the court.

These incidents made headlines in the newspapers. The Commission continued to take evidence and reported in due course, but two Commissioners resigned and the landlords refused to take part in the proceedings.

The case was Carson's last professional appearance in Ireland.

WESTMINISTER

When Parliament resumed on 31 January 1893, Balfour led off for the Conservatives. His speech did not end until 11.30 p.m. and by the time Carson rose to make his maiden speech there were only fifteen minutes left before the adjournment at midnight. He used the time to comment on and criticise the first six months of Morley's office as Chief Secretary. As regards Morley's claim that there had been a diminution in crime,

Carson contended that this was due to the repeal of the Crimes Act.

When he resumed his speech the following day, Carson referred to the payment of agricultural rents, which Morley had said were now being paid more consistently than ever before, and declared that the payment of rents in Ireland did not depend on the condition of tenant farmers but on whether Nationalist leaders had told them to pay. He castigated the Evicted Tenants Commission and its Chairman's decision not to allow him to cross-examine John Roche, MP. In explanation of why he had wished to cross-examine Mr Roche, he said he had been present at a trial in Dublin where it had been shown that Mr Roche had been involved in grave matters relating to the Clanricarde estate but had refused to give evidence. Carson alleged that Roche had made a speech inciting tenants to attack Lord Clanricarde's land agent, as a result of which the agent's body had been found shortly afterwards riddled with bullets. Carson added that, from information he had received, Mr Roche had stated he was among those who helped to resist the Sheriff at an eviction.

At this juncture Mr Roche arrived and interjected to say that he had not been present at the eviction for the purpose of resisting it, but admitted he had been present and indeed was proud to have been present.

'I make no charge against the honourable Member,' Carson replied. 'I am not accusing him of resisting the eviction, but having regard to the fact that he was there and proud of it, I suggest that at least I was entitled to put one question in cross-examination.' This caused some laughter.

Carson then referred to another speech by Mr Roche in which he had exhorted tenants to throttle a certain landlord 'until the glass eye fell out of his head'. Roche rose indignantly and denied that he had told the tenants to throttle the landlord, but admitted that 'in the heat and excitement of the moment' he had said that by adhering loyally to their pledges they would throttle him, and that he hoped 'they would not loose their grasp until the glass eye fell out of his head'.

'Well,' remarked Carson, 'I really will leave it to the House whether that was a matter upon which one might have been allowed to put a question to the witness.' This caused further laughter, and Roche did not intervene again.

The concluding portion of Carson's speech criticised the release of certain prisoners and referred to the 'miserable Home Rule Bill'.

When he concluded his speech, which had lasted for over an hour, Carson was cheered for several minutes. Balfour patted him on the back and Gladstone said it was the best maiden speech he remembered. The *Times* devoted a leading article to his speech and said that Carson had 'made his points with convincing conciseness and lucidity'.

THE ENGLISH BAR

Soon afterward Carson rented furnished rooms at 19 Bury Street, off St James's Street, convenient to the Houses of Parliament. He applied for re-admission to the Middle Temple so that he could practise in England, and was called to the English Bar in April 1893. Briefs began to trickle in. Though he was a Queen's Counsel in Ireland, he rated only as a junior counsel in England.

Carson's English law practice steadily increased as his abilities and successes became widely known, and he took part in many interesting law cases over the years. Unfortunately there is not enough space here to give an account of many of these. A few will be mentioned, but for others the reports in H. Montgomery Hyde's biography of Carson are well worth reading.

THE SECOND HOME RULE BILL, 1893

Under Gladstone's Home Rule Bill of 1886 no Irish members were to be elected to Westminster, but the Prime Minister changed his mind on this point and the 1893 Bill provided for 80 Irish members to be elected to Westminster (as distinct from those to be elected to the new Irish Parliament). The powers of the Home Rule Parliament would be limited. Defence, foreign affairs, postal services, currency, and customs were matters reserved to the Westminster Parliament.

During the summer of 1893, the Bill was discussed by the Commons, taking up 200 hours of parliamentary time. Redmond, leader of the Irish Party, was dissatisfied with the Bill and said: 'No man in his senses can any longer regard it as either a full or final or satisfactory settlement of the Irish question. 'Carson attended the House regularly and moved amendments. He came up against seasoned Liberal members – Gladstone, Asquith and Morley, and also Irish Nationalists such as Redmond, Dillon, O'Brien and Healy. At one stage there were disorderly scenes in the House when T.P. O'Connor called Joseph Chamberlain 'Judas'.

The Bill was passed with a majority of 34 votes, but the House of Lords, a bastion of Conservatism, rejected it by an overwhelming 378 votes. Gladstone was disappointed but hardly surprised. It was his final attempt to devolve a form of Home Rule to Ireland, and he retired shortly afterwards. His successor as Prime Minister was Lord Rosebery, who favoured the abolition of the veto powers held by the House of Lords but was not fully committed to Irish Home Rule.

In November 1893, the popular weekly magazine *Vanity Fair* published a character sketch of Carson:

Having more knowledge of Ireland than most Members of Parliament, he contrives, though he has not yet made a great name as a statesman, to say even more distasteful things about the oppressed Nationalists than the most brutal of Saxons. He is a bold and sinuous person, who pays no heed at all to the persuasions of the Nationalists who so prettily chide him for his want of patriotism. He seems to like the disgrace of being stigmatised as Mr Balfour's Crown Prosecutor; nor is he put out when he is openly said to be as big a blackguard as ever was Peter the Packer ... yet he is not without virtue. He has not much of a practice in England; but he has appeared in a case which arose out of a modern Labour trouble, and it is possible that he will get more clients. For he is a hard-working, painstaking, lynx-eyed practitioner who can speak strongly. He is a lean, pale-faced Irishman, who has as much wit and as much ability as Irishmen often have. He has not fattened even on robust Unionism.

In 1894 Carson applied to the Lord Chancellor to be recognised as a Queen's Counsel in England but was informed that there was no precedent for the appointment of a QC with only a year's practice at the English Bar; the usual period was nine years. Carson was annoyed at this rebuff but, due to public criticism, the Lord Chancellor relented and Carson became QC in England soon afterwards.

He spoke against the Evicted Tenants Bill, which aimed at restoring to their lands Irish tenants who had been evicted up to fifteen years earlier for non-payment of rents, and accused Morley of 'putting a premium on illegality'. His speech was highly praised, but the Bill was passed by the Commons before being rejected by the House of Lords.

OSCAR WILDE

In 1895 Carson received a brief that was to make him famous as a cross-examining counsel: it requested him to defend the Marquess of Queensbery against a charge of criminal libel brought by Oscar Wilde, who was then at the height of his fame. Carson knew Wilde, as they had attended Trinity College at the same time, but he was no friend of his. Their interests and outlook were quite different. Carson was a serious-minded Unionist politician and Queen's Counsel, whereas Wilde was a writer and playwright whose wit and flamboyant appearance were renowned, and whose politics tended towards Irish nationalism. They had met in London on only one occasion, when Wilde's carriage nearly knocked down Carson when he was crossing the Strand. Wilde got out and shook hands with Carson. 'Fancy you being a Tory and Arthur Balfour's right-hand man! You're coming along, Ned,' said Wilde, and then suggested that Carson should dine with him some day. This off-hand invitation came to nothing: if it had, Carson might have refused to accept the brief, as he made it a rule never to appear against a person from whom he had received hospitality. At first, Carson did not wish to accept the brief but Queenberry's solicitors prevailed upon him to do so.

Wilde's charge of criminal libel arose out of a card left for him by Queensberry at Wilde's club, on which Queensberry had written: 'To Oscar Wilde posing as a somdomite' (meaning 'sodomite').

The charge of criminal libel brought by Wilde against the Marquess of Queensberry opened in the Old Bailey on 3 April 1895, with Wilde being represented by Sir Edward Clarke, QC, MP and Queensberry by Edward Carson, QC, MP.

As the chapter on Oscar Wilde contains an account of the trials, including Wilde's libel case against Queensberry, it is unnecessary to go over the ground here, except for a few brief comments.

Wilde's performance in the witness box showed his gift of oratory and his lively wit, and his replies to Carson caused laughter in court on many occasions. His wit and eloquence did not save him, however, from Carson's penetrating cross-examination, which lasted several hours. Carson, of course, had the benefit of knowing that the weight of evidence was on his side, in the shape of several young men who were prepared to go into the witness box and give evidence against Wilde.

When the evidence against Wilde began to mount up, the libel charge was withdrawn by Sir Edward Clarke to avoid further revelations, but soon afterwards, Wilde was arrested and charged with committing acts of 'gross indecency'. Carson declined to take any part in these criminal proceedings against Wilde, though he could have had the leading brief, according to Montgomery Hyde.[2]

When the jury failed to agree on a verdict at the end of that criminal trial and the prosecution were trying to fix a date for a new trial, Carson approached the Solicitor-General, Sir Frank Lockwood (who was well known to him), and said: 'Cannot you let up on the fellow now? He has suffered a great deal.' Lockwood replied that he could not do that, as it would be alleged that the case had been abandoned because of certain other names, including Lord Rosebery's, mentioned in Queenberry's letters.

The retrial resulted in a guilty verdict against Wilde, for which he was imprisoned for two years. The shame and disgrace of his conviction and imprisonment ruined his life.

CONSERVATIVES IN POWER AGAIN

In mid-1895 the Liberals were defeated in a House of Commons vote and, when a general election was held, the Conservatives achieved power with a majority of 133. Lord Salisbury became Prime Minister for the third time, and Balfour became First Lord of the Treasury and Leader of the House of Commons. Carson has been tipped for a law office but did not get one; instead, he spent the next five years as a back-bencher, which allowed him more time to expand his legal practice.

Carson's colleague representing Trinity, David Plunkett, QC, was raised to the peerage and his parliamentary seat was taken by the historian W.E.H. Lecky. Carson, as the senior Member for Trinity College, was sworn in as a member of the Irish Privy Council on 5 April 1896.

During the new Parliamentary session, Carson had a serious difference of opinion with Conservative party leaders, arising out of a new Land Bill introduced by the new Chief Secretary for Ireland, Gerald Balfour, Arthur's brother. The Bill extended the scope of the 1881 Act and speeded up the purchase of land, in accordance with recommendations of a committee that had been chaired by Morley. Carson had been a leading member of that committee but had withdrawn when he felt that his proposals were not receiving fair consideration. He believed that the Bill betrayed the interests of landlords, and felt so strongly about this that he openly criticised the government. 'Each successive Government has thought it necessary from time to time,' he said, 'to bring in a Bill dealing with the Irish land policy, and no matter how the law might have been settled, to take a small slice of what remains to the landlord. It is part of the everlasting attempt to make peace in Ireland by giving sops to one party at the expense of the other.'

His amendments to the Bill were resisted and there were harsh exchanges with the government. Arthur Balfour disagreed with Carson's approach and made this clear when he said: 'I cannot help regretting the line which my right honourable friend is taking. I cannot understand him taking the view he has taken, and expressing it with the trenchant hostility which has characterised his remarks.'

Carson insisted on his amendments being voted on and was supported by 40 or more Unionists, but to no avail. Eventually he ceased pursuing his amendments and left the House, followed by Lecky, Colonel Saunderson and a few others. But he did not absent himself completely from the remaining stages of the Bill; indeed, he spoke on amendments submitted by other members, and it was during these discussions that he openly disagreed with Arthur Balfour's approach to the land problem and virtually accused him of duplicity. 'I call it a transition when a right honourable Member at one time professes certain principles as those which ought to be embodied in an Act of Parliament, and when he is on the other side of the House says that it is not necessary that they should be put into the Bill of his own Government.'

This accusation stung Balfour, who defended his actions and appealed to followers of the government to support the Bill. Carson did not do so; in fact he told the Conservative chief whip that he intended to act independently from then on. The friendly relations between Carson and Balfour were restored in due course, but Balfour felt that Carson had unnecessarily raised opposition by landlords to the 1896 Land Bill.

HOME LIFE AND SUCCESS

By the late 1890s, Carson was one of the most successful and highly paid lawyers in England. His fees were now at the same rate as those charged by Rufus Isaacs, a leading counsel who often appeared for the other side when Carson took briefs. Carson's earnings in 1899 totalled £20,000, an enormous sum in those days.

He and his wife were invited to many dinners and house parties. Lord and Lady Londonderry were particularly friendly with them, since Lord Londonderry had been Lord Lieutenant in Ireland. Carson also attended the Garden Party held at Windsor Castle to mark the Diamond Jubilee of Queen Victoria. He was now a highly respected figure in English society.

When his wife and children joined Carson in London they stayed at first in lodgings near Marble Arch, but when his earnings increased they purchased a large house in Rutland Gate, and also a house in the village of Rottingdean on the Sussex Downs, where they stayed on weekends and during holidays. It was there he became acquainted with the artist Edward Burne-Jones, the writer Rudyard Kipling, and Stanley Baldwin, a future Prime Minister.

Their eldest son, Harry, who reached the age of eighteen at the end of 1898, left school and was restless and extravagant. He failed to settle into a career, and Carson paid his fare to South Africa, whence he started farming in Southern Rhodesia. On the outbreak of the South African war Harry enlisted in Rhode's cavalry and later in the South Staffordshire Regiment.

Meanwhile, Mrs Carson found that her life in London was lonelier than it had been in Dublin. Her husband spent most of his time in Parliament or in the law courts, and the younger children were away at school for long periods. She felt neglected. Her husband's hypochondria and his bouts of exhaustion and depression – his doctors said he was suffering from neurasthenia – did not help her situation. Alvin Jackson, in his recent short study of Carson[7], comments as follows on Carson's 'vulnerable health and his profound sense of mortality':

> As a child he was diagnosed as having a weak heart ... As a young man he contracted typhoid and came close to death ... In his mid-twenties he was also plagued by gallstones ... But, to a very great extent, his ill-health, and his anxiety, were self-induced. He worked too hard ... Overwork and professional insecurity made Carson liable to anxieties concerning his health and his prospects, and this led frequently to intense depression ... Carson's depression seems also to have been rooted in his personal circumstances. His first marriage, to Annette Kirwan, was broken only by her death in April 1913. Annette never fully adjusted to Carson's meteoric rise to professional and political prominence, and in particular she hated their move to London in 1892–3. She felt that she was socially out of her depth, and she resented the extent to which her husband was lionised in the Conservative salons. She felt, with some justification, that she was neglected by Carson.'

A pen-picture of Carson is given by F.S.L. Lyons in his *Ireland since the Famine*:[5]

> Tall, grim, hatchet-faced, with a sallow complexion and a saturnine expression, he looked, and frequently was, a dyspeptic pessimist. He was, in addition, a hypochondriac who enjoyed his ill health to the full, though this did not prevent him, like many hypochondriacs, from getting through an immense amount of work and living to a ripe old age on the strength of it. In the House of Commons, as in the courts, he made his impact by his conciseness and clarity, his ruthlessness in argument, his impatience of compromise. He had, besides, a flair for the theatrical or flamboyant gesture which was out of place in parliament (though he used it even there to good effect), but which enabled him in the years after 1910 to play like a virtuoso upon the emotions of mass-audiences, especially in Ulster.

CATHOLIC UNIVERSITY EDUCATION

During his period as Chief Secretary for Ireland Balfour had raised in the Commons the question of providing some system of university education for Catholics, but the reaction from Ulster Unionists and English Conservatives was so unfavourable that he dropped it. Carson, however, was personally in favour of the idea and wrote to Balfour: 'It would be better and safer to give the Roman Catholics the necessary money and charter and allow them to work out their own scheme on purely denominational lines.'

In the House of Commons he said:

> I often think that Members of this House, who meet habitually in England, do not thoroughly understand that the Irish Catholics are a

people passionately devoted to their religion. They are a people who will not accept any institution in relation to the education of their children which is in conflict with their views; and, this being the fact, and all other expedients having been tried, what can be the use of believing that the aim of university education should be the aim of secularism, when the great bulk of the Catholic people in Ireland will not accept and could not accept that solution?

These opinions showed understanding and independence of mind on Carson's part, but it was not until the Irish Universities Act of 1908, passed by the Liberal government during Augustine Birrell's term as Chief Secretary for Ireland, that this problem was resolved.

In May 1900 Balfour told Carson that he and the Prime Minister, Lord Salisbury, would like him to fill the vacancy for Solicitor-General in England. Though Carson knew that this would mean a reduction in his income, he accepted the office. Thereupon, he was elected a Bencher of the Middle Temple and was knighted.

CHANGES IN PARLIAMENT

In 1902 Arthur Balfour, aged 54, became Prime Minister in place of Lord Salisbury, who had resigned for health reasons. Carson remained on as Solicitor-General but there were a number of other changes. Lecky disliked parliamentary life and resigned the seat he held on behalf of Trinity, which was then taken by J. H. Campbell, KC. In one of his last letters as an MP, Lecky wrote: 'We are having a most dreary session of persistent Irish obstruction – skilfully carried out – involving division on nearly every item, and bringing with it very late nights and a general dislocation of the Parliamentary machine.'

A new member of the House was Winston Churchill, then aged 28, who sat on the benches behind Carson.

When Wyndham's famous Land Bill of 1903 was introduced, Carson gave it only qualified support. In a speech at Oxford, he said: 'They call this the last Irish Land Bill. They talk of a permanent solution. I have been hearing of a last Irish Land Bill and of a permanent solution all my life, and I have no doubt that I shall hear of them again.' As a result of this speech, Carson had to send to the Prime Minister, a letter of explanation, which he ended with the words: 'I need hardly add that, so long as I have the honour of serving under you, I never could intentionally do a disloyal act.'

It was around this time that Carson began annual visits, with his wife, to the spa at Homburg, near Frankfurt in Germany, which had been popularised by King Edward VII. These visits were originally intended to relieve his aches and pains, but they also became social occasions.

ALASKA

In 1903 Carson was nominated as one of the British government's advocates at an arbitration tribunal set up to resolve a dispute between the USA and Great Britain as to the exact territorial boundary between Canada and Alaska, particularly along the deeply indented Pacific coastline of British Columbia.

In the eighteenth century, Alaska had been claimed by the Tsar as part of the Russian empire. This led to territorial disputes between Russia, Britain and the USA, which were resolved (it was thought) by a treaty in 1825 between Russia and Britain, which described the boundary between Canada and Alaska as following 'the tops of the mountains running parallel to the coast', from the Portland Canal in the south to Mount St Elias in the north. In 1867 Russia sold the Alaskan territories to the USA for seven million dollars, subject to the continuation of the terms of the 1825 treaty. Canadians were not too happy at this new situation, but it didn't seem to matter greatly to them until gold was discovered in the Yukon in 1896 and American prospectors began to wander into what the Canadians regarded as their territory. The precise borders of Alaska suddenly became important.

Efforts to reach agreement broke down, but in 1903 the British, Canadian and American governments agreed to set up a commission to resolve the territorial dispute. The commission would consist of six jurists, three to be nominated by the USA and three by Britain. The American government nominated three political figures (much to the annoyance of the Canadians, who did not regard them as jurists) and the British government nominated Lord Chief Justice Alverstone (who would preside) and two distinguished Canadian lawyers.

The problem area was the deeply indented coastline of British Columbia, with its many inlets and islands, which had to be reconciled with the treaty requirements that the boundary should follow the tops of the mountains parallel to the coasts, northwards from the Portland Canal. The arbitration commission sat for nineteen days, receiving submissions by lawyers from both sides, including Carson. Their findings were issued a few weeks later and there was consternation in Canada when it was learned that Lord Chief Justice Alverstone had agreed with the US interpretation of the 1825 treaty. The Commission's findings meant that the US gained this deeply indented coastal area. The two Canadian members refused to sign the document.

Carson was disappointed at the failure of his efforts to convince the commission of the British position, and Canadians felt that political expediency had triumphed.

In 1905 Carson received a letter from the Lord Chancellor offering him a High Court judgeship. He did not accept the offer because he wished to remain in politics; he also wished to resume private practice at the Bar after the pending general election, when the Liberals were expected to win, as indeed they did.

At the end of 1905 Balfour resigned as Prime Minister and the King requested the Liberal leader, Sir Henry Campbell-Bannerman, to form a government, marking the end of ten years of Conservative rule.

LIBERAL LANDSLIDE

The general election of January 1906 resulted in a huge Liberal victory; they got 377 seats, giving them an overall majority of 84. Many out-going Conservative MPs lost their seats, including Arthur Balfour who, however, was elected in another constituency soon afterwards. The Conservatives and Unionists were reduced to 157 seats, the Irish Nationalists got 83 seats, and the Labour Party 53 seats. This situation meant that the Liberal government did not have to depend on the votes of the Irish Party to get legislation through the House – until 1910, that is, when another election gave the Irish Party the balance of power.

Carson, with a safe seat in Trinity College, found himself playing a more prominent role in party politics when he returned to Westminister. One of the new Members was Captain James Craig, aged 35, Unionist MP for East Down. Craig succeeded Colonel Saunderson, who was very ill, as principal spokesman for the Ulster Unionists, and afterwards became Carson's right-hand man.

PRIVATE PRACTICE AGAIN

As Carson was no longer an officer of the Crown he was able to resume private practice at the Bar, which earned him a great deal of money. One of his cases, known as 'The Gaiety Girl Divorce Case', shows Carson in an unusually relaxed mood.

A young man named Francis Bryce, an officer in the British army, met a pretty young woman named Mabel Duncan, a member of the Gaiety musical comedy group. He fell in love with her, married her in 1898 against the advice of his parents, resigned his army commission, and started business on the Stock Exchange. Mabel was a vivacious and sociable woman and the marriage went well, though Mr Bryce found himself attending more race meetings and other festivities with his wife then he really wished.

During Oxford Commemoration Week in 1905 they met a rich young university student named Harold Pape. This young man soon became infatuated with Mabel, who was a good deal older than himself, and she and her husband found themselves being invited to stay with the Pape family. Harold Pape was an amateur horse rider and, while Mr Bryce was attending to stocks and shares, Harold and Mabel often attended race meetings together. Mabel told her husband that she had been with a lady friend at those meetings.

Some time later, Mr Pape and the Bryces went to a county ball in Exeter, where Harold danced a lot with Mabel, and Mabel's husband took an interest in a young lady who was referred to in the case as Miss A. In due course, Mr Bryce's mother mentioned to her son that people were talking about what seemed like an affair between Mabel and Harold Pape. Frank Bryce heeded his mother's warning and consulted a solicitor, who engaged detectives to watch the alleged erring pair.

While her husband was away in July 1906, Mabel visited some friends, Dr and Mrs Ellison, in Windsor and, with another lady, stayed in a nearby hotel. It transpired that Mr Pape had also booked a room in the same hotel. The following month, Mabel visited the Ellisons again, in Bembridge where they were on holiday, and Mr Pape stayed in a nearby hotel. The detectives reported that one afternoon, while the Ellisons were out, Mr Pape had been in the house with Mabel when she was changing her dress. To cap it all, Mr Bryce discovered a bundle of love letters from Harold Pape to his wife. This was too much for him and he instructed his solicitors to institute proceedings for divorce on the grounds of adultery between Mabel and Harold Pape. Mabel did not wish her marriage to Frank Bryce to be dissolved, nor did Harold Pape wish to marry Mabel, so they decided to contest the petition for divorce and to deny that adultery had ever taken place.

The trial opened on 4 May 1907 and lasted fifteen days. This seems a long time for a relatively straightforward case, but then Mr Bryce was represented by two senior counsel, Mabel was represented by Rufus Isaacs, and Harold Pape was represented by Edward Carson.

In opening the case for the plaintiff, Mr Henry Duke, KC, relied on the incidents referred to above, the love letters, and the evidence of a former chauffeur of the Bryces who said in testimony he had seen Mabel and Harold Pape 'cuddling and kissing like lovers'.

When Rufus Isaacs cross-examined Mr Bryce he raised the latter's relationship with another lady, Miss A., suggesting that it was this which had caused the trouble between himself and his wife and which had also led to Mr Bryce facilitating his wife's meetings with Mr Pape.

During Caron's cross-examination of Mr Bryce, the latter said that

when the four of them were going to the theatre together he had suggested to his wife that she and Miss A. should go together in a hansom
cab and that Mr Pape and himself would go in another hansom, but his
wife had replied that 'that was absurd as there would be no one to help
her out of the cab or pay the cabman'.

When Carson enquired why they could not have gone together in a
four-wheeler, Bryce replied: 'No one ever goes in a four-wheeler to the
theatre.' Carson commented: 'Well, perhaps I am out of date myself.'

When the four of them had gone punting on the river, Bryce admitted
he had been in a punt with Miss A. for nine hours, during which period
his wife was in another punt with Mr Pape. He explained he had punted
towards Reading.

CARSON: How far?

BRYCE: About a mile.

CARSON: What, in nine hours! What else did you do?

BRYCE: I sat and read, smoked and lunched – the usual things everybody does on the river. (*Laughter*)

CARSON: Nine hours is a long time, and you knew that all the time
your wife was with the co-respondent. I take it that was what usually
occurred on these river trips?

BRYCE: Yes, it was the ordinary way – it was natural.

CARSON: The natural way to treat your wife?

BRYCE: I treated the co-respondent as a friend. I was not using him as
a convenience.

CARSON: Could you not have obtained a boat that held four people?

BRYCE: From the point of view of comfort it was impossible to go four
in a punt.

CARSON: Then it was for comfort and not for convenience that you
occupied separate punts?

When Miss A., a pretty young woman of nineteen, gave evidence, she
claimed to have a bad memory and that she was unable to remember
many of the incidents. Carson then questioned her about the time she
had spent in the punt with Mr Bryce.

CARSON: Did you see Mrs Bryce, your chaperone, during all these
hours?

MISS A.: No.

CARSON: Is it the usual way to treat a chaperone?

MISS A.: She told me to go and I went.

CARSON: Oh, I see. She said to you, 'Go with my husband and amuse
him for six or seven hours, and be a good girl,' and so you, like a good
girl, obeyed?

MISS A.: I was told to go and I went.

CARSON: I am not blaming you. I only want to know what occurred.

The chauffeur who had seen Mrs Bryce and Mr Pape 'cuddling and kissing like lovers' was the next witness. He told Carson that he was not shocked at this behaviour, as he had often seen such things before.

CARSON: Where?

CHAUFFEUR: Everywhere. In England, Ireland, Scotland and Wales.

CARSON: Oh, please leave Ireland out! ... Is cuddling and kissing, in your experience, an epidemic all over the United Kingdom? (*Laughter*)

The injured wife, Mrs Mabel Bryce, then gave evidence and created a good impression. She was questioned about Mr Pape's letters and the following exchange took place:

COUNSEL: When Mr Pape wrote: 'I want you tonight awfully, awfully,' what did you understand?

MRS BRYCE: I thought he wished me to be with him.

JUSTICE DEANE: But did you not understand by that something improper?

MRS BRYCE: No, my Lord; he so often put into his letters: 'I wish you were here.'

JUSTICE DEANE: But 'tonight'. You are a married woman and understand these things.

MRS BRYCE: I looked upon the words as a figure of speech.

Mr Harold Pape, aged 24, gave evidence and admitted he had been in love with Mrs Bryce, but denied adultery. The jury dismissed the petition for divorce, but added that the conduct of Mr Pape was deserving of severe censure.

CONFLICT WITH THE HOUSE OF LORDS

The Liberal government held power for the next ten years, up to May 1915, when a coalition government was formed during the First World War, and was in fact the last Liberal government elected in Britain. They initiated many measures of social reform (for example, non-contributory old-age pensions) but were eventually supplanted by the Labour Party. Some of their measures were opposed by the Conservative Party, and the House of Lords, which had a built-in Conservative majority, came into serious conflict with the House of Commons by rejecting or severely amending a number of the Liberal Bills. In 1906 they so drastically altered the government's Education Bill that it had to be dropped. This led to a declaration by the then Prime Minister (H. Campbell-Bannerman) that 'a way must be found, and a way will be found, by which the will of the people, expressed through their elected representatives in this House, will be made to prevail'.

On 24 June 1907, Campbell-Bannerman formally introduced a resolution in the Commons that 'in order to give effect to the will of the people, as expressed by their elected representatives, the power of the other House to alter or reject Bills passed by the House must be restricted by law, so as to secure that, within the limits of a single Parliament, the final decision of the Commons should prevail'. [8] After three days' debate the motion was carried by 432 votes to 147. Despite these clear warnings, the Lords were unrepentant. In 1908 they rejected the government's Licensing Bill, which sought to reduce the number of public houses (with compensation payable).

At this stage, Mr Campbell-Bannerman resigned because of ill-health and died shortly afterwards. Herbert Asquith took his place as Prime Minister, and Lloyd George became Chancellor of the Exchequer. This set the scene for the constitutional conflict between the Lords and the Commons that had been brewing for some time.

The crunch came when the Lords rejected Lloyd George's budget in 1909. Faced with the need to raise extra funds to pay for old-age pensions and funds to build extra warships to counteract growing German naval power, the government's budget proposed to increase income tax from nine pence to fourteen pence, impose a super-tax of sixpence in the pound on incomes above £5,000, introduce land taxes, raise death duties, and increase liquor licences and duties on spirits and tobacco. In the Commons these proposals were strenuously resisted by the Conservatives – 42 parliamentary days were spent on the committee stage of the Finance Bill, during which Carson played an active role in the opposition. But the Liberal majority prevailed. The impositions on liquor licences and on spirits were unpopular in Ireland, and the Irish Party voted against the Bill's second reading. However, they decided to abstain on the third reading; they did not wish the government to be defeated, as this would put the prospect of Home Rule at risk.

When the Finance Bill reached the House of Lords it was rejected by 350 votes to 75. This was an unprecedented step and was a direct challenge to the House of Commons. The Liberal government decided to call an immediate general election on the issue of whether the House of Lords had a right to reject legislation passed by the elected House of Commons.

The result of this election, in January 1910, was a reduction in the Liberal seats from 377 to 275, and an increase in the Conservative/Unionist seats from 157 to 273. Nevertheless, the Liberals were still the largest party (if only by a whisker) and, with the support of Labour and the Irish Nationalists, remained in office and set about re-introducing their budget, which the Irish Party supported this time. The House of Lords, when confronted with the budget for a second time, decided to be sensible and allow it to pass.

A few months later the government placed on the Commons order paper the following three proposals to restrict the powers of the Lords:

* that the Lords could not amend or reject a money bill;

* that any other Bill which had been passed by the Commons in three successive sessions would automatically become law, even if rejected by the Lords, provided that two years had elapsed since its first introduction;

* that the maximum duration of Parliaments should be reduced from seven years to five.

The Irish Nationalists, who now held the balance of power, warmly welcomed these proposals, which, if implemented, meant that Home Rule was now achievable within a few years. Redmond had, as a result of hard bargaining, reached an understanding with Asquith that the Liberals would introduce a new Home Rule Bill as soon as the veto power of the House of Lords had been overcome.

King Edward VII, whom Asquith had briefed about these constitutional difficulties, died in May 1910, and was succeeded by George V, then aged 45. The government decided to make a last effort to reach a compromise agreement with the Conservatives on the powers of the Lords, and for several months in 1910 a succession of top-level meetings were held between Liberal and Conservative leaders. (Carson and Redmond, who were not involved in these meetings, were worried that compromises unacceptable to their respective, and opposing, positions would result from these meetings.) The two parties failed to reach an agreement, however, and the government decided to ask the King to dissolve Parliament so that the issue could be put before the electorate. Asquith also obtained from the King a promise (given reluctantly and to be kept secret for the time being) that if the Liberals were returned to power, and if the Lords continued to veto government legislation, he would agree to create sufficient additional peers to ensure that the legislation would be passed by the House of Lords.

The election of December 1910 left the position of the parties (Liberals 272, Conservatives and Unionists 271, Irish Nationalists 83, Labour 42) virtually unchanged, and the Liberals remained in government.

Asquith went ahead with the Parliament Bill to restrict the powers of the Lords and, despite strong Conservative opposition, it was passed by the Commons on 15 May 1911. When it came before the Lords they gave it a second reading without a division, but then proceeded drastically to amend it so as to negative its purpose. Asquith informed the King that the time had now come when he, as leader of the government, would need to inform the opposition of the King's agreement to create additional peers to ensure that this Bill was enacted. The King agreed to keep his promise, though he disliked having to do so, and Asquith informed Balfour of his agreement. This news led to a Conservative storm of protest, so much so that when Asquith rose to speak in the Commons shortly afterwards he was howled down for a period of half an hour.

Many of the Lords vowed to oppose the Bill to the bitter end, while others advised caution, worried by the threat of the creation of perhaps 300 or more additional Liberal peers; Asquith had a list of 249 names already prepared. When the day of reckoning arrived in the Lords on 10 August, there were splits in the ranks of the Conservative peers. Many stuck to their guns and voted against the Bill, but a large number abstained and 37 others voted with the government. The Bill was thus carried by 131 votes to 114. The threat had worked without the necessity of creating additional peers.

All this was very unwelcome news to Carson, who could see that it would be now be legally possible for the Liberal government to have a new Home Rule Bill enacted within the following two or three years.

CHAIRMAN OF THE IRISH UNIONISTS

For some years up to 1910, the chairman of the Irish Unionists in Parliament had been Walter Long, who represented a South Dublin constituency, but in the January 1910 election he was elected by a London constituency. As it was the custom for the chairman of the Irish Unionists to be an MP holding an Irish seat, the Irish Unionists agreed unanimously to invite Carson to become their chairman. He accepted the offer, knowing that it would entail much extra work. On the day the new Parliament met, 21 February 1910, he was formally elected chairman and told the Ulster Unionists: 'I dedicate myself to your service whatever may happen.'

In the subsequent government reshuffle, Winston Churchill became Home Secretary and made clear his support for Home Rule. It was Churchill's father, Lord Randolph Churchill, who had openly supported the Ulster Unionists in their opposition to Gladstone's Home Rule Bill of 1886, but Winston, who had been a Conservative at the beginning of his political career, had transferred his allegiance to the Liberals in 1904. He was therefore regarded as a turncoat and was subjected to much personal criticism by the Unionists. (Churchill reverted to Conservatism in later years and achieved fame as Prime Minister during the Second World War.)

In his first speech as Home Secretary, Churchill defended the government's proposals on Home Rule. Carson's sarcastic reply was: 'I have no doubt if the right honourable gentleman had remained a member of the Conservative Party and had seen any political advantage to be gained from the introduction of Home Rule, or from opposition to Home Rule, he would have been equally willing to adopt the particular view that suited his particular interests for the moment.' Carson went on to taunt the Irish Nationalists for swallowing the budget because they viewed it as a step towards Home Rule. He castigated the government for their announced intention of going ahead with a new Home Rule Bill, and said:

> You have had it twice rejected, and now, by your bargaining with the Irish Nationalists, for the sake of your budget, for the sake of remaining in office, you want to sneak this Bill through, breaking up the United Kingdom, without the people having an opportunity of expressing an opinion upon it, which they have expressed so emphatically upon former occasions.

The reference to 'sneaking the Bill through' was hardly justified, as the Liberal Party's support for Home rule was well known.

THE ARCHER-SHEE CASE (THE WINSLOW BOY)

As a front-bench speaker for the Conservatives and chairman of the Irish Unionists, Carson was kept busy with political affairs. But he continued his law practice and, around this time, agreed to take on the job of trying to rectify a wrong done to thirteen-year-old boy, George Archer-Shee, who had been discharged from the Royal Naval College at Osborne, in the Isle of Wight, for allegedly stealing and cashing a postal order for five shillings. Carson's success in clearing the boy's name, despite legal impediments, was widely acclaimed. Many years later, in 1946, the English playwright, Terence Rattigan, wrote a successful play, called *The Winslow Boy*, about the case, and this was later made into a film.

His unrelenting efforts to defend, and ultimately to vindicate, the boy's innocence shows Carson at his best. Hyde's biography[2] contains an excellent report of the case.

FAMILY PROBLEMS

Around 1910–11, Mrs Carson's health began to deteriorate and, in addition, some of the children, now grown up, worried Carson. Harry, the eldest, had returned from South Africa with a wife, but found it difficult to settle into a regular occupation. He joined the yeomanry, where his extravagant habits caused problems. His brother, Walter, was a midshipman in the navy, but his father found it difficult to understand him. Gladys was an intelligent young woman, but unfortunately contracted tuberculosis. While undergoing treatment in a Swiss sanatorium she fell in love with an American man, whom Carson did not like. In a letter to Lady Londonderry, to whom he wrote regularly, he commented: 'My children are a rum lot.'

A few months later, in June 1911, when Carson's health was troubling him again, his doctor sent him to Baden-Baden for a four-week course of treatment. He liked the place but was bored stiff. What exasperated him was the fact that much of the House of Lords debate on the Parliament Bill took place while he was in Baden-Baden. In a letter dated 3 June to Lady Londonderry he said: 'I feel very despondent about the Home Rule campaign ... I hope the Lords will stand firm and let the Radicals make their filthy Peers and then become ridiculous.' On 25 June he wrote:

> 'The surroundings here are exquisitely beautiful. I never saw such foliage and trees and the views are wonderful, but of course to me it is miserable lonely and I am not able to walk much. I quite despair of getting fit. I have done too much work and am suffering for it in consequence. I am very depressed about the Home Rule question. It seems to me as if everything was helping it on ... There is nothing to write about from this place. It is 'treatment' all day long, but whether it is of any use remains to be seen.'

ULSTER DEFIANCE

In January 1911 Carson had visited Belfast to preside at a meeting of the Ulster Unionist Council, of which he was now Vice-President. Formed in 1905, the Council represented Unionist Clubs and Associations, and Orange Lodges, throughout Ulster. Carson was now recognised by the vast majority of Protestants in Ulster as one of their two main leaders (the other being James Craig) in the struggle against Home Rule.

In July, Craig and Carson agreed that steps would have to be taken to show the government the extent of public opposition in Ulster to any form of Home Rule for Ireland. Craig undertook to arrange a monster meeting in Belfast, which Carson would address. In a letter to Craig on 29 July, Carson wrote:

> What I am very anxious about is to satisfy myself that the people over there really mean to resist. I am not for a mere game of bluff, and unless men are prepared to made great sacrifices which they clearly understand the talk of resistance is no use ... Personally I would be prepared to make any sacrifice, my time, my business, money, or even my liberty, if I felt assured we would not in the end be abandoned. I am glad to

have so good and true a friend as you to work with, and, if we get sufficient help, we ought to be able to call a halt.

Craig lived in a house called Craigavon on the south shore of Belfast Lough, with large grounds and a sloping lawn that could be used as a natural amphitheatre for meetings. It was here that a huge gathering was held on the afternoon of Saturday, 23 September 1911, attended by members of Orange Lodges, County Grand Lodges, Unionist Clubs, and the Women's Association. It was estimated that about 100,000 people took part. After the passing of a resolution welcoming Carson as their leader, he addressed the gathering:

> I know the responsibility you are putting on me today. In your presence I cheerfully accept it, grave as it is, and I now enter into a compact with you, and every one of you, and with the help of God you and I joined together – I giving you the best I can, and you giving me all your strength behind me – we will yet defeat the most nefarious conspiracy that has ever been hatched against a free people. But I know full well that this Resolution has a wider meaning. It shows me that you realise the gravity of the situation that is before us, and it shows me that you are here to express your determination to see this fight out to a finish.

> Mr Asquith, the Prime Minister, says that we are not to be allowed to put our case before the British electorate. Very well. By that determination he drives you in the ultimate result to rely upon your own strength, and we must follow all that out to its logical conclusion ...That involves something more than that we do not accept Home Rule.

> We must be prepared, in the event of a Home Rule Bill passing, with such measures as will carry on for ourselves the government of those districts of which we have control. We must be prepared – and time is precious in these things – the morning Home Rule passes, ourselves to become responsible for the government of the Protestant Province of Ulster.

> We ask your leave at the meeting of the Ulster Unionist Council to be held on Monday, there to discuss the matter, and to set to work, to take care, so that at no time and at no intervening space shall we lack a Government in Ulster, which shall be a Government either by the Imperial Parliament or by ourselves.

These sentiments were enthusiastically applauded and, two days later, 400 delegates of the Ulster Unionist Council met in Belfast, under the chairmanship of Lord Londonderry, to decide what should be done. They promised unwavering support for their leaders and appointed a Commission of five men 'to take immediate steps, in consultation with Sir Edward Carson, to frame and submit a Constitution for a provisional government of Ulster, having regard to the interests of the Loyalists in other parts of Ireland: the powers and duration of such provisional government to come into operation on the day of the passage of any

Home Rule Bill, to remain in force until Ulster shall again resume unimpaired her citizenship in the United Kingdom.' The five members of the Commission were: Captain James Craig, MP; Colonel Sharman Crawford, MP; Thomas Andrews, a well-known Liberal-Unionist; Colonel R.H. Wallace, a prominent member of the Orange Institution; and Edward Sclater, Secretary of the Unionist Clubs.

From this time on, Carson became more and more committed to the Ulster cause. Until then his opposition to Home Rule had been motivated by a determination to keep the whole of Ireland within the United Kingdom. But after 1911 the efforts of the Ulster Unionists gradually turned towards excluding Ulster from the scope of Home Rule, and Carson thus found himself reluctantly supporting a revised policy that would mean leaving Unionists in other parts of Ireland to fend for themselves.

Arthur Balfour resigned as leader of the Conservatives in November 1911, because of ill health, and Bonar Law succeeded him as a compromise candidate. (Carson had been approached to put his name forward but declined.) Bonar Law, aged 53, had been born in Canada, but his father came from Antrim and he himself had been brought up among Scottish Presbyterians. His whole outlook was sympathetic towards the Ulster Unionists.

Meanwhile, the Liberals and Irish Nationalists were scornful of the threats of the Ulster Unionists. Churchill referred to the 'squall which Sir Edward Carson was trying to raise in Ulster – or rather in that half of Ulster of which he has been elected Commander-in-Chief', and added: 'We must not attach too much importance to the frothings of Sir Edward Carson. I daresay when the worst comes to the worst we shall find that civil war evaporates in uncivil words.'

Churchill made himself even more unpopular by announcing that he proposed to visit Ulster at the invitation of the Ulster Liberal Association, to speak in support of Home Rule with John Redmond and Joseph Devlin, Nationalist MP for West Belfast. The Ulster Liberals had booked the Ulster Hall for that meeting, to be held on 8 February 1912, and this raised a storm of protest. The Hall was owned by Belfast Corporation and it had been there that Churchill's father had roundly condemned Home Rule in 1886. The Standing Committee of the Ulster Unionist Council adopted a resolution which 'observed with astonishment the deliberate challenge thrown down' by the holding of a Home Rule meeting in the centre of the loyal city of Belfast, 'and resolves to take steps to prevent its being held'.

After Carson had addressed two mass meetings in Liverpool and a large meeting in the Free Trade Hall in Manchester, he travelled on to Belfast because of the crisis developing there.

The government discovered that the Ulster Unionist Council had booked the Ulster Hall for the night preceding the Home Rule meeting, with the intention of continuing to occupy it into the following day, to stimy the Home Rule meeting. Churchill decided that it would be unwise to insist on the Ulster Hall being used for their meeting and wrote to Lord Londonderry telling him that, in the circumstances, he would ask the Ulster Liberal Association to arrange the meeting, on the same day, in another venue in Belfast. A suitable large hall was not available and the meeting was held in a large marquee in Belfast Celtic's football ground. The Ulster Unionist Council appealed for calm on the day of the meeting, but the government decided to take no chances and sent military reinforcements to the area.

Churchill, accompanied by his wife, secretary and two Liberal MPs, arrived at Larne, where a hostile crowd greeted him, and travelled to Belfast by train. When he was being driven from the Grand Central Hotel in Belfast that afternoon, on his way to the football ground, a huge crowd gathered along the route and the occupants of the car were booed, hissed and threatened until the car reached the nationalist area, when the mood of the people changed completely. The meeting passed off peacefully. Carson had stayed in Belfast that day, in case of trouble, but was able to return to London after congratulating the Ulster Unionist Council on the satisfactory and peaceful termination of the day's proceedings.

THE KING INTERVENES

While these meetings and demonstrations were taking place, King George V became personally concerned at the trend of events, which seemed to be heading towards civil conflict. He explained his worries to Asquith and, after a cabinet meeting on 6 February 1912, Asquith reported to the King that the government had discussed whether the Ulster counties with large Protestant majorities should be allowed to contract out of the Bill. His memo to the King informed him that the cabinet had agreed to the following conclusions:

(a) that the Bill as introduced should apply to the whole of Ireland;

(b) that the Irish leaders should from the first be given clearly to understand that the government held itself free to make such changes in the Bill as fresh evidence of facts, or the pressure of British opinion, may render expedient;

(c) that if, in the light of such evidence or indication of public opinion, it becomes clear as the Bill proceeds that some special treatment must be provided for the Ulster counties, the government will be ready to recognise the necessity either by amendment of the Bill, or by not pressing it on under the provisions of the Parliament Act. In the meantime, careful and confidential enquiry is to be made as to the real extent and character of the Ulster resistance.[4]

This memo indicated that, though Asquith was pressing ahead with the Home Rule Bill without excluding Ulster, he was leaving himself with plenty of room for manoeuvre.

After Balfour had spoken to the King about the Conservatives' views, the King suggested to Asquith that a conference between leaders of the Liberal and Conservative parties should be held, to try to reach a settlement. This conference, extending over several weeks, was held towards the end of 1913, but was unsuccessful. Balfour sought permanent exclusion of Ulster, whereas Asquith was prepared to consider only a temporary exclusion.

PROTEST MEETINGS

Craig and Carson continued to hold protest meetings and about 100,000 people attended a meeting on 9 April 1912 in the Royal Agricultural Society's showgrounds in Balmoral. Bonar Law was present with a large number of MPs from England and Scotland. The platform party, which reviewed a lengthy parade by the Ulster Volunteers, comprised Bonar Law, Carson, Lord Londonderry and Walter Long.

The tone of the meeting may be gathered from the following exhortations in Bonar Law's speech:

> You must trust in yourselves. Once again you hold the pass, the pass for the Empire. You are a besieged city. The timid have left you; your Lundys have betrayed you; but you have closed your gates. The Government have erected by their Parliament Act a boom against you to shut you off from the help of the British people. You will burst that boom. That help will come, and when the crisis is over men will say to you in words not unlike those used by Pitt – you have saved yourselves by your exertions and you will save the Empire by your example.

A Resolution against Home Rule was adopted, and Carson and Bonar Law grasped each other's hands as a sign of solidarity. In a letter to Lady Londonderry a few days later, Carson said that the proceedings at Balmoral seemed like a dream and the meeting was the most thrilling experience he had ever had.

THE HOME RULE BILL

Two days after the Balmoral demonstration, the (third) Home Rule Bill, similar to the 1893 Bill, was introduced by Asquith. It proposed to set up an Irish Parliament of two Houses, with an Executive, but the Parliament's powers were to be confined to internal Irish affairs; even control of police was to remain with Westminster for a while. The Bill stipulated that the supreme authority of the UK Parliament 'over all persons, matters, and things in Ireland' was retained, and Irish representation in Westminster was to continue, though with reduced numbers. Despite the limited parliamentary powers in the Bill, a Nationalist convention in Dublin on 23 April welcomed it. Irish public opinion seemed to welcome it but the Sinn Fein leader, Arthur Griffith, condemned the Bill as inadequate.

On the second reading a few weeks later the Bill was carried by a majority of 101 votes (including the Irish Nationalists and Labour). When the committee stage was reached in June, an amendment to exclude the counties of Antrim, Armagh, Derry and Down was put down by a Liberal back-bencher, one of whose comments was: 'Orange bitters and Irish whiskey will not mix.'

This amendment posed a problem for the Ulster Unionists. If they supported it they could be accused of deserting the Irish Unionists living outside these four counties, but if they opposed it and subsequently resorted to force to take control of these counties, they could be accused of duplicity. They decided to support the amendment for two reasons: (a) the exclusion of several north-eastern counties might make Home Rule unworkable and thus unacceptable to the Irish Party; and (b) to indicate that, in the last resort, they were prepared to settle for the exclusion of the north-eastern counties. Some government speakers taunted them with deserting Unionists in other parts of Ireland. Carson replied in words that showed his Dublin roots:

> Is it desertion? I do not agree. Let me say for myself, and in no egotistical way, that as a Dublin man – the Solicitor-General was very anxious to know my pedigree – I should be the very last, with all my relatives living in the south and west of Ireland, and in various places, who would for one moment consent to what I believe would be in the slightest degree a desertion of any part of Ireland.

After a three-day debate the amendment was defeated by 69 votes.

The fact that the government was not prepared to accept a proposal to exclude even the predominantly Unionist north-eastern corner signified to Carson that they were determined to apply Home Rule to the whole of Ireland, irrespective of the wishes of the Ulster Unionists, and shortly afterwards he announced that this would be accepted as a declaration of war.

The anti-Home Rule campaign continued and intensified to the extent that Bonar Law, at a meeting at Blenheim Palace on 29 July, vehemently condemned the Liberal government, referring to it as 'a revolutionary committee which has seized upon despotic power by fraud'. The Conservatives, he declared, 'would not be bounded by the restraints that would influence them in an ordinary constitutional struggle', and that, even if the Bill were carried through the Commons, 'there are things stronger than parliamentary majorities'. He added:

> If an attempt were made to deprive these men [Ulster Protestants] of their birthright – as part of a corrupt parliamentary bargain – they would be justified in resisting such an attempt by all means in their power, including force ... I can imagine no length of resistance to which Ulster can go in which I should not be prepared to support them, and in which, in my belief, they would not be supported by the overwhelming majority of the British people.[5]

Such expressions from a leader of the Conservative Party were unprecedented and were tantamount to inciting civil war. Redmond, however, regarded these threats as bluff and blackmail, and told Asquith so, but Asquith was worried about the growing tension over Home Rule. Gradually he, and his government, began to conclude that some form of exclusion for the north-east counties (perhaps a temporary exclusion for a few years) would have to be considered if the risk of civil strife was to be avoided.

ULSTER'S SOLEMN LEAGUE AND CONVENANT

After the Balmoral demonstration it was suggested that further demonstrations should be held at which those attending would be asked to sign a solemn and binding commitment against Home Rule. Carson liked the idea and asked Craig to prepare a suitable wording. The result was the famous Solemn League and Convenant which read as follows:

> Being convinced in our consciences that Home Rule would be disastrous to the material well-being of Ulster as well as the whole of Ireland, subversive of our civil and religious freedom, destructive of our citizenship, and perilous to the unity of the Empire, we, whose names are underwritten, men of Ulster, loyal subjects of His Gracious Majesty, King George V, humbly relying on the God whom our fathers in days of stress and trial confidently trusted, do hereby pledge ourselves in solemn Covenant throughout this our time of threatened calamity to stand by one another in defending for ourselves and our children our cherished position of equal citizenship in the United Kingdom, and in using all means which may be found necessary to defeat the present conspiracy to set up a Home Rule Parliament in Ireland. And in the event of such a Parliament being forced upon us we further solemnly and mutually pledge ourselves to refuse to recognise its authority. In sure confidence that God will defend the right we hereto subscribe our

names. And further, we individually declare that we have not already signed this Covenant. God Save the King.

The Covenant was approved at a meeting of the Ulster Unionist Council in Belfast on 23 September, 1912. Carson addressed the delegates:

How often have I thought over this Covenant. How many hours have I spent before it was published in counting the cost that may result. How many times have I thought of what it may mean to all we are about here. Does any man believe that I lightly took this matter in hand without considering with my colleagues all that it may mean either in the distant or the not too distant future? No, it is the gravest matter in all the grave matters in the various offices I have held that I have ever had to consider. But the more I consider it, the more I believe it to be right. I at all events am prepared to go to the end.

At this, the crowd shouted: 'We will back you!'

Carson then went on a tour, speaking about the Covenant, which culminated in ceremonies in Belfast on Saturday, 28 September. At first, there was a religious service in the Ulster Hall, conducted by ministers from the Protestant churches, followed immediately by a solemn gathering in the City Hall, where Carson was the first person, followed by various religious and political leaders, to sign the Covenant. The public were then admitted to sign copies. By the end of that day over 80,000 people had signed, and by the end of the campaign it was estimated that over 400,000 Ulster men and women had signed.

When Parliament met that autumn Asquith moved a 'guillotine' motion laying down time limits for the various stages of the Bill. (However, it allowed 25 days for the committee stage debate, which does not seem unduly restrictive.)

On 1 January 1913, Carson moved an amendment to exclude the province of Ulster from the Bill. In a speech which Asquith described as 'very powerful and moving', Carson made it clear that even if Ulster were excluded, the Unionists would continue to oppose Home Rule for Ireland, and warned that the Covenant would not be abandoned without force. Redmond opposed the amendment, saying: 'Ireland for us is one entity.' Asquith rejected the amendment, saying: 'No Government could allow so undemocratic a claim as that put forward by Ulster to veto Home Rule.' The amendment was defeated by 97 votes.

When the Bill reached the third stage a fortnight later, Carson was absent, tending his sick wife, who had suffered another stroke. (She was to die on 6 April 1913, aged 57.)

The Bill passed the Commons on 16 January 1913, by a majority of 109 votes, but two weeks later it was rejected by the Lords, by 326 votes to 69. The second circuit of the Bill, as provided for in the Parliament Act, took place during March–July 1913, and the Lords rejected it again.

BYE-ELECTION IN DERRY

Soon after the Lords' rejection of the Bill, there was a bye-election in the city of Derry, which the Nationalist Party won. Gwynn's comments on this episode were:

> The Nationalist and Unionist forces in Derry City had for years been almost equally divided, and every effort was now made by both sides. The Nationalists found a strong candidate in a Protestant Liberal, who agreed to become a pledge-bound member of the Nationalist Party; and after a contest, conducted with tremendous excitement, which focused the attention of the whole English press, the seat was captured by the Nationalists. The victory was all the more significant because it turned the balance between the Nationalist and Unionist representation in the province as a whole. Henceforth there were seventeen Home Rule Members for the province as against sixteen Unionists. No greater blow to the pretensions of the Orangemen to speak for all Ulster could have been delivered at the time. The argument which Redmond had stated so often had been most remarkably vindicated.[8]

In September, 500 members of the Ulster Unionist Council met in the Ulster Hall to approve of the setting up of a provisional government, in the event of the Home Rule Bill becoming law. This *de facto* government would have 77 members, with a commission of five acting as its Executive. Carson would be chairman of the Executive.

Three days later, 15,000 members of the Ulster Volunteer Force paraded in Balmoral, reviewed by a retired Indian Army officer, Lieutenant General Sir George Richardson, who was now commander of the force. Carson, Craig and Lord Londonderry stood near the saluting base. The proceedings ended with the unfurling of a huge Union Jack and the singing of 'Rule Britannia' and 'God Save the King'.

The Liberals were tending towards some form of temporary exclusion for north-east Ulster, but the Irish Party was not prepared to compromise on this issue. In a speech in Limerick on 12 October, Redmond said: 'Irish Nationalists can never be assenting parties to the mutilation of the Irish nation. Ireland is a unit ... The two-nation theory is to us an abomination and a blasphemy.'

On 14 October, Bonar Law had the first in a series of confidential meetings with Asquith, but the Prime Minister would not agree to the exclusion of the six north-eastern counties. He made this clear at a meeting in Leeds on 27 November when he said: 'We are not dissatisfied with the Government of Ireland Bill as it stands. We are not going to be frightened or deflected by menaces of civil war. We are not going to make any surrender of principle. We mean to see the thing through.'

Carson was invited to attend some of the talks between Asquith and

Bonar Law. He was unyielding and said to Asquith at one stage: 'I have no doubt, Mr Prime Minister, you have thought out very carefully what you intend to do when they resist your Bill in Ulster and when the first five hundred Ulstermen are shot down in Belfast.' Asquith exclaimed: 'My God! Five hundred! I tell you that if one Ulsterman was shot in such a quarrel it would be a disaster of the first magnitude.'

Shortly afterwards, Carson wrote to Asquith to clarify what he meant by the 'exclusion' of Ulster from Irish Home Rule:

> I thought that it was always apparent that, when the exclusion of Ulster was discussed, I meant that Ulster should remain as at present under the Imperial Parliament and that a Dublin Parliament should have no legislative powers within the excluded area. Ulster would therefore send no members to the Dublin Parliament, but would continue as at present to send members of the Imperial Parliament. This would of course involve that the administration of Ulster should be under the control of the Imperial Parliament. I do not think I can say anything more specific.

GUN RUNNING

The Ulster Volunteers had a few thousand rifles, but not nearly enough for a force of 100,000 men. Captain W.B. Spender, a staff officer in the UVF, was given the task of procuring arms, and got in touch with Major Fred Crawford, a fanatical enthusiast for the Unionist cause (he had signed the Covenant with his own blood), who had already obtained many of the rifles held by the Volunteers. Crawford had contacts in Germany and was given approval for the purchase of between 20,000 and 30,000 rifles and several million rounds of ammunition, plus a small steamer to bring them to Ulster.

Crawford set off for Hamburg and, on his way through London, called on Carson to find out precisely where Carson stood in regard to the importation of arms for the Volunteers. He told Carson that once he had embarked on this course there could be no turning back, and enquired whether Carson was prepared to back him up to the finish. If not, he would not go ahead with it.

Carson looked him straight in the eye and said: 'Crawford, I'll see you through this business, if I should have to go to prison for it.' Crawford was satisfied.

That meeting occurred in February 1914, and on 8 March the second reading of the Home Rule Bill (within its third circuit of Parliament) began in the Commons. Asquith and Birrell had prevailed upon Redmond to accept an amendment to the effect that any Ulster county could, by a vote of its parliamentary electors, exclude itself from the operation of the Act for a period of six years, after which period they would be brought within Home Rule unless Parliament had decided otherwise in the meantime. Asquith announced this compromise when moving the second reading of the Bill, but Carson would have none of it. 'So far as Ulster is concerned,' he said, 'be exclusion good or bad, Ulster wants the question settled now and for ever. We do not want sentence of death with a stay of execution for six years.' He added that if the time limit were omitted he would submit the amended Bill to a convention in Belfast. The time limit of six years was retained.

THE CURRAGH INCIDENT

In March 1914 the Commander-in-Chief in Ireland, Sir Arthur Paget, was instructed to take precautions to safeguard military depots in Ulster, to prevent possible raids for arms. He was summoned to London and was met by Colonel Seely, Secretary for War, Churchill and Birrell, and later by Sir John French, Chief of the Imperial General Staff. French informed Sir Henry Wilson, Director of Military Operations, of his discussion with Paget. Wilson, who sympathised with the Ulster Unionists, met Carson that night at a dinner and told him that the government intended to spread troops all over Ulster. Wilson expressed the opinion that if the government wanted to crush Ulster they would have to mobilise the whole army. He added for good measure that a large proportion of officers would refuse to coerce Ulster.

In the Commons the following day Carson referred to rumours about army contingents being sent to Ulster, and accused Churchill of trying to provoke the Ulster people. That night Carson took the boat-train to Belfast where he was received with honours by Craig and two companies of Volunteers, led by General Richardson.

Meanwhile, Sir Arthur Paget had returned to Dublin, where he briefed his senior officers about the War Office's proposals to secure the safety of the North. Unfortunately, his briefing was inaccurate and let some army officers to believe that the government proposed to undertake immediate military operations in Ulster.

At the Curragh military base, Brigadier-General Hubert Gough, an Ulsterman and commander of the Cavalry Brigade, plus 58 other officers, reported that they would prefer to be dismissed rather than carry out orders against Ulster. When Asquith learned of this development, he arranged a meeting with Seely, Churchill and the military chiefs to diffuse the situation. The meeting achieved this, but not without difficulties. In the end, General French and General Ewart resigned because of the military insubordination. The Secretary of State for War, Colonel Seely, also resigned. Asquith himself took temporary control of the War Office. But the whole episode reflected badly on the government.

LANDING OF ARMS

Meanwhile, Major Crawford had purchased 30,000 rifles and three million rounds of ammunition from a dealer in Hamburg, together with a small steamer named *Fanny* (which had a Norwegian captain and crew) on to which the arms were loaded in Danish waters.

After various adventures and misadventures, the arms were transhipped off the Welsh coast to a small coal vessel, the Clydevalley (renamed Mountjoy II), which arrived at Larne on the night of 24 April 1914. The arms were packed in small bundles for easy handling, and the Ulster Volunteers succeeded in unloading and distributing them during that night. Some smaller consignments were landed at Donaghadee and Bangor.

News of the landing was telegraphed to Carson and Lord Londonderry in London. The newspapers highlighted the story, and Asquith was asked to make a statement. He described the gun-running as a 'grave and unprecedented outrage', and assured the House of Commons that the government would take 'appropriate steps to vindicate the authority of the law'. The Irish Attorney-General was asked to prepare information against Carson and the others involved so that proceedings could be taken against them. On further consideration, however, the government decided not to institute legal proceedings, a decision influenced by views, expressed by the King, Birrell and Redmond, that it would make matters worse to press charges against Carson and his co-conspirators.

HOME RULE – FINAL STAGES

In Parliament the Home Rule Bill was awaiting its final passage. Asquith met Bonar Law and Carson on 5 May to discuss possible compromises, but no progress was made. One change did emerge, however: instead of an exclusion clause being incorporated in the Bill, exclusion would be provided for in a separate Amending Bill which (hopefully) could be enacted at the same time as the main Home Rule Bill (or Government of Ireland Bill, was its correct title). Asquith announced this proposal in the House on 12 May, without indicating what the terms of the Amending Bill would be. Bonar Law protested that the House had a right to know what the Amending Bill would contain before the main Bill was passed, but Asquith disagreed.

The main Bill was finally passed by the Commons a fortnight later.

In June the Amending Bill was introduced in the House of Lords (rather than in the Commons) to test the response there. It consisted of the proposal Asquith had already made known to the Conservatives, i.e., that each county in Ulster could, by plebiscite, opt out of Home Rule for a period of six years. This did not satisfy the House of Lords, who amended it to provide for the permanent exclusion of the whole province of Ulster, without a plebiscite. The Bill, so amended, was returned to the Commons on 14 July.

The Liberals believed that there was no justifiable case for excluding the whole of Ulster from Irish Home Rule, seeing that five of the nine Ulster counties had Nationalist majorities. If the Ulster Unionists had a sustainable case on religious and demographic grounds for excluding the predominantly Protestant and Unionist counties in Ulster, they could not similarly justify excluding counties with Nationalist majorities.

A census held in 1911 had shown that the population of Ulster was 1,581,696 people, of whom 690,816 were Catholics and 890,880 were non-Catholics. The percentage of non-Catholics (i.e., predominantly Protestant and Unionist) in each of the nine counties was as follows:[9]

Co. Antrim	79.5%
Co. Down	68.4%
Co. Armagh	54.7%
Co. Derry	54.2%
Co. Tyrone	44.6%
Co. Fermanagh	43.8%
Co. Monaghan	25.3%
Co. Donegal	21.1%
Co. Cavan	18.5%

These percentages show why the Liberals felt that there was a reasonable case for excluding counties Antrim, Down, Armagh and Derry, but no case for excluding Monaghan, Donegal and Cavan. The problem counties were Tyrone and Fermanagh, where Catholics formed 55 or 56 per cent of the population. (It is true that not all Catholics were Nationalists, nor that all Protestants were Unionists, but experience in Ulster showed that the vast majority of Catholics were Nationalists and the vast majority of Protestants were Unionists.)

In view of the continuing impasse, Asquith agreed to a suggestion by the King that a conference between all the Party leaders should be held in Buckingham Palace, under the chairmanship of either himself or the Speaker of the House of Commons. This conference was held, with the Speaker as chairman, from 21 to 24 July, 1914. Those present were

Asquith, Lloyd George, Redmond and John Dillon on one side, and Bonar Law, Lord Lansdowne, Carson and Captain Craig on the other. Under discussion were the areas to be excluded and the period for which those areas could be excluded. The conference got bogged down on the first point and never reached the second.

On the second day, Asquith wrote a letter to a close friend which showed his dejection:

> We sat again this morning for an hour and a half, discussing maps and figures, and always getting back to that most damnable creation of the perverted ingenuity of man – the county of Tyrone. The extraordinary feature of the discussion was the complete agreement (in principle) of Redmond and Carson. Each said: 'I must have the whole of Tyrone, or I die; but I quite understand why you say the same.' The Speaker, who incarnates bluff unimaginative English sense, of course cut in: 'When each of two people say they must have the whole, why not cut it in half?' They would neither of them look at such a suggestion.
>
> Lloyd George and I worked hard to get rid of the county areas altogether and proceed on Poor Law Unions which afford a good basis of give and take. But again both Irish lots would have none of it. Nothing could have been more amicable in tone or more desperately fruitless in result. We agreed to meet again tomorrow, when we shall make a final – though I fear futile – effort to carve out a 'block'. I have rarely felt more hopeless in any practical affair: an impasse, with unspeakable consequences, upon a matter which to English eyes seems inconceivably small, and to Irish eyes immeasurably big. Isn't it a real tragedy?[4]

On 24 July the Speaker informed the House that the Conference had been unable to reach agreement on the area to be excluded. Asquith then announced that the Amending Bill would be introduced on 30 July.

Meanwhile important events were happening elsewhere. On 26 July a consignment of arms (smaller than the quantity landed in Ulster) was landed in board daylight at Howth Harbour, a few miles north of Dublin, and collected by the Irish Volunteers, a nationalist organisation established in November 1913. The authorities in Dublin Castle immediately sent troops to seize the arms, but they were too late. When the troops were marching back to barracks in Dublin they were jeered by a hostile but unarmed crowd. The troops opened fire; three people were killed and 38 wounded.

1914–18 WAR

In Sarajevo, Serbia, on 28 June 1914, the Austrian Archduke Francis Ferdinand was assassinated by a terrorists. The Austrians, having decided that Serbia must be taught a lesson, sent an ultimatum and then a declaration of war. Germany agreed to support Austria, and Russia felt obliged to support Serbia. When Russia mobilised, Germany declared war on Russia and also on France, Russia's ally. The German plan of war, already prepared, was first to attack and defeat France and then to attack Russia. The Germans invaded neutral Belgium on their way to attack France and this brought an immediate response from Britain, who decided to come to the defence of Belgium and France. Britain declared war on Germany on 4 August and sent an expeditionary force of 100,000 men to France to halt the German invaders. Preparations for a full-scale war thus became the main preoccupation of the British government.

When Bonar Law and Carson met Asquith on 30 July and learned of the imminence of war, they suggested that the Amending Bill should be postponed. After consulting his colleagues and Redmond, Asquith agreed that Home Rule should be put into cold storage until the end of the war.

Shortly afterwards Carson was queried about the future role of the Ulster Volunteers and replied that a large number of them would be willing to serve for home defence, and many would be willing to serve elsewhere. Redmond informed the Commons that the National Volunteers would be prepared to defend the coasts of Ireland 'in comradeship with our brethren in the north'.

By this stage Carson's two sons had joined the forces: Harry the army and Walter the navy. An Ulster Division was formed from the Ulster Volunteers and went for training in England before proceeding to France, unaware of the awesome fate that was to befall them in the battle of the Somme in July 1916.

Difficulties and differences about Home Rule persisted. Bonar Law and Carson pressed Asquith to defer enacting the Home Rule Bill, whereas Redmond continued to press for its placing on the statute book even though it would not come into force until the end of the war. On 15 September, Asquith informed the Commons that the Home Rule Bill would be signed by the King and become law, but that its operation would be suspended until the end of the war. He also announced that the Amending Bill would be introduced in the next session. Bonar Law was outraged at this news, alleging that the government had taken advantage of the Unionists to betray them. At the end of his speech he walked out of the chamber, followed by Carson and his supporters.

Carson was absent when the Home Rule Bill received the Royal Assent in the House of Lords on 18 September – for a very good reason. On the previous day he had married Miss Ruby Frewen, a young Englishwoman whom he had first met in August 1912 at the spa in Homburg. The wedding had been kept secret and only a few close friends were present.

Carson was 60 and his bride just 30, but theirs turned out to be a happy marriage.

WAR DUTIES

The Conservatives agreed to support the Liberal government in the war against Germany, but tensions rose when the numbers of dead and wounded continued to rise. One of the earliest military disasters was the failure of the Dardenelles campaign against the Turks early in 1915, with great loss of life. There was much criticism of the conduct of the war with the result that a Coalition government was formed in May 1915. Asquith remained as Prime Minister and Lloyd George became Minister of Munitions; Bonar Law became Colonial Secretary; and Balfour became First Lord of the Admiralty. Churchill (who had been First Lord) was demoted to Chancellor of the Duchy of Lancaster; Arthur Henderson (Labour) became Secretary of State for Education, and Carson became Attorney-General. Redmond was offered a seat in government but refused. He objected to Carson being included in government on the grounds that, as leader of the Ulster Unionists, he had threatened resistance to the forces of the Crown and to decisions of Parliament. Asquith refused to budge.

Carson's position in government did not last long, however, as he became disillusioned with the manner in which the War Council was conducting its business, and he resigned in October 1915. He returned to the back benches, where he became chairman of a group of Conservatives who kept the government under constant surveillance.

The number of volunteers joining the army at the outset of the war was huge, with the result that the armed forces in Britain soon totalled about one million men; but the casualties in France were so enormous that towards the end of 1915 the imposition of compulsory military service came before government. Carson strongly favoured conscription, as did Lloyd George, but Asquith temporised because so many groups, including the Irish Party and the Labour Party, were opposed to it. Nevertheless, the conscription of young men was imposed in 1916, though not in Ireland because of the strength of opposition there, including objectives by the Irish Party and the Catholic hierarchy.

EASTER RISING, 1916

After the Easter Rising, which sought an Irish republic, the government decided to review the 1914 Home Rule Act and to make another attempt at a settlement. Lloyd George was given the task of persuading Carson and Redmond to reach a settlement, and achieved this in a manner that let to a grave misunderstanding of his proposals as far as Redmond was concerned. Lloyd George prepared a document which proposed that the Government of Ireland Act of 1914 should be brought into operation 'as soon as possible' for the 26 counties, but with the six north-eastern counties excluded, and that after the end of the war an Imperial Conference should consider this matter again.

When Lloyd George sent these proposals to Carson he enclosed a note which said: 'We must make it clear that at the end of the provisional period Ulster does not, whether she wills it or not, merge in the rest of Ireland.' The sending of this partisan note was a breach of faith by Lloyd George as far as the Irish Party was concerned.

When Lloyd George's proposals came before the Cabinet at the end of June they were fiercely opposed by some members, particularly Lord Landsdowne, a Kerry Unionist landlord who was the government's spokesman in the House of Lords, where he announced that the exclusion of the six counties would be 'permanent and enduring'. The end result was that the Home Rule proposals were deferred once again, a move that greatly undermined Redmond's reputation in Ireland, where Sinn Fein was rapidly gaining public support. The days of the Irish Parliamentary Party were numbered.

Carson too was disappointed with the deferment of the proposals which, after an onerous effort, he had prevailed upon the Ulster Unionists to accept as the only tolerable settlement available. In a letter to his wife he said: 'The people who oppose this settlement don't realise how we fought to get Ulster excluded, and what an achievement it is to have got that.'

ASQUITH OVERTHROWN

Lloyd George was still dissatisfied with the conduct of the war, which had become bogged down in trench warfare on the western front. He suggested to Asquith that a small War Committee should be set up, of which he (Lloyd George) would be chairman. Asquith was prepared at first to consider the idea, but soon turned it down, saying that it would cut across the Prime Minister's responsibilities. This led to difference of opinion within the government, particularly among Conservative ministers, who felt that a change at the top was needed. When Asquith became aware of this loss of support, he resigned so that Lloyd George could form a government. Carson, who had been critical of Asquith's leadership for a long time, welcomed this development.

When Lloyd George was forming the new government he offered Carson the post of Lord Chancellor. Carson declined, because he wished to be more involved in the prosecution of the war, and was then appointed First Lord of the Admiralty. (Lloyd George revealed in later years that he had wished to make Carson a member of the War Cabinet, as minister without portfolio, but had been 'overridden by the personal prejudices of the majority of the Conservative leaders against Carson. They all admired but disapproved of him'.)

Carson's attitude in the Admiralty was to let the senior naval staff carry out their duties; but this did not satisfy Lloyd George. When, in February 1917, the Germans intensified the war at sea by authorising their submarines to sink all ships, whether British or neutral, Lloyd George became convinced that convoys of ships escorted by warships would be the most effective defence against submarines. This idea was put to the admirals who, Lloyd George felt, were reluctant to adopt it. Carson defended the admirals who, he said, would use convoys when sufficient escort shops were available. Lloyd George came under pressure from Sir Douglas Haig, Commander-in-Chief in France, who was alarmed at the increasing number of ships being sunk by the German submarines, and who felt that Carson was not suitable for the job of First Lord of the Admiralty. (He later formed a more favourable opinion of Carson.) In July, Lloyd George told Carson that he wished him to vacate the Admiralty and become a member of the War Cabinet. Carson demurred but was persuaded by Lloyd George to accept the change, and acted as Minister for Propaganda.

IRISH CONVENTION, 1917

When the USA entered the war against Germany in 1917, the US government raised the question of independence for Ireland, for which there was widespread support among Irish-Americans. Lloyd George suggested holding a Convention representing all sectors in Ireland to see whether agreement could be reached between them. Meetings of the Convention, chaired by Horace Plunkett, were held in Trinity College, Dublin, for several months from mid-1917. The Convention contained 95 delegates representing the churches, trade unions, commercial bodies, local government, Irish Nationalists and Irish Unionists. Sinn Fein refused to attend.

Lord Midleton, leader of the Southern Unionists, seemed to be prepared to compromise, but the Ulster Unionists continued to insist on permanent exclusion of the six north-eastern counties, which Redmond would not tolerate. Thus no agreement was reached. Redmond resigned from the Convention in January 1918, and died two months later.

Carson, who said the Convention had caused him a lot of trouble, resigned from the government in January 1918, as he felt that to continue as a member of the War Cabinet would be inconsistent with his position as chairman of the Ulster Unionists, now that the Home Rule question had come to the fore again.

POST-WAR YEARS

When the war ended, the outgoing coalition government decided to remain together for the general election held in December 1918. Lloyd George and Bonar Law issued a joint manifesto in which they said that they would explore all practical paths towards settling the Irish question, on the basis of self-government, but that there could be no complete break between Ireland and the British Empire and no forcible submission of the six north-eastern counties to a Home Rule parliament.

Carson decided to compete for a seat in Ulster instead of in Trinity College, and was invited to go forward for a seat in the new Duncairn division of north Belfast. There, he spoke in favour of the coalition and praised Lloyd George's work as Prime Minister during the war. The votes cast were:

Sir Edward Carson (Unionists)   11,637
Major W.H. Davey (Nationalist)   2,449
Dr H.M. MacNabb (Sinn Fein)   249

The Irish Unionists had 26 members elected, mostly in Ulster. The most significant result of the 1918 election, however, was the success of Sinn Fein, who won 73 seats, whereas the Irish Nationalist Party held on to only six seats out of 68 seats in the outgoing Parliament. The coalition, embracing Conservatives and quite a number of Liberals, got 478 seats, a huge majority. The Asquithian Liberals, who had gone forward as part of the opposition, attained only 27 seats. Labour won 59 seats. (From this time on, Labour gradually supplanted Liberals in Parliament.)

DÁIL ÉIREANN

The elected Sinn Fein members refused to have anything to do with the Westminster Parliament and set up their own assembly (Dáil Éireann) in Dublin. All elected Irish representatives were invited to attend, including the Irish Unionists, but not surprisingly, the Unionists ignored this invitation, as did the remnant of the Irish Party. The Sinn Fein members (apart from those in prison) met in the Mansion House in Dublin on 21 January 1919 and appointed members of a government. They declared the independence of Ireland in the following words:

> Now, therefore, we, the elected representatives of the ancient Irish people in National Parliament assembled, do, in the name of the Irish nation, ratify the establishment of the Irish Republic and pledge ourselves and our people to make this declaration effective by every means at our command.

This Declaration of Independence and the efforts of the newly appointed government to act as the lawful government of Ireland inevitably brought about a state of war between Dáil Éireann and the British government. As far as the Sinn Fein government was concerned, Home Rule was put aside and complete Irish independence was now the objective.

NEW COALITION GOVERNMENT

Lloyd George remained on as Prime Minister and offered Carson a Cabinet post. Carson, now aged 64, declined the offer, as he wished to return to practise at the Bar. James Craig, who had had a minor post in the outgoing government, became Parliamentary Secretary to the Ministry of Pensions.

The problem now confronting Carson and the Ulster Unionists was that the 1914 Home Rule Act, which was on the statute book and awaiting implementation, might be brought into operation without the promised amendment excluding the six Ulster counties. Carson therefore continued to devote his time to this problem. When addressing an Orange gathering in Belfast on 12 July 1919, he reiterated the same message of defiance: 'If there is any attempt to take away one jot or title of your rights as British citizens and the advantages which have been won in this war of freedom, I will call out the Ulster Volunteers.'

This flamboyant speech was criticised in England, where Lloyd George decided he would make yet another effort to resolve the Irish problem. A Cabinet Committee was set up with prominent Unionist Walter Long as chairman, and their recommendations led to the Government of Ireland Bill, 1920.

INTERLUDE

On 17 February 1920, Mrs Carson gave birth to a baby boy whom they called Edward. This birth gave great joy to both parents, and the bashful father was cheered when he next entered the House of Commons.

GOVERNMENT OF IRELAND ACT, 1920

The following week the Government of Ireland Bill was introduced in the Commons. It provided for the repeal of the Home Rule Act of 1914 and, in its place, the establishment of two separate subordinate parliaments, one covering the six counties of Northern Ireland and the other covering the remaining 26 counties of Ireland, each with its own elected membership. However, the Bill made it clear that Westminster would have ultimate sovereignty and would continue to control foreign affairs, defence, posts and telegraphs, income tax and customs and excise. The Bill stipulated that Northern Ireland would elect thirteen representatives to Westminister, and Southern Ireland would elect 33 members. The Bill also provided for a Council of Ireland comprising twenty representatives each from the Dublin and Belfast parliaments, 'with a view to the eventual establishment of a parliament for the whole of Ireland, and to bring about harmonious action between the parliaments and governments of Southern Ireland and Northern Ireland'.

The Bill was not favourably received in Ireland. Sinn Fein wanted an independent Irish republic for the whole of Ireland, not a parliament with limited powers for only 26 counties. The Irish Uionists had never sought Home Rule for part of Ulster but wished to remain an integral part of the United Kingdom. Nevertheless, the Bill had a definite attraction for Ulster Unionists in that it placed them outside the jurisdiction of the Dublin government. Carson consulted his colleagues to determine their attitude towards the Bill. One of the main points of discussion was whether they should put down an amendment to include Donegal, Monaghan and Cavan as part of Northern Ireland, but this was decided against as it was evident from previous polls that, in an all-Ulster assembly, Unionists would have a majority of only one or two seats over Nationalists and Republicans. This would be too small a margin for comfort.

The Bill passed the Commons by a large majority, the only opponents being the Labour members, the Asquithian Liberals, and the remnants of the Irish Party. The Ulster Unionists abstained from voting, but Carson made a speech in which he lamented the breaking-up of the Union between Great Britain and Ireland:

> Ireland is mad to give up her representation in this House. Every injustice and every harm committed on Ireland ... was inflicted before the Union and not since the Union, and none of them would be possible

with the present representation of Ireland in the Imperial Parliament ... I cannot vote for Home Rule and I will not vote for Home Rule. At the same time I shall do nothing to prevent this Bill from becoming law.

A few days later, when the Bill was due to be considered by the House of Lords, Carson clarified the Ulster Unionists' views in a letter to the Lord Chancellor, which the latter read out in the Lords:

With reference to the Government of Ireland Bill which will be before the House of Lords next week, I observe that it is frequently stated that no one in Ireland wants the Bill passed into law. May I say, with the full consent of all my colleagues in Ulster, that this is a fallacy. It is quite true that we are all of the opinion that to maintain the Union is the soundest policy, but we recognise that under the existing circum-stances, and especially having regard to the fact the Act of 1914 is upon the Statute Book, it is not possible to secure that position as it at present stands. Ulster wants peace, and above all things to be removed from the arena of party politics in the Imperial Parliament, and we have therefore made up our minds that in the interests of Ireland, Great Britain, and the Empire, the best and only solution of the question is to accept the present Bill and endeavour to work it loyally.

The Bill was passed and received the Royal Assent in December 1920. Arrangements were to be made, in accordance with the Act, to hold elections in Northern and Southern Ireland for the purpose of forming the two new Parliaments. The Ulster Unionists invited Carson to be the leader of the party but he declined, on the grounds that a younger man would be more suitable for the position. Sir James Craig thus became the new Unionist leader. Craig (later Lord Craigavon) was a wealthy Belfast man, a Unionist MP since 1906, with strong attachments to Ulster.

Carson, when relinquishing his chairmanship of the Ulster Unionists, made the following wise remarks, which unfortunately were largely ignored during the subsequent history of Northern Ireland:

From the outset, let us see that the Catholic minority have nothing to fear from the Protestant majority. Let us take care to win all that is best among those who have been opposed to us in the past. While main-taining intact our own religion, let us give the same rights to the religion of our neighbours.

NORTHERN IRELAND

The first election in Northern Ireland, on 21 May 1921, with a high poll of 89 per cent, resulted in the election of 40 Unionists, six Sinn Feiners, and six Irish Nationalists. Craig was appointed Prime Minister and formed a government of Unionists (something which continued to be the pattern for the following 50 years).

At the same time, an election was also held in 'Southern Ireland', which resulted in almost a clean sweep for Sinn Fein and republican candidates, who were unopposed. But they boycotted the proposed Southern Ireland parliament, with the result that the 26 counties continued to be governed from London via Dublin Castle (though the republican Dáil Éireann also claimed jurisdiction) until the Irish Free State was established in 1922.

A few days after the election, Carson was made a Lord of Appeal in the House of Lords, under the title of Lord Carson of Duncairn (a life peerage). He bought a large old house, with twenty acres of land, not far from Ramsgate, where he hoped to spend weekends with his wife and young son before retiring there.

When King George V opened the new Northern Ireland Parliament in Belfast on 22 June 1921, Carson did not attend; he felt he could not absent himself for a week from his legal duties in the Lords. Mrs Carson attended in his place. King George made an appeal 'to all Irishmen to pause, to stretch out the hand of forbearance and conciliation, to forgive and forget, and to join in making for the land they love a new era of peace, contentment and goodwill'. Lloyd George wrote to De Valera, as the chosen leader of the majority of people in Southern Ireland, inviting him to attend a conference in London 'to explore to the utmost the possibility of a settlement'. A truce in the vicious warfare between the two sides was agreed upon, and negotiations began which ended in the Anglo-Irish Treaty of 6 December 1921, granting Dominion Status to a new autonomous Irish Free State. The Treaty applied to the whole of Ireland, but Northern Ireland was given the right to opt out within a short period, which it did. The Treaty also provided for a Boundary Commission to 'determine in accordance with the wishes of the inhabitants, so far as may be compatible with economic and geographic conditions, the boundaries between Northern Ireland and the rest of Ireland'; but this proved to be a dead letter in the long run.

The ratification of the terms of the Treaty led to a serious and tragic split between the Irish representatives in Dáil Éireann (64 for, 57 against) and a short but brutal civil war ensued.

When Carson read the terms of the Treaty he remarked: 'I never thought I should live to see the day of such abject humiliation for Great Britain'; and when the Treaty was discussed in the House of Lords on 14 December 1921, he made it the subject of his maiden speech there. He denounced the Treaty as a betrayal and severely criticised the coalition government for surrendering to murderers. These are some of his remarks, spoken with venom:

> I speak for a good many. I speak – I can hardly speak – for all those who, relying on British honour and British justice, have in giving their

best to the service of the State, seen themselves now deserted and cast aside without one single line of recollection or recognition in the whole of what you call peace terms in Ireland ...

And do you think either we or the country are going to be taken in by this manufactured glorification of what you are pleased to call the Treaty between Great Britain and Ireland? No, we are not. We tell you, if you want to pass it, go and ask the country, but you will not dare. That is the last thing you will do, or the last thing you care about. And all this comes from the long continuance in office of a Coalition Government which was formed for entirely different objects and entirely different purposes ...

They (Articles of the Treaty) were passed with a revolver pointed at your head. And you know it. You know you passed them because you were beaten. You know you passed them because Sinn Fein with the army in Ireland has beaten you. Why do you not say so ...

At that time, I did not know, as I know now, that I was a mere puppet in a political game. I was in earnest, I was not playing politics. I believed all this. I thought of the last thirty years, during which I was fighting with others whose friendship and comradeship I hope I will lose from tonight, because I do not value any friendship that is not founded upon confidence and trust. I was in earnest. What a fool I was! I was only a puppet, and so was Ulster, and so was Ireland, in the political game that was to get the Conservative party into power. [2]

He severely criticised members of the government, particularly Lord Curzon, Foreign Secretary and Leader of the House of Lords, Lord Birkenhead (Lord Chancellor), and Austen Chamberlain, Leader of the House of Commons; the latter two were signatories to the Treaty. His vitriolic, even vindictive, remarks shocked many members, though they pleased a few diehards.

Montgomery Hyde classified the speech as 'perhaps the most brutally frank oration ever delivered in that assembly as well as a masterpiece of concentrated invective'. It was the speech of a disillusioned and disappointed man. Nevertheless, the Lords approved the Treaty by a large majority.

Whether Carson was justified in feeling betrayed is doubtful. An observer can reasonably believe that Carson's intransigent opposition to Home Rule, over a long period of years, left him in a vulnerable position should his tactics fail, as they ultimately did. In the years up to 1914 the limited form of Home Rule which the Liberals were prepared to give Ireland was acceptable to the majority of the Irish people, but was not acceptable a few years later, when complete national independence became the demand.

Carson failed to comprehend the legitimacy of the demand for Irish independence, and he fought tooth and nail against a form of Home Rule which gave only limited powers to a subordinate Irish parliament. While demanding exclusion from Irish Home Rule for Ulster Unionists, he rejected the claim for exclusion from Northern Ireland of the Nationalist majorities in counties Tyrone and Fermanagh. The form of Home Rule which the Irish Party had fought for would have maintained the supremacy of Westminster, but the Ulster Unionists would have none of it, even though they eventually accepted Home Rule for Northern Ireland.

CONSERVATIVES REGAIN POWER

The coalition government was still in power towards the end of 1922, but by the time another general election became imminent many Conservatives were dissatisfied. Carson was openly critical of the coalition and was instrumental in negating Austen Chamberlain's wish to have the next election contested by it. With Carson's support, Bonar Law succeeded in having a motion adopted by the Conservative Party in favour of the Conservatives contesting the next election as a separate party. Lloyd George resigned immediately and Bonar Law was asked to form a government, becoming Prime Minister on 23 October 1922. A general election a few weeks later resulted in a Conservative majority.

Carson's comment on the downfall of the coalition was: 'Mr Austen Chamberlain, then supposed to be a Unionist leader, has said that it was from the moment of the signing of this Treaty that the coalition began to topple down. Of course it was, and I am glad of it. It is the just reward of the treachery of which he was at the head, and so may it always be.'

Shortly afterwards, the Irish Free State Constitution Bill, giving effect to the Treaty, was passed by both Houses of Parliament. In the Lords, Carson showed his detestation of the measure. Referring to the civil war then convulsing Ireland, he remarked:

> To those who were loyal to you in Ireland, it has been a year of hell. It is still hell ... During that year almost every house of any importance in Ireland has been burnt down. Men have been taken out of their beds because they served you in the war ... or as those whom you selected to put down crime – taken out one after the other and shot dead. All law has vanished from Ireland. All protection is at an end in Ireland ... I personally can thank God that nearly all my relatives have been able to come away, and that is the only consolation they can have as a reward for having been loyal subjects of the Crown.[1]

Aside from his judicial functions in the Lords, Carson took part in a number of discussions there. For example, he tried, but failed, to persuade the British government to legislate for the return of the Lane pictures to Dublin, and he introduced a Bill to control money-lending, a topic in which he had a personal interest, as his eldest son had fallen foul of money-lenders in an effort to clear off gambling debts.

CARSON'S RELIGIOUS BELIEFS

In December 1927 an interesting matter occupied the House of Lords when the approval of an alternative Prayer Book for use in the Church of England came before Parliament. Carson did not agree with the proposal, as he felt it went too far in extending the tenets of belief. His comments on the proposal give an insight into his religious views. Colvin's biography[1] reports Carson's contribution as follows:

> Carson being an Irishman brought up in the Church of Ireland, it was almost inevitable that he should take the Protestant or 'Low Church' side, but even his friends were unprepared for the strength of his conviction. Carson's life, indeed, had always glowed round a core of earnest faith. As a law student at Trinity College he used to preach at street corners of a Sunday night; his religion was something very deep and very dearly cherished. 'Remember,' he said in the House of Lords on this occasion, 'that religion is a thing that you learn at your mother's knee. I say that without disrespect to any of the right reverend prelates. Any religion I ever learned was from my mother, and it is to me one of the most precious possessions.'

> So it was that after venturing 'as a member of a sister Church, the Irish Church, which has, up to this time, been in communion with the Church of England, to ask your Lordships to hear me for a few moments,' Carson proceeded to deliver one of the strongest and most eloquent speeches of the debate against the alternative prayer-book. He took the view that any change in a book which generations had loved and honoured would merely disturb belief without harmonising practice. Why, he asked, was a proposal to legalise illegalities to be called reform? Better disestablishment than surrender to schismatics who were seeking to undermine the Reformation ...

> To his friend Dr D'Arcy, the Primate, Carson wrote at length on the subject. 'What I have very strongly felt,' he wrote, 'was that a good deal of the change in the alternating common service, coupled with the Reservation provisions, would leave it open to those who wish to defy the rubrics to make a justification for going much further than was contemplated by the book of the deposited belief and in my view an alternative Communion Service goes to the very root of disunity. I do not think the Bishops understand how deep the feeling amongst the masses is, even amongst those who, one might say, are not much concerned in religion in an active sense, that any change which may lead to a modification of the Reformation Settlement should be opposed.

Montgomery Hyde's biography[2] contains the following additional interesting remark by Carson on that occasion:

Let me make this one confession at the outset. It is the first time in my life – and I am a very old man – that I have ever felt grateful to Mr Gladstone for disestablishing the Irish Church, and for this reason – whatever your Parliament may do here in relation to the Prayer Book, it will not bind the Irish Church, which can still go on cherishing the precious heritage of the Reformation.

LAST YEARS

In 1929 Carson's health deteriorated and he resigned his position as Lord of Appeal. Carson had been an outstanding prosecuting and defence counsel but was not regarded as a great Law Lord. Colvin says, at the end of his biography: 'It is the testimony of Bench and Bar and the officers of the Court that Carson was rather a competent than a great judge, rather a shrewd than a profound lawyer.'[1]

Carson continued to a member of the House of Lords. When the Statute of Westminster was passed in 1931, giving the Dominions extensive powers of self-government, he argued that it should not apply to the Irish Free State because of the Treaty; but the government would not accept this line of argument.

When the Fianna Fáil party under De Valera came to power in 1932 and began to dismantle the Treaty, Carson felt that his warnings had been borne out. In his last important speech in the Lords, he expressed his disillusionment with party politics, perhaps to an exaggerated extent:

> I only came into public life because I cared for my fellow Loyalists in Ireland. I went all through my public life doing my best for them, and I saw them in the end betrayed; but at all events betrayed under the pretext that certain safeguards were provided. Now I have lived to see every one of these safeguards absolutely set at naught and made useless. That is not a pleasant political career ... Every single promise we have made to the Loyalists in Ireland has been broken, every pledge of law and order destroyed, everything that makes life and property safe has gone, and now the last remnant is to be taken away.

In 1932 Carson attended the official opening of the new Parliament Building at Stormont in Belfast. In the following year he attended the dedication of a bronze statue of himself in front of the Parliament Buildings, where it still stands in impressive display.

He was then living in retirement at Cleve Court, near Ramsgate, with his wife and young son Ned. His eldest son, Harry, and his younger daughter, Gladys, had died, but his other son and married daughter visited him from time to time. Many of his old friends had passed away and his visits to London became infrequent. He felt old and depressed.

In March 1934, aged 80, Carson appeared in the House of Lords for the last time. In June 1935 he contracted bronchial pneumonia but pulled through. A few weeks later, in a letter to a friend, he said: 'I have had a real rotten time and indeed I grow in strength very slowly if at all. I have not been in London this year and 2 or 3 times outside my 'demesne'. I have found the hot weather very exhausting but I must still hope. I go out every day and sit in the garden and watch the birds!'

He grew weaker and by October was confined to his room. He was found to be suffering from leukaemia, and died peacefully on 22 October 1935.

Craig (Lord Craigavon), Prime Minister of Northern Ireland, announced that Carson would be given a state funeral, with burial in St Anne's Cathedral, Belfast. His body was brought by naval vessel through Belfast Lough, placed on a gun-carriage, and paraded to St Anne's, where his body was entombed. The Church of Ireland Primate officiated at the funeral service.

BIBLIOGRAPHY

(1) Edward Marjoribanks and Ian Colvin, *The Life of Lord Carson*; three volumes. Gollancz, London, 1932, 1934 and 1936.
(2) H. Montgomery Hyde, *Carson*. Heinemann, 1953, and Constable, London, 1974.
(3) A.T.Q. Stewart, *Edward Carson*. Gill & MacMillan, Dublin, 1981.
(4) Roy Jenkins, *Asquith*. Collins, London, 1964 and 1978.
(5) F.S.L. Lyons, *Ireland since the Famine*. Weidenfeld & Nicolson, 1971, Fontana, 1973.
(6) Jonathan Bardon, *A History of Ulster*. Blackstaff Press, Belfast, 1992.
(7) Alvin Jackon, *Sir Edward Carson*. Dundalgan Press, Dundalk, 1993.
(8) Denis Gwynn, *The Life of John Redmond*. Harrap, London, 1932.
(9) Patrick Buckland, *Ulster Unionism and the Origins of Northern Ireland 1886–1922*. Gill & MacMillan, 1973.

Acknowledgements

For permission to reproduce photographs, drawings and paintings we would like to acknowledge with thanks:

SECTION 1

Yeats

Yeats in the early 1930s (Bord Fáilte)

W.B. Yeats, a portrait by his father, John Butler Yeats (National Gallery of Ireland)

Yeats's Dublin birthplace, 5 Sandymount Avenue (Photo Pat Tutty, courtesy of Vivien Igoe)

Lilly (Susan) Yeats by John Butler Yeats (National Gallery of Ireland)

Jack Yeats, the painter, as formidable a talent as his brother (Bord Fáilte)

Georgiana Hyde-Lees, Mrs Yeats (Photo courtesy Brian Seed; by permission of Michael Yeats)

Yeats, with his children Michael and Anne, in the garden on Thoor Ballylee in the 1920s (By permission of Michael Yeats)

Thoor Ballylee, Yeats's symbolic home in Galway (Bord Fáilte)

Yeats the Magus, the engraved frontispiece by Edmund Dulac for *A Vision* (Peter Costello)

How the Poets Passed: the famous caricature of Yeats and AE as public figures. It was said that Yeats set out from 82 Merrion Square to call on AE, just as AE left 84 Merrion Square to call on Yeats. Neither found the other at home (Peter Costello)

Yeats during his last years (Bord Fáilte)

Joyce

James Joyce, a portrait by Pavel Tchelitchev (National Gallery of Ireland)

James Joyce as the youngest boy at Clongowes (Couresty Fr Bruce Bradley SJ)

Joyce (standing 2nd from the left) with his college contemporaries (Curran Papers, UCD)

Nora Barnacle, photographed in Galway in 1903, the year before she ran away with Joyce (Cornell Joyce Collection)

James Joyce, photographed by his friend Con Curran. Asked what he was thinking, he replied, 'I was wondering if you would lend me five shillings.' (Curran Papers, UCD)

The Volta, Dublin's first cinematograph, opened by Joyce in 1909 (Peter Costello)

Joyce in Trieste with his son Giorgio (Croessmann Collection, University of Southern Illinois)

Lucia Joyce, the Joyces's daughter, with other student dancers in Paris (Poetry Collection, Lockwood Memorial Library, SUNYAB)

James Joyce in 1918 (Bord Fáilte)

Four generations of Joyces (Gisèle Freund, with permission of John Hillelson Agency)

Swift

Dean Swift, portrait by Charles Jervas (National Gallery of Ireland)

The house in Hoey's Court behind Dublin Castle in which Swift was born (Central Catholic Library)

St Patrick's Cathedral, a contemporary drawing by W. H. Bartlett (Courtesy estate of Dr Robert Wyse Jackson)

Esther Johnson, Swift's 'Stella'; portrait by James Lathem (National Gallery of Ireland)

Hester van Homrigh, Swift's 'Vanessa' by Philip Hussey (National Gallery of Ireland)

St Patrick's Hospital, the original aspect photographed at the turn of the century before the recent modernisation (Central Catholic Library)

Gulliver in Lilliput: inflatable model of Gulliver landed on Dollymount beach during the Dublin Millenium celebrations in 1988.

Swift's memorial, with its famous inscription in St Patrick's cathedral (Bord Fáilte)

FATHER BROWNE'S AUSTRALIA
E. E. O'Donnell

'a master photographer with an unerring eye.'
London *Independent*

'the most important documentary historian of this century.'
Irish Times

Next in the acclaimed **Father Browne** series, following on *Father Browne's Ireland, Father Browne's Dublin, The Genius of Father Browne*, and *A Life in Pictures*.

Affected by gassing in WWI, Fr. Browne was sent on a voyage to Australia for health reasons. He spent two years (from 1925 - 1927) taking over 900 photographs and this volume presents the cream of the collection from the developing cities to the wild Outback.

0-86327-443-9

FATHER BROWNE'S CORK

Here are flashing insights on the personalities of Cork men, women and children; panoramic shots of land and sea, featuring, for example, the Mizen cliffs and Garnish Island; famous Great Houses and churches; pictorial slices of history, and many instances of what can only be described as `curiosities'...

0-86327-489-7

These books are available from all good bookshops or direct from
WOLFHOUND PRESS,
68 Mountjoy Square,
Dublin 1.
Tel: 8740354 Fax: 8720207.